Weight Watchers
Program
Cookbook

Weight Watchers®

Program

Cookbook

by

JEAN NIDETCH

HEARTHSIDE PRESS, INCORPORATED • PUBLISHERS
GREAT NECK, NEW YORK 11021

Contents

Acknowledgements

We gratefully acknowledge recipe contributions received from our franchises located in the following areas:

GREATER BIRMINGHAM, ALABAMA
CENTRAL CALIFORNIA
NORTHERN CALIFORNIA
ORANGE AND SAN DIEGO, CALIFORNIA
OTTAWA, CANADA
COLORADO
EASTERN CONNECTICUT
WASHINGTON, D. C.
CENTRAL FLORIDA
GREATER MIAMI, FLORIDA
NORTHEAST FLORIDA
PALM BEACH COUNTY, FLORIDA
GREATER ATLANTA, GEORGIA
CENTRAL ILLINOIS
CHICAGO, ILLINOIS
GREATER WICHITA, KANSAS
MAINE
BALTIMORE, MARYLAND
TWIN CITIES, MINNEAPOLIS AND ST. PAUL, MINNESOTA
BERGEN COUNTY, NEW JERSEY
NORTH JERSEY
ADIRONDACKS, NEW YORK
CAPITOL DISTRICT, NEW YORK
SOUTHERN TIER, NEW YORK
SYRACUSE, NEW YORK
COLUMBUS, OHIO
OREGON
CENTRAL PENNSYLVANIA
PUERTO RICO
CHARLESTON, SOUTH CAROLINA
GREATER MEMPHIS, TENNESSEE
NASHVILLE, TENNESSEE

CORPUS CHRISTI, TEXAS
DALLAS, TEXAS
EL PASO, TEXAS
WEST TEXAS
SALT LAKE CITY, UTAH
BURLINGTON, VERMONT
GREATER PUGET SOUND, WASHINGTON
SOUTHERN WISCONSIN

as well as contributions received from our own operations in New York City; Saginaw, Michigan; West Germany; and South Africa.

A special thanks to Felice Lippert, Director of Food Research at Weight Watchers, International, and her staff, without whom this book would not have been possible.

And finally, we pay tribute to Nedda Anders, Editor of Hearthside Press, Inc. and her staff, who have played so important a role as publishers of the *Weight Watchers Program Cookbook*.

Introduction

First a nostalgic word about the original cookbook published in 1966: many of its recipes fit the revised Weight Watchers Program, and you may continue to enjoy them—perhaps even more so when you realize that to make space for new material, those unique and delectable dishes have not been repeated. So cherish your first book.

The Weight Watchers Program, introduced in 1963, was a boon to the overweight, helping hundreds of thousands of people lose millions of unhealthy, unsightly pounds. In 1972 a revised Program was introduced, which incorporated the latest findings in nutritional information. At that time we also introduced the Leveling Plan, developed to help those people who found that the last 10 pounds before goal were the hardest to lose. The new Leveling Plan provides the extra impetus so necessary if you are to shed that stubborn weight. It leads you to our Maintenance Plan, to be followed when you've reached your goal weight. It's the plan that helps keep you trim forever.

This three-in-one Program has had outstanding results, especially as it now includes the foods that temptation is made of. Who will want to cheat when foods such as spaghetti, rice, potatoes, mayonnaise, and all the delicious new dishes which can be made from them, are "legal?" (By the way, I'd better explain that "legal" is not a reference to law, but rather denotes foods and cooking methods acceptable on our Program.)

Many other innovations have taken place since 1966. Under the continued direction of Albert Lippert, Chairman of the Board, our company has grown tremendously. In our home office, a Food Research Division, headed by Felice Lippert, was created to answer your questions and help in the development and testing of new recipes. There, the staff, including a medical advisor, nutritionists and chefs, works to serve the public—researching, evaluating and compiling information about overweight and obesity.

No weight-control organization in the world is as large—or, I think, as knowledgeable about and as attuned to the problems of the overweight—as we are. And so, since overweight is a problem around the world, the world has beaten a path to our door—you will now find Weight Watchers classes throughout the United States, and in Puerto Rico, Canada, England, Sweden, West Germany, Italy, Australia and South Africa; soon, in other countries.

We have branched out to reach the overweight in other ways too. In 1968 we introduced the *Weight Watchers Magazine,* and today it has a readership of more than two million people a month. Another innovation was the licensing of food companies to produce pre-portioned foods. Thus, you will find in your supermarket freezer fish luncheons and dinners galore, plus turkey, veal, chopped sirloin and other foods. They differ from the commercial TV dinners in offering more of the important (costlier too!) fish and meats and less of the fillers.

We also authorize the marketing of beverages with the low-calorie count that fits into our needs. For members-on-the-go, there are single-serving packets of sugar substitutes, instant non-fat dry milk powder, and instant chicken, beef, and onion broth mixes. Spurred on by America's sweet tooth, our licensed producers have developed marvelous frozen desserts, and an unbelievably delicious fruit snack. We have many other goodies in store for you too—so now, if you "cheat," it won't be because you had no choice on the grocery shelves.

For me, personally, there have been many changes too. I have been told that there are few success stories as sudden and as amazing as mine; I described most of it in my book *The Story of Weight Watchers,* published in 1970. Yes, it is thrilling for me, a formerly fat housewife in a size 44 dress, with no claim to distinction, to know that I founded the world's largest organization of its kind. It's fun to be on national television, to crowd auditoriums when I lecture, to have keys to cities presented to me by mayors, to meet governors (Wisconsin's governor even proclaimed a Jean Nidetch day as part of a Weight Watchers Week). We've been written into the U. S. Congressional Record too.

But above all, my life seems truly significant when I remember that through the Weight Watchers Program so many fat, unhappy people have been born again into thin, happy people. Maybe, this time, it will happen to you . . . or to someone you love.

Jean Nidetch

FOUNDER OF WEIGHT WATCHERS

January 1973

Weight Watchers strongly urges you to consult your physician before and during your participation in the Program.

The Basic Program; Including Menu Plans

Please follow the Program as given. Eat only the foods listed in your Menu Plan, in the quantities and weights specified and at the meals named. Never skip a meal. Foods may be combined in varied ways, as described in our recipes, but remember to count all ingredients. Keeping a daily food record as outlined later in this book will help you do this.

1. DIETETIC PRODUCTS
For the most part, dietetic products are not permitted. The exceptions are the artificial sweeteners, carbonated beverages (see p. 235) and imitation and/or diet margarines (see p. 213).

2. USE AS DESIRED
A number of condiments and seasonings, such as herbs, spices, certain prepared sauces, and beverages, may be used as desired. See p. 235 for a complete list. Note that the products listed under #2A are unlimited; those listed under #2B are limited.

3. VEGETABLES (UNLIMITED AND MODERATE AMOUNTS)
Use fresh, frozen or canned vegetables as listed on p. 244. They may be taken at luncheon, dinner or between meals, but be sure to include at least one #3 vegetable at luncheon. The #3A vegetables are unlimited; the #3B vegetables must be measured (daily, up to 4 cups raw or 2 cups cooked, except for cucumbers, peppers, dill pickles and tomatoes, which are counted). Vary your selections from day to day.

4. VEGETABLES (LIMITED)
Select one vegetable or a combination of several (totaling 4 ounces daily) from the list on p. 286, at noon or evening meal. Vary your selection from day to day. A serving is 4 ounces, weighed after the vegetable is cooked and drained (suggestions for using liquid drained from cooked vegetables are given on p. 284).

5. FRUIT
See your Menu Plan for the amount of fruit you are allowed.

Choose one fruit or juice daily at breakfast. Fruits are divided into 3 groups; see pp. 128-130 for lists and details.

6. FISH, MEAT AND POULTRY

FISH: You must use a minimum of 5 fish meals weekly; follow your Menu Plan for amounts. Fish is divided into 2 categories; choose from the shellfish group only once a week, if desired. You may broil, bake, roast, panbroil, braise, poach or steam fish. See p. 91-92 for further details.

MEAT AND POULTRY: These are divided into Group B and Group C meats. Choose from Group B meats, which may be broiled, baked or roasted, only 3 times a week; choose from Group C meats, which may be broiled, baked, roasted, panbroiled, braised, poached or steamed, as desired. Follow your Menu Plan; see p. 164-165 for lists and further details.

7. LIVER

You must eat liver at least once a week; if you have it more often, count it as a Group C meat. Choose from chicken, calf, lamb, steer, beef, turkey, rabbit or venison liver at noon or evening meal. See p. 152 for further details.

8. BREAD AND CEREAL

BREAD: You may have bread at mealtime only, following your Menu Plan. Use packaged, presliced, enriched white bread, or 100% whole wheat bread (without honey or molasses). Each slice should weigh about 1 ounce. No thin-sliced, dietetic or specialty breads. See p. 23 for further details.

CEREAL: You may have one ounce (or the cup measure equivalent) of any ready-to-eat or uncooked (but not presweetened) cereal, following your Menu Plan. You must have cereal with skim milk. When cereal is selected, your slice of bread may be taken at breakfast or at another meal. See p. 24 for further details.

9. DAILY CHOICE

By omitting one slice of bread from your menu, you may substitute one item from this group. See p. 54 for list of permitted substitutions and further details.

10. FATS

Daily, but at mealtime only, you must use one tablespoon of any one of the fats listed on p. 213 (or 2 tablespoons of imitation—diet

—margarine). The fat may be used in a spread, salad dressing, or sauce; it may also be used in cooking—full details are given on p. 213.

11. EGGS AND CHEESE

EGGS: Use 4 eggs a week for morning or noon meals only. Cook them in shell, poach or scramble without fat. See p. 73 for additional rules.

CHEESE: You may eat cheese as indicated on your Menu Plan, at morning or noon meals only. Do not use more than 4 ounces of hard cheese weekly. Any hard or sliceable cheese, or any soft cheese such as cottage, pot, farmer and ricotta may be used. Further details on p. 40.

12. MILK

See your Menu Plan for amounts of milk permitted; you may have skim milk, evaporated skimmed milk or buttermilk, as described on p. 196. Milks labeled "skimmed milk products" are not allowed on Program.

13. Do not eat or drink the following (except, of course, for "legal" recipes as given in this book):

Alcoholic beverages, beer, wine
Bacon or back fat (fat back)
Beans, dried
Butter
Cake, cookies, crackers, pies
Candy, chocolate
Catsup, chili sauce
Coconut or coconut oil
Corn
Cream, sweet or sour
Cream cheese
Fried foods
Fruit, dried, canned in syrup or dietetic
Ice cream, ice milk, ices and sherbets
Jams, jellies, or preserves
Luncheon meats
Muffins, biscuits
Non-dairy creamers or toppings
Olives or olive oils

Pancakes, waffles
Peanut butter
Peanuts, other nuts
Peas, dried (black-eyed, crowder, chick, etc.)
Pizza
Popcorn, potato chips, pretzels
Pork, pork products
Puddings, custards, flavored gelatin desserts
Raw fish or meat
Rolls, specialty breads
Salad dressings
Sardines
Smoked fish (except finnan haddie and salmon)
Smoked meat
Soda pop, ades, punch
Soups
Sugar
Syrups

MENU PLAN FOR WOMEN

MORNING:
Juice or fruit
Choice of
>Cheese, 1 ounce hard or 2 ounces farmer
>>or ¼ cup cottage or pot cheese
>or Fish, 2 ounces
>or Egg, 1
>or Cereal, 1 ounce with skim milk

Bread, 1 slice
Beverage, if desired

NOON:
Choice of
>Fish, meat or poultry, 4 ounces
>or Cheese, 2 ounces hard or 4 ounces farmer
>>or ⅔ cup cottage or pot cheese
>or Eggs, 2

#3 vegetable, at least 1
#4 vegetable, 4 ounces, if desired
Bread, 1 slice
Beverage, if desired

EVENING:
Choice of
>Fish, meat or poultry, 6 ounces

#4 vegetable, 4 ounces (if not eaten at noon meal)
#3 vegetable, reasonable amounts
Beverage, if desired

DAILY
1 tablespoon vegetable oil, vegetable-oil margarine or mayonnaise
>or 2 tablespoons imitation (or diet) margarine

2 glasses (8 fluid ounces each) skim milk
>or 1 glass (8 fluid ounces) evaporated skimmed milk
>or 1½ glasses (12 fluid ounces) buttermilk

3 fruits
2 #3 vegetables
4 ounces #4 vegetable

WEEKLY
Liver at least once
3 selections from Item #6, Group B
4 eggs
Fish at least 5 times

OPTIONAL DAILY
Bouillon or broth
Tomato Juice
Coffee or Tea
Water

MENU PLAN FOR MEN

MORNING:
Juice or fruit
Choice of
      Cheese, 1 ounce hard or 2 ounces farmer
          or ¼ cup cottage or pot cheese
      or Fish, 2 ounces
      or Egg, 1
      or Cereal, 1 ounce with skim milk
Bread, 2 slices
Beverages, if desired

NOON:
Choice of
      Fish, meat or poultry, 4 ounces
      or Cheese, 2 ounces hard or 4 ounces farmer
          or ⅔ cup cottage or pot cheese
      or Eggs, 2
#3 *vegetable,* at least 1
#4 *vegetable,* 4 ounces, if desired
Bread, 2 slices
Beverage, if desired

EVENING:
Choice of
Fish, meat or poultry, 8 ounces
#4 *vegetable,* 4 ounces (if not eaten at noon meal)
#3 *vegetable,* reasonable amounts
Beverage, if desired

DAILY:

1 tablespoon vegetable oil, vegetable-oil margarine or mayonnaise
       or 2 tablespoons imitation (or diet) margarine
2 glasses (8 fluid ounces each) skim milk
    or 1 glass (8 fluid ounces) evaporated skimmed milk
       or 1½ glasses (12 fluid ounces) buttermilk
5 fruits
2 #3 vegetables
4 ounces #4 vegetable

WEEKLY:

Liver at least once
3 selections from Item #6, Group B
4 eggs
Fish at least 5 times

OPTIONAL DAILY:

Bouillon or broth
Tomato Juice
Coffee or Tea
Water

MENU PLAN FOR YOUTH

MORNING:

Juice or fruit
Choice of
     Cheese, 1 ounce hard or 2 ounces farmer
       or ¼ cup cottage or pot cheese
  or Fish, 2 ounces
  or Egg, 1
  or Cereal, 1 ounce with skim milk
Bread, 1 slice
Skim milk, 1 glass (8 fluid ounces), if desired

NOON:

Choice of
     Fish, meat or poultry, 4 ounces
  or Cheese, 2 ounces hard or 4 ounces farmer
     or ⅔ cup cottage or pot cheese
  or Eggs, 2

#3 vegetable, at least 1
#4 vegetable, 4 ounces, if desired
Bread, 2 slices
Skim milk, 1 glass (8 fluid ounces), if desired

EVENING:
Choice of
Fish, meat or poultry, 6 ounces
#4 vegetable, 4 ounces (if not eaten at noon meal)
#3 vegetable, reasonable amounts
Skim milk, 1 glass (8 fluid ounces), if desired

DAILY:
1 tablespoon vegetable oil, vegetable oil margarine or mayonnaise
       or 2 tablespoons imitation (or diet) margarine
4 glasses (8 fluid ounces each) skim milk
       or 2 glasses (16 fluid ounces) evaporated skimmed milk
       or 3 glasses (8 fluid ounces each) buttermilk
5 fruits
2 #3 vegetables
4 ounces #4 vegetable

WEEKLY:
Liver at least once
3 selections from Item #6, Group B
4 eggs
Fish at least 5 times

OPTIONAL DAILY:
Bouillon or broth
Tomato Juice
Water

MENU SUGGESTIONS FOR ONE WEEK

Follow your Menu Plan as to the amounts permitted; complete Program requirements where necessary.

Breakfast

Monday	Broiled Grapefruit (p. 136), grilled cheese (1 slice bread, 1 ounce hard cheese), beverage
Tuesday	½ cup orange juice, tarragon poached egg (add tarragon vinegar to poaching water), toast, beverage
Wednesday	One cup strawberries, 1 ounce ready-to-eat cereal and skim milk (½ cup)
Thursday	½ cantaloupe, French Toast (p. 73), beverage
Friday	Sliced ripe peach, Not-So-Danish Pastry (p. 47), beverage
Saturday	1 cup tomato juice, Apple Spiced Oatmeal (p. 35), beverage
Sunday	Honeydew melon wedge, smoked salmon platter with 2 ounces smoked salmon on bed of shredded lettuce, 1 medium tomato, sliced and sprinkled with minced chives, Melba Toast Triangles (p. 24), pot of hot coffee or other beverage

Luncheon

Monday	Shrimp Oreganata (p. 126), mixed green salad with Basic French Dressing (p. 227—use 1½ teaspoons vegetable oil) and Croutons (p. 24) made from ½ slice bread, fruit, beverage
Tuesday	Broiled flounder filet, broccoli, bread, Skinny Devil (p. 237), Apricot Buttermilk Mold (p. 133)
Wednesday	Tuna Waldorf Salad (p. 118) in Croustades (p. 28), tomato juice, Lemon Dessert Gelatin Whip (p. 240)
Thursday	Open-face sliced turkey sandwich with garnish of watercress, Potato Salad (p. 64), Cranberry Gelée (p. 136), beverage
Friday	Spinach and Ricotta Gnocchi (p. 47), hearts of lettuce with Thousand Island Dressing (p. 227), Raspberry Italian Ices (p. 146), beverage

Saturday   Artichoke heart cocktail with Herb Spread (p. 223), Mushroom Omelet (p. 80), bread, "Margarita" in a Frosted Glass (p. 237), Pineapple-Peach Sherbet (p. 144)

Sunday   Pizzaiola (p. 42), tossed green salad with Tangy French Dressing (p. 220), Fruit Shake (p. 204)

Dinner

Monday   ½ grapefruit, Poached Salmon (p. 96), sprinkled with dill, steamed zucchini, Hawaiian Beets (p. 289), Fluffy Chocolate Pie (p. 241), beverage

Tuesday   Celery Bisque (p. 246), Mediterranean Lamb Chops (p. 178), Mint Jelly (p. 240), Baked Winter Squash with margarine (p. 301), cooked cauliflower, Cherry Coupe (p. 134), beverage

Wednesday   Mock Split Pea Soup (p. 256), broiled hamburger with Mock Bearnaise Sauce (p. 225), hot sauerkraut or Swedish Coleslaw (p. 261), Water-Fried Onion Rings (p. 295), bread, Baked Apple (p. 130), Hot Mint Tea (p. 238)

Thursday   Calf Liver with Scallion Sauce (p. 156), rice, wax bean salad with tarragon or garlic vinegar (p. 220), Coffee Ice "Cream" (p. 197), beverage

Friday   Chicken Soup (p. 238) with minced dill, or Watercress Soup (p. 253), Gefilte Fish (p. 107) bordered with cooked carrots and green pepper rings, Horseradish Sherbet (p. 252), Poached Fruit (p. 141), beverage

Saturday   Mock Wonton Soup (p. 239) or Chinese Cabbage Soup (p. 264), Chicken Chow Mein (p. 185—including Chinese "Fried" Noodles), English Mustard, Soy Sauce, Pineapple Bavarian Cream (p. 200), hot Oolong Tea

Sunday   Horse's Neck Highball (p. 237), Platter of Crudités (p. 253) with Mock Hollandaise Sauce (p. 225), Roast Beef (p. 166), Puree of Peas (p. 299), Blender Quick Chocolate Ice "Cream" (p. 198), beverage

USING OUR RECIPES

Recipe directions may sometimes look as if they're taking the long way around, but remember, they're all shortcuts to your goal weight! Never try to "get away with" using one pan when we call for two (you may have one less pot to wash, but you'll still have that pot around your middle). Always take the trouble to measure and weigh — don't think you can judge portions by eye.

Divide Evenly

Because of the importance of measuring and weighing on our Program, always follow these rules for recipes for more than one serving: Mix ingredients well, and divide the mixture evenly so every portion has an equal amount of each ingredient. Also, in recipes where the liquid as well as the solid part has to be divided evenly, as in soups:

1) drain the liquid and set aside,
2) divide solid ingredients evenly, and
3) add equal amounts of the liquid to each portion.

Think of the little extra care as "indulging" yourself . . . to a new slim figure and a happier life.

Bread and Cereal

You can't live by bread alone, but it's the basic ingredient for our croutons, crumb piecrusts, canapés, fruitcake and bread puddings. There are even matzo recipes for Passover. And cereal lovers will find a few crunchy concoctions, too. If you're a breakfast sweet-treater, you'll be getting up a little earlier to prepare our Blueberry Muffins or Cannoli. If you like to bake, you won't know whether to transform our simple Piecrust into an Apple, Key Lime, Cherry or Chocolate Meringue Pie; all included here. Party-givers, spread the table with our Party Bread Cases or Bread Lilies. Your guests will feel positively pampered. And so will the kids, when you serve our Fudge Ice "Cream" Roll at their next birthday party.

RULES FOR USING BREAD

1. Amounts:

> WOMAN: 1 slice for breakfast, 1 for lunch
> MAN: 2 slices for breakfast, 2 for lunch
> YOUTH: 1 slice for breakfast, 2 for lunch, 1 for dinner

2. The only breads we permit are the enriched white or 100% whole wheat breads made without honey or molasses. No thin-sliced, dietetic or specialty breads, or breads labeled whole wheat which are not 100% whole wheat (i.e., those made with a mixture of flours).

3. The bread must be eaten at mealtime only; never between meals.

4. *Exceptions:* When you are having cereal for breakfast, you may either have your bread at breakfast, or transfer a slice to another meal. You may also omit one slice of bread from the menu for one of the Daily Choices (but don't do this more than 2 or 3 times a week).

RULES FOR USING CEREAL

1. Cereal may be taken only at breakfast and only with skim milk (a minimum of ½ cup). If you select cereal, you must omit the cheese, egg or fish from your breakfast menu.

2. Ready-to-eat or uncooked cereals are allowed, except the pre-sweetened varieties.

3. The allowed cereal must be weighed on the scale: 1 ounce is allowed. If you are using a cooked cereal, weigh out your ounce before cooking. Then measure the equivalent cup measure for future use.

4. Remember that if cereal is eaten, 1 slice of your required bread may be transferred to another meal, or may be taken at breakfast if preferred.

HOW TO MAKE BREAD CRUMBS

To make the fine, dry, even crumbs we use for piecrusts or sauces, and for topping foods, put two-day-old or slightly stale bread (or fresh bread dried out in 250° F. oven) in blender and blend. To make the coarse crumbs we call for in a light-textured stuffing, pull apart two-day-old bread with a fork.

CROUTONS, BREAD STICKS, MELBA TOAST, ETC.

> 1 slice enriched white bread, cut into any desired shape
> Seasonings to taste (garlic powder, dehydrated onion flakes
>   reconstituted in water, coarse salt, caraway seeds, aniseed,
>   dried herbs, paprika, etc.)
> 1 tablespoon bouillon (optional)

Tear bread into crumbs for croutons; cut into 5 strips for bread sticks; into squares or triangles for melba toast. Bake on aluminum foil pan until bread is crisply toasted, then season heavily with choice of seasonings. Or sprinkle toast with bouillon, dip into seasonings placed in a small bowl and return to oven for a few minutes to dry. Makes 1 serving.

TWOFERS

Sandwiches are not taboo, so enjoy your quota of bread. Arrange your sandwich filling decoratively on one slice of bread, open-face style. Or you can get crafty (just this once) and have "2" slices of bread, and count only 1! Remember the "Twofers" I told you about in the first edition of *Weight Watchers Cookbook?* You cut the bread horizontally to make 2 very thin slices of bread. Pile on sandwich filling. I know it makes you feel good just to see bread on both sides of your sandwich. Or on the day cereal is eaten, you may transfer your one slice of bread from breakfast to make a sandwich with two slices of bread.

BREAD LILIES

1 slice white enriched bread, cut horizontally to make 2 slices
1 recipe Green Grape Jelly (p. 138—count 1 cup seedless grapes)

Flatten bread with rolling pin. Roll, starting at one corner, into a cone shape. Fasten with toothpick and chill. Serve filled with Jelly as a dessert or meat accompaniment. Makes 1 serving.

BREAD STUFFING

There are dozens of ways to use this stuffing. Think of it as a filling for precooked green pepper, tomato, squash or eggplant cases. Bake it in a casserole to accompany your Thanksgiving day bird. Or tuck it under your cooked chicken or fish just before serving.

1 cup diced celery
1 cup chicken bouillon
2 slices day-old bread, cut into coarse crumbs
1 teaspoon salt
Dash pepper
½ teaspoon each thyme, coriander and savory

Cook celery in bouillon until celery is soft and bouillon almost evaporated. Add to bread cubes with seasonings. Moisten with more water or bouillon if dressing seems dry. Makes 2 servings.

CINNAMON TOAST

>1 slice enriched white bread
>1 teaspoon margarine
>Artificial sweetener to equal 2 teaspoons sugar
>¼ teaspoon cinnamon
>Dash nutmeg (optional)

Toast bread lightly in toaster, spread with margarine. Combine sweetener and cinnamon (nutmeg too, if desired), sprinkle on toast, and place toast under broiler for approximately ½ minute, until cinnamon is melted. Makes 1 serving.

VARIATION
Lemon Spice Toast: Prepare cinamon toast as above, adding a dash of grated lemon rind or dehydrated lemon peel to cinnamon-sweetener mixture before sprinkling on toast.

FRUITCAKE

>1⅓ cups instant non-fat dry milk
>½ cup orange juice
>6 small slices pineapple (canned in its own juice) plus 6 table-
> spoons juice
>2 cups frozen cranberries, thawed and chopped
>2 medium apples, peeled, cored and grated
>Artificial sweetener to equal 1½ cups sugar
>2 tablespoons lemon juice
>2 teaspoons cinnamon
>1 teaspoon vanilla or maple extract
>8 slices bread, toasted and made into crumbs

Combine dry milk, orange and pineapple juices and whip with electric mixer until stiff. Add pineapple (cut into chunks), cranberries, apples, sweetener, lemon juice, cinnamon and extract; blend thoroughly. Add bread crumbs and mix well. Line the bottom of a 9x9-inch square cake or loaf pan with brown paper, add fruit mixture and bake for 1 hour at 350° F. Cool on rack, loosen sides with a knife, then invert on a plate. Makes 8 servings.

CANNOLI (ITALIAN PASTRY)

"Pastry" Cases

 2 slices enriched white bread, cut horizontally into twofers
 2 tablespoons cream-flavored dietetic carbonated beverage
 ½ teaspoon vanilla extract
 4 cardboard tubes, each 1½ x 4½ inches, wrapped in
  aluminum foil

Filling

 1⅓ cups ricotta cheese, well drained
 Artificial sweetener to equal ½ cup sugar
 1 teaspoon vanilla extract
 ½ teaspoon orange extract

Prepare "Pastry" Cases: Flatten the twofers with a rolling pin. Combine beverage and vanilla extract and sprinkle over twofers. Roll each slice around a paper tube. Bake at 400° F. for 15 minutes until bread is golden brown. Remove bread from tube and return to oven for 5 minutes more, or until inside is lightly toasted.

Prepare Filling: With an electric mixer, beat ricotta until smooth, add remaining ingredients and continue to beat until light. Spoon equally into prepared "pastry" cases. Chill in refrigerator until very cold. Makes 2 luncheon servings.

BLUEBERRY MUFFINS

 1 slice bread, made into crumbs
 ⅓ cup instant non-fat dry milk
 ½ teaspoon baking soda
 1 tablespoon water
 1 egg, separated
 Artificial sweetener to equal 2 teaspoons sugar
 ½ cup blueberries

Place crumbs, dry milk and baking soda in bowl. Add water, egg yolk, sweetener and blueberries. Fold in stiffly beaten egg white. Pour into non-stick muffin tins and bake at 350° F. for 12 to 15 minutes. Makes 1 serving.

CROUSTADES (PARTY BREAD CASES)

Remove crusts from 1 slice of bread and cut into 4 pieces. Flatten and extend each piece by rolling it with a rolling pin. Press into muffin tin (about 1-inch diameter per cup) and bake at 375° F. for about 10 minutes, or until golden brown. May be filled with chopped liver; flaked tuna fish; broiled ground beef—all weighed first. Place crusts in blender and blend to make crumbs. Sprinkle crumbs on top of filled croustades; garnish with a rolled strip of pimento, if desired. Makes 1 serving; 4 croustades.

FUDGE ICE "CREAM" ROLL
Who needs cookies hidden in the bathroom hamper with recipes like this —

> 4 slices bread, made into fine crumbs
> 2 tablespoons instant non-fat dry milk
> 4 eggs
> Artificial sweetener to equal 2 tablespoons sugar
> 2 tablespoons chocolate extract
> ½ teaspoon vanilla extract
> Few drops brown food coloring
> Ice "Cream" Filling (below)

Combine bread crumbs and dry milk; set aside. Combine remaining ingredients except Ice "Cream" Filling in blender and blend until smooth. Add bread crumb mixture, and blend until thoroughly mixed. Pour batter onto an 11 x 14-inch baking sheet; spread out evenly. Bake at 400° F. for 8 minutes, then immediately roll up in damp towel. Allow to cool, then chill thoroughly and prepare Ice "Cream" Filling (below). When filling is ready, unroll chocolate roll carefully. Spread filling to within one inch of edges of chocolate roll. Reroll, wrap in aluminum foil. Freeze immediately. You can slice the roll into 4 equal portions, wrap each one separately and refreeze. Makes 4 servings.

Ice "Cream" Filling

> 2 cups evaporated skimmed milk, chilled in freezer till crystals
>   form
> Artificial sweetener to equal 5 tablespoons sugar
> 1½ teaspoons vanilla extract
> Dash salt

Whip partially frozen milk with electric mixer. Add other ingredients, stir. Freeze in ice cube trays. Rewhip several times when slightly hard to keep ice from forming.

CHOCOLATE CAKE WITH PINEAPPLE SAUCE

Chocolate Cake

> 4 eggs, separated
> Artificial sweetener to equal 10 teaspoons sugar
> ¼ cup water
> 4 slices enriched white bread, made into fine crumbs
> 8 teaspoons chocolate extract
> Few drops brown food coloring (optional)

Pineapple Sauce

> ½ medium pineapple, peeled and cored
> Artificial sweetener to equal 2 tablespoons sugar
> 2 tablespoons water

Preheat oven to 350° F. In mixing bowl, combine egg yolks, sweetener and water. Whip until light, add bread crumbs and mix. Beat egg whites with electric mixer until stiff peaks form. Add extract and food coloring and beat another two minutes. Carefully fold egg white mixture into yolks. Pour into a 9 x 9-inch pan lined with wax paper. Bake at 350° F. for 30 minutes. Meanwhile, prepare sauce by combining all ingredients in blender. Run at medium speed for one minute, or until pineapple is finely chopped and mixture is of even consistency. Serve each portion of cake with a quarter of the Pineapple Sauce. Makes 4 luncheon servings.

COCONUT BREAD PUDDING

    1 cup skim milk
    1 egg
    Artificial sweetener to equal 6 teaspoons sugar
    ½ teaspoon vanilla
    1 teaspoon coconut extract (optional)
    1 slice enriched white bread, cubed
    Cinnamon to taste
    Hot water

Combine all ingredients except bread, cinnamon and hot water in blender and blend. Pour mixture into small baking dish. Place bread cubes on top and press in. Sprinkle with cinnamon. Set dish in another pan holding ½ inch of water and bake at 350° F. for about 50 minutes or until a knife comes out clean when inserted in mixture. Makes 1 serving.

NOTE: For a fluffier pudding, separate egg yolk and white. Beat white separately until stiff, fold into blended mixture and bake as above.

VARIATIONS

Rhubarb Bread Pudding: Add 1 cup diced raw rhubarb, sprinkled with cinnamon, to the pudding and bake as directed above.

Orange Bread Pudding: Use ½ cup skim milk and ½ cup orange juice (omit 1 cup milk). Season with 1½ teaspoons dehydrated orange peel and ¼ teaspoon orange extract (omit coconut extract and cinnamon). Follow directions above.

PIECRUST (SMALL)

    2 slices fresh enriched white bread, made into crumbs
    Artificial sweetener to equal 2 teaspoons sugar
    ¼ teaspoon vanilla extract
    3 tablespoons water

Place bread crumbs in mixing bowl. Add sweetener, extract and water. Mix to a smooth paste. Press into 8-inch pie pan and bake at 400° F. for 15 minutes or until brown and crisp. Makes 2 servings.

PIECRUST (LARGE)

For a 9- or 10-inch piecrust, use 3 slices toast, ¼ cup water, ½ teaspoon vanilla extract, and artificial sweetener to equal 3 or 4 teaspoons sugar. Follow directions above. Makes 3 servings.

GLAZED FRUIT PIES

1 small piecrust (p. 30 — count ½ slice bread per serving; don't bake piecrust, just refrigerate)
Fruit Filling (see below)
Glaze

    1 teaspoon gelatin
    ¼ cup dietetic carbonated beverage (any flavor)
    2-3 tablespoons hot liquid left from cooking fruit (see below), or (for raw fruit fillings) hot dietetic carbonated beverage
    Few drops food coloring (optional)

Prepare piecrust and filling, and transfer filling to crust. Make glaze by softening gelatin in beverage and dissolving in hot cooking liquid or hot beverage. (Add food coloring, if desired.) Spread glaze evenly over fruit filling. Serve pie immediately or refrigerate and serve chilled. Makes 4 servings.

RAW FRUIT FILLINGS

Banana: Slice 4 medium bananas and sprinkle with lemon juice to prevent discoloration. Use a drop or two of yellow food coloring in the glaze.

Mandarin: Use 2 cups mandarin orange sections with dash of cherry extract, if desired. Use orange-flavored beverage in the glaze.

Pineapple: Crush 8 small slices pineapple (canned in its own juice); use as a filling. Use 8 tablespoons juice for the glaze, and add yellow food coloring to the glaze.

COOKED FRUIT FILLINGS

Spicy Apple: Peel (reserve peelings), core and slice 4 medium apples. Cover with citrus-flavored dietetic carbonated beverage and bring to boil. Cook covered until apples are just tender (don't overcook). Transfer apples to piecrust and reserve cooking liquid. When preparing glaze, add apple peelings to cooking liquid and cook at high heat until reduced to 3 tablespoons liquid. Strain;

add ¾ teaspoon apple pie spice (or cinnamon and dash nutmeg) and artificial sweetener to liquid. Prepare glaze as above. You may also add a dash apple pie spice to the piecrust.

Apricot: Cook 12 sliced apricots in cream-flavored dietetic carbonated beverage to cover. Transfer fruit to piecrust and reserve cooking liquid for making glaze.

Peach or Plum: Cook 4 medium peaches or 4 large plums in orange-flavored beverage; add almond extract if desired. Add yellow food coloring to peach glaze and red to plum.

Strawberry: Cook 4 cups hulled strawberries in water just long enough to draw juices; sweeten artificially if you wish. Color.

KEY LIME PIE

Most Northerners are surprised to learn that Key Lime Pie is yellow — it's the skin of the lime that's green, not the juice.

> 1 large (9-inch) baked Piecrust (p. 31—count 1 slice bread per serving)
> 1 envelope (1 tablespoon) unflavored gelatin
> ½ cup cold water
> 3 eggs, separated
> 4 tablespoons fresh lime or lemon juice
> 1½ teaspoons grated lime or lemon rind
> Artificial sweetener to equal 12 teaspoons sugar
> ¼ teaspoon salt
> ⅓ cup instant non-fat dry milk
> ⅓ cup ice water
> Few drops green food coloring

Cool baked piecrust. Sprinkle gelatin in cold water to soften. Combine in medium saucepan the slightly beaten egg yolks, 3 tablespoons of the lime or lemon juice, rind, sweetener, salt and softened gelatin. Cook over low heat, stirring constantly until liquid is warm and gelatin dissolved. Remove from heat. Cool. In small bowl, combine and beat dry milk powder, ice water and remaining tablespoon lime or lemon juice until stiff peaks form. Fold into gelatin mixture with few drops green food coloring. Beat egg whites until stiff peaks form. Fold gently but thoroughly into gelatin mixture. Fill pie shell. Cool in refrigerator till set. Brown quickly under broiler. Makes 3 servings.

CHERRY PIE

    1 slice enriched white bread, made into crumbs
    ½ cup sweet cherries, pitted
    ¼ cup water
    Artificial sweetener to equal 1 tablespoon sugar, or to taste
    ½ envelope (1½ teaspoons) unflavored gelatin
    Drop cherry extract
    1 teaspoon imitation (or diet) margarine

Sprinkle ¾ of the crumbs into the bottom of a small, round oven-proof dish. Cook cherries in small saucepan with water, sweetener, and gelatin. When cherries are soft, add cherry extract, and pour over crumbs in pan. Top with remaining crumbs. Bake at 350° F. until brown. Remove from oven, top with margarine, put back in warm oven to melt margarine and serve at once. Makes 1 serving.

CHOCOLATE MERINGUE PIE

    1 small (8-inch) Piecrust (p. 30—count 1 slice bread per
        serving)
    1 envelope (1 tablespoon) unflavored gelatin
    2 cups skim milk
    Artificial sweetener to equal 2 tablespoons sugar
    ¼ teaspoon salt
    2 eggs, separated
    1 tablespoon chocolate extract
    ½ teaspoon vanilla extract
    ½ teaspoon imitation butter flavoring
    1 tablespoon brown food coloring, or red and green for brown
    ⅛ teaspoon cream of tartar

Cool baked piecrust. In saucepan over very low heat, combine gelatin, skim milk, sweetener to equal 2 teaspoons sugar and ⅛ teaspoon salt. Bring to simmering temperature, stirring to dissolve gelatin. Beat egg yolks slightly, add a few teaspoons of hot milk to beaten egg yolks, then stir yolks into milk. Cook until mixture thickens slightly, then remove from heat; stir in extracts, butter flavoring and coloring. Pour into piecrust and refrigerate till firm. Beat egg whites, remaining sweetener, remaining salt and cream of tartar until mixture stands in stiff, glossy peaks. Spoon on pie in 4 equal mounds. Broil about 4 inches from source of heat for 30 seconds, or just until meringue is slightly browned. Serve at once, or refrigerate and serve well-chilled. Makes 2 luncheon servings; supplement as required.

VARIATION
Mocha Meringue Pie: Replace skim milk with 2 cups strong coffee; use only 1½ teaspoons chocolate extract and 1½ teaspoons maple extract. Follow recipe above.

SQUASH CHIFFON PIE

> 1 small (8-inch) baked Piecrust (p. 30—count ½ slice bread per serving)
> 4 cups yellow squash (crookneck)
> ½ cup orange juice
> 2 envelopes (2 tablespoons) unflavored gelatin
> Artificial sweetener to equal 8 tablespoons sugar
> ½ teaspoon vanilla extract
> ½ teaspoon each cinnamon and nutmeg

Prepare piecrust, bake and set aside to cool. Wash and slice squash. Cook in lightly salted boiling water until soft (about 10 minutes); drain. Meanwhile, pour orange juice into blender and sprinkle gelatin on top to soften. Add sweetener, vanilla, and hot cooked squash. Turn on blender to mix well. Transfer mixture to piecrust. Sprinkle top with cinnamon and nutmeg and refrigerate till firm. Makes 4 servings.

VARIATION
Squash-Pineapple Chiffon Pie: Put 3 large slices pineapple (canned in its own juice) plus 6 tablespoon juice into blender; puree till crushed. Fold into squash mixture above, before transferring to piecrust. Makes 4 servings and includes 1 fruit for each serving.

CEREAL

Easiest breakfast to prepare is a bowl of cereal garnished with fresh fruit. Try adding any one of these to your 1 ounce cereal with skim milk:

½ cup strawberries, blueberries or raspberries
3 apricots, sliced
1 medium nectarine, or 1 medium peach, sliced or diced
2 small slices pineapple (canned in its own juice) plus 2 tablespoons juice
1 medium banana, sliced
1 medium pear, sliced

You may poach some of the above fruits too, using just enough water to cover, and sweetener to taste; stir poaching liquid into cereal too. Flavorings like raspberry, coconut, or nut extract, and spices like cinnamon, cardamon or nutmeg add zest to breakfast cereals too.

APPLE SPICED OATMEAL

1 ounce uncooked oatmeal
½ medium apple, cored, peeled and sliced very thin
¼ teaspoon cinnamon
¼ teaspoon nutmeg
1 teaspoon orange extract
1 tablespoon imitation (or diet) margarine
Brown sugar replacement to taste (optional)
½ cup skim milk

Be sure to weigh the cereal before it is cooked. Cook cereal according to package directions, but add the sliced apple. Stir cinnamon and nutmeg, extract and margarine into cooked cereal, mix well and serve hot with skim milk and brown sugar replacement, if desired. Makes 1 serving.

PASSOVER RECIPES
(*Substituting matzo for bread*)

During (and only during) Passover, you may use one-half board of regular or whole wheat matzo in place of 1 slice bread. Egg matzo is "illegal."

MATZO FRY (A MATZO OMELET)

> 1 matzo board
> Boiling water
> 2 eggs, well beaten
> ¼ teaspoon salt
> Dash of pepper
> Artificial sweetener to taste
> Cinnamon

Break matzo into 2-inch pieces and place in colander. Scald by pouring boiling water over them. Drain quickly to prevent sogginess. Add eggs, salt and pepper to the matzo. Heat a large non-stick skillet. Add the egg mixture and cook over low heat to golden brown on one side, then turn carefully and brown on the other side. Sprinkle with artificial sweetener and cinnamon, if desired. Divide evenly. Makes 2 servings.

MATZO OMELET WITH APPLE FILLING

> 2 eggs
> ½ cup skim milk
> ¼ teaspoon salt
> 1 matzo board
> Apple Filling (recipe below)

Combine eggs, milk and salt; beat well. Break matzo into small pieces and add to egg mixture, mixing lightly. Let stand to soften matzo. Pour mixture into heated non-stick skillet, cover; cook over moderate heat 5-8 minutes. Turn the pancake and finish cooking for another 2 minutes. Remove from pan. Spread evenly with Apple Filling and roll. Sprinkle with artificial sweetener. Makes 2 servings.

Apple Filling

    2 medium apples, peeled, cored and diced
    6 tablespoons water
    ½ teaspoon cinnamon
    Artificial sweetener to taste (optional)

Combine all ingredients in saucepan and cook until apples are tender. Remove from heat. Stir with a fork to smooth out the mixture, but allow some apples to remain in pieces. Makes 2 servings.

LUKSHEN KUGEL (PUDDING)

    1 matzo board, broken into pieces
    2 eggs
    ½ cup skim milk
    Dash of salt
    2 cups cream-flavored dietetic carbonated beverage
    ⅔ cup cottage cheese
    1 medium apple, peeled, cored and coarsely grated
    Artificial sweetener to equal 4 teaspoons sugar, or to taste
    Cinnamon

Place matzo in blender container and blend into fine crumbs. Add 1 egg, half of the milk and salt and blend until smooth. Pour small amount of batter into a hot, non-stick skillet, covering entire surface. Cook until slightly brown on one side, turn and cook 10-15 seconds longer. Repeat until all of the batter has been used. Makes 3-4 blintzes.

Cut blintzes into ¼-inch strips to resemble noodles. Bring beverage to a boil, add blintz strips and cook for about 2½ minutes. Drain. Combine with cottage cheese and apple, and toss. Place in small baking dish. In a bowl, beat remaining egg lightly, and combine with remaining milk and sweetener. Pour over cheese-and-blintz mixture. Toss and sprinkle with cinnamon. Bake at 350° F. for about 15-20 minutes or until kugel is firm. Makes 2 servings.

VARIATION
Passover Blintzes: Make 4 blintzes following directions above. Fill blintzes with ⅔ cup cottage cheese and artificial sweetener to equal

1 teaspoon sugar. Fold to enclose stuffing and bake on non-stick baking sheet at 375° F. till heated. Makes 2 luncheon servings.

CARROT MATZO KUGEL (PUDDING)

12 ounces grated carrots
1½ matzo boards, made into crumbs
3 eggs, slightly beaten
1 tablespoon dehydrated onion flakes
1 teaspoon salt
1 tablespoon vegetable oil
1 cup chicken bouillon
2 teaspoons minced parsley

Combine all ingredients and mix well. Pour into 1½-quart baking dish. Bake in a moderate oven (325° F.) for 50 minutes or until firm. Makes 3 servings.

MATZO BALLS FOR SOUP

2 matzo boards, crumbled
¾ teaspoon salt
4 eggs, separated
4 quarts rapidly boiling water
4 servings Chicken Soup (p. 238)
Chopped parsley for garnish

Place matzos in blender and blend to make fine meal. Add salt. Beat egg whites until stiff, and beat egg yolks separately until smooth and lemon-colored. Fold whites into yolks, then fold in matzo meal. Refrigerate for 1 hour. With wet hands, divide mixture into 12 equal portions and shape each portion into a ball. Drop into water and cook 20-25 minutes. Remove balls with slotted spoon, and add to hot chicken soup. Garnish with parsley. Makes 4 servings.

NOTE: In any recipe for more than one serving, divide mixture evenly, following the directions on page 22.

Cheese

You can do so much with an ounce or two of cheese! On our list are some that are mild and mellow, nippy or salty, sweet and nutlike or sharp and pungent. Use your favorites in dips, open-faced sandwiches, au gratin, in salads, soups, quiches, soufflés, rarebits, ragouts. Yes, even in pizza, in my own special version of a "dumpling," and wonder of them all — a cheesecake.

You'll discover how to make our Sour Cream and a delicious spreadable Cream Cheese, "legal" because it has a cottage-cheese base. And, having learned that, you can then serve that most luscious of all French cheese dishes, Coeur a la Crême.

Keep a variety on hand for convenience. Storage of cheese is no trick at all when you know how. The enemies are evaporation of moisture, and mold that wasn't planned at the cheesemakers. To keep hard or semi-hard cheeses from drying out, always cover the cut side tightly; it will retain freshness for several weeks. You cannot expect such longevity for soft cheeses. Use them within a few days.

Hard cheeses can be kept even longer by freezing. Divide into serving amounts, because, once unfrozen, the cheese should be used promptly. Wrap airtight in small packages, or grate and store in convenient sizes, freeze in freezer, then use for cooking following your Menu Plan.

A foreign name doesn't necessarily mean imported. Many cheeses that originated abroad are now manufactured in the United States but still go by their foreign names.

RULES FOR USING CHEESE

1. Amounts:

> BREAKFAST: 1 ounce hard or 2 ounces farmer or ¼ cup cottage or pot cheese

> LUNCH: 2 ounces hard or 4 ounces farmer or ⅔ cup cottage or pot cheese.

2. Do not use more than 4 ounces of hard (or semi-hard) cheese weekly.

3. Cheeses are "illegal" if they are soft enough to spread evenly and not hard enough to slice easily. Do not use cheese products or cheese spreads.

4. Any hard or sliceable cheese and any soft cheese which does not spread smoothly are approved. Follow your Menu Plan. The following cheeses are permitted:

Hard or Semi-Hard

AMERICAN CHEESE—MILD TO SHARP

BLEU—SHARP AND SPICY

CANADIAN SLICES

CHEDDAR—MILD TO SHARP

COLBY AND COON (TYPE OF CHEDDAR)—MILD TO SHARP

EDAM—MILD AND NUTLIKE

FARMER—(COLBY-TYPE)— AVAILABLE IN CANADA

FETA—SLIGHTLY SALTY

MONTEREY JACK (MONTEREY, OR JACK CHEESE)—MILD

MOZZARELLA—MILD

MUENSTER—MILD TO MELLOW

PARMESAN—SHARP, PIQUANT

PORT DU SALUT (OKA)—MELLOW TO ROBUST

RICOTTA SALATA

ROMANO—SHARP, SALTY

ROQUEFORT—SHARP AND SPICY

STILTON—PIQUANT, SPICY

SWISS—SWEET, NUTLIKE

TILSIT—MILD TO SHARP

Soft

BASKET

COTTAGE (SKIM MILK VARIETY PREFERRED)

FARMER

POT

RICOTTA

CHEESE AND CLAM BOWL
Serve with raw vegetables for the noon meal.

⅓ cup cottage cheese
2 teaspoons lemon juice
1 teaspoon Worcestershire
2 teaspoons minced parsley
2 ounces minced clams

Blend cottage cheese, lemon juice, Worcestershire and minced parsley in a blender (or mash well by hand). Stir in clams. Chill in small serving bowl at least 30 minutes. Makes 1 luncheon serving.

CREAMY ROQUEFORT DRESSING

1 ounce Roquefort or bleu cheese
1 tablespoon water
1 tablespoon vegetable oil
1 tablespoon wine vinegar
Salt and pepper
Dash dry mustard and celery seed

Mash Roquefort or bleu cheese with a fork; stir in water and vegetable oil. Add wine vinegar and seasonings. Serve on fruit or on green salad. Makes 1 luncheon serving; supplement as required.

CHEESE AND EGG DUMPLINGS

1 slice bread, made into crumbs
1 egg, beaten slightly
1 ounce grated cheddar cheese
Dash salt and pepper
1 recipe hot Chicken Soup (p. 238)

Combine bread crumbs with beaten egg, cheese, salt and pepper. Mix well and refrigerate for 30 minutes or more. Shape into small cheese dumplings and drop into hot soup. Simmer covered for 10 minutes. Makes 1 luncheon serving.

TOMATO AND FETA CHEESE SALAD
Feta is a Greek cheese made from sheep or goat milk.

1 clove garlic (optional)
2 medium tomatoes
1 tablespoon dehydrated onion flakes, reconstituted in 1 tablespoon water
½ teaspoon salt
1 tablespoon vegetable oil
2 ounces feta cheese, cut up

Rub small salad bowl with cut garlic. Dice tomatoes and sprinkle with onion flakes, salt and oil. Top with feta cheese. Makes 1 luncheon serving.

FARMER CHEESE-BERRY

2 ounces farmer cheese
1 slice bread, lightly toasted
½ cup strawberries
¼ teaspoon vanilla extract

Spread farmer cheese on toasted bread and set under broiler until top browns. Mash strawberries, season with vanilla and serve over cheese toast. Makes 1 breakfast serving.

PIZZAIOLAS—A DELICIOUS LUNCH
These little pizzas can also be made with 1 medium sliced tomato instead of thickened tomato juice. I like to hide the seasoning under the cheese, where the heat won't scorch it and make it bitter.

1 slice enriched white bread
½ cup tomato juice, cooked down to half volume
Dash of oregano, garlic powder and basil or Italian seasoning spice
2 ounces hard cheese, cut up

Toast bread lightly, spread with thickened juice, sprinkle on seasoning and add cheese. Broil until cheese is melted. Makes 1 serving.

VARIATIONS

Tuna Pizza: Follow recipe above, but use only 1 ounce hard cheese. Combine 2 ounces tuna fish with seasonings, distribute over tomato juice, top with cheese and proceed according to directions.

Roasted Pepper Pizza: Toast one slice of bread. Flatten a pimento on toast; add slices of ½ medium tomato seasoned with a dash red hot sauce and a pinch of Italian spices or rosemary. Cover with 2 ounces of hard cheese, sliced thin. Broil until cheese is melted and bubbly brown.

REUBEN SANDWICH

    1 slice 100% whole wheat bread
    2 ounces sliced cooked white meat turkey
    ¼ cup drained sauerkraut
    1 ounce sliced Swiss cheese
    Watercress
    ½ medium dill pickle, sliced
    Radish roses

Toast bread lightly. Arrange slices of turkey on the toast. Spread sauerkraut over turkey and top with cheese. Bake at 450° F. or put under broiler until the sandwich is thoroughly heated and cheese is melted. Garnish with watercress, dill pickle and radish roses. Makes 1 luncheon serving.

CHEESE RAREBIT FOR ONE
You may omit toast and serve rarebit on a sliced tomato.

    2 ounces grated hard cheese
    ¼ cup Tomato Sauce (½ cup tomato juice reduced by half)
    Dash of salt and cayenne pepper
    1 slice toast

In a saucepan set over low heat, melt cheese. Stir in Tomato Sauce. Season with salt and pepper. When thoroughly hot, serve on toast. Makes 1 luncheon serving.

CHEESE AND POTATO RAGOUT
Remember to omit bread when you use potato.

>   1 medium (3-ounce) potato, boiled and diced
>   ½ cup fresh mushrooms, sliced and cooked
>   2 tablespoons shredded pimento
>   Salt and pepper
>   ½ cup skim milk
>   2 ounces grated sharp cheddar or Swiss cheese
>   Dash paprika or cayenne pepper

In a shallow pan, make layers of potato, mushrooms and pimento and sprinkle with salt and pepper. Pour in milk, top with cheese and sprinkle with paprika. Bake at 325° F. until bubbly. Makes 1 luncheon serving.

VARIATIONS
1. Replace or supplement potatoes with other cooked (or canned) vegetables such as 1 cup broccoli, asparagus, cauliflower, or replace with ½ cup cooked enriched rice or lima beans.

2. Bake the cheese-potato mixture in 2 parboiled medium green peppers. Omit mushrooms so you do not exceed daily allowance of #3B vegetables.

CREAMY LUNCHEON ASPIC

>   1 envelope (1 tablespoon) unflavored gelatin
>   ½ cup cold water
>   1⅓ cups cottage cheese
>   2 tablespoons mayonnaise
>   1 teaspoon Worcestershire
>   Few drops red hot sauce
>   Salt

Sprinkle gelatin over cold water in small saucepan. Place over low heat, stirring constantly until gelatin dissolves. Remove from heat. Combine remaining ingredients in blender container, and puree until smooth. Add to gelatin mixture; mix well. Pour into small ring mold which has been rinsed in cold water. Refrigerate to chill. Unmold and fill center with greens or other unlimited (#3A) vegetables. Makes 2 servings.

ENCHILADA

½ cup Catsup (p. 215—count 1½ cups or 12 fluid ounces tomato juice)
1 tablespoon dehydrated onion flakes
1 medium tomato, chopped
½ clove garlic, minced
1 tablespoon chopped green chili peppers
Dash artificial sweetener
½ teaspoon ground cumin
¼ teaspoon salt
¼ teaspoon oregano
¼ teaspoon basil
2 ounces shredded Monterey Jack cheese
1 slice bread, toasted

Put all ingredients (except cheese and toast) in saucepan and simmer for 15 minutes. Dip toast in mixture and moisten both sides. Put coated toast in small ovenproof serving dish and top with shredded cheese and remaining sauce. Bake at 350° F. for 15 to 20 minutes. Makes 1 serving.

CHEESE SOUFFLE

1 ounce finely diced or grated cheese (Swiss, Parmesan or cheddar)
½ cup skim milk
½ slice bread, made into crumbs
1 egg, separated
Dash salt, cayenne, dry mustard or grated nutmeg

Combine cheese, skim milk and bread crumbs in small saucepan and heat slowly until cheese is melted. Remove from heat and add slightly beaten egg yolk, salt, cayenne and mustard (or nutmeg). Beat egg white until stiff. Fold gently into cheese mixture. Transfer to small casserole and bake about 30 minutes in 375° F. oven until puffy and well browned. Makes 1 luncheon serving.

CHILE RELLENOS (Stuffed Peppers Mexicano)

4 green chiles, or roasted pimentos
1 ounce Monterey Jack cheese
1 egg, separated
1 tablespoon water
Pinch salt
1 slice bread, made into crumbs
1 cup tomato juice
1 clove garlic
Dash of cayenne or oregano

Remove seeds from chilies. (Or use long "fingers" of roasted pimentos folded in half lengthwise.) Cut cheese into strips and stuff into chilies. Mix egg yolk with water. Beat egg white with salt until it is very stiff. Fold yolk into stiff egg whites. Add crumbs, stir. Dip chiles into batter. Refrigerate ½ hour. Heat tomato juice with remaining ingredients. Cook chiles in tomato juice mixture until they're thoroughly heated. Makes 1 luncheon serving.

CHEESE AND ONION QUICHE (PIE)

1 small (8-inch) Piecrust (p. 30—count 1 slice bread per serving)
8 ounces onion, cut into thin slices
1 cup water
½ envelope instant chicken broth and seasoning mix
2 ounces sharp cheddar or Swiss cheese, shredded
2 eggs, beaten
½ cup evaporated skimmed milk
½ teaspoon salt
¼ teaspoon pepper
¼ teaspoon nutmeg

Cool piecrust. Preheat oven to 400° F. Water-fry onions in saucepan with water and broth mix. When onions are translucent, transfer to piecrust. Arrange cheese over onions, combine remaining ingredients, and pour into pie shell. Bake on lowest rack of oven for 10 minutes. Reduce temperature to 325° F. and bake until custard is set, about 45 minutes more. Makes 2 luncheon servings.

SPINACH AND RICOTTA GNOCCHI (DUMPLINGS)

>1 cup cooked, drained chopped spinach
>⅓ cup ricotta cheese
>Salt and pepper
>1 egg, beaten
>1 slice bread, made into crumbs
>Dash nutmeg

Squeeze out liquid from spinach. In small saucepan over low heat cook spinach, with cheese, salt and pepper. Stir frequently to prevent burning. When mixture is hot, remove from heat, stir in egg, bread crumbs and nutmeg, mixing well. Chill for 2 hours or longer. Drop by rounded teaspoonfuls onto non-stick baking sheet (or sheet lined with aluminum foil), and bake at 400° F. for 15 minutes or until browned. Serve hot. Makes 1 luncheon serving.

NOT-SO-DANISH PASTRY

>¼ cup cottage cheese
>Artificial sweetener to equal 1 teaspoon sugar
>Dash of cinnamon
>½ teaspoon flavor extract (vanilla, coconut, black walnut, etc.)
>1 slice toast

Mix cottage cheese with sweetener, cinnamon and flavor extract. Spread on toast and place under broiler until bubbly and hot. We think this tastes somewhat like a fresh-baked cheese Danish. Makes 1 serving.

VARIATIONS

1. Use imitation butter flavoring and add ¼ teaspoon dehydrated orange peel. Roll freshly-made toast with rolling pin to flatten, then cut diagonally in half. Divide cheese mixture over toast halves, roll up, secure with toothpicks and bake in preheated oven, at 375° F., for 10 minutes.

2. Omit sweetener and flavoring, combine cheese with caraway seeds and salt, spread on toast — and think of rye bread.

CHEESE AND RATATOUILLE FONDUE (NO EGG)

> 1 slice bread, made into crumbs
> 2 ounces finely diced or grated hard cheese
> 1 serving Ratatouille (p. 270—count ¾ daily allowance of
> #3B vegetables)
> ½ cup skim milk
> 1 garlic clove

Combine first four ingredients and mix well. Rub inside of small casserole with cut clove of garlic, add the cheese mixture and bake at 375° F. until piping hot and bubbly. Or put all of these ingredients except the garlic clove into a blender and turn on motor to make a smooth mixture. Transfer to garlicky casserole and bake as directed. Makes 1 luncheon serving.

CHEESE LATKES (PANCAKES)

You don't have to be Jewish to enjoy latkes. They're a great treat even without the blueberry topping; with it — yummy. Use any approved fruit in season as a topping.

> 1 egg, well beaten
> ⅓ cup cottage cheese
> ⅓ cup skim milk
> ¼ teaspoon salt
> 1 slice bread, made into crumbs
> Blueberry Topping (see recipe below)

Combine the ingredients and mix well. Drop by spoonfuls onto hot non-stick pan. Brown lightly on both sides. Serve with Blueberry Topping. Makes 1 serving.

Blueberry Topping

> ½ cup blueberries
> 1 tablespoon water
> Artificial sweetener to equal 2 teaspoons sugar

Combine the ingredients, cover and simmer slowly until berries are soft. Makes 1 serving.

HOMEMADE SOUR CREAM (FROM COTTAGE CHEESE)

⅔ cup cottage cheese
¼ cup butermilk, skim milk or water
½ teaspoon lemon juice
Salt (optional)

Combine all ingredients in blender and run until smooth. Remove from blender container and serve immediately or refrigerate. Excellent dressing for crisp salad greens, cooked vegetables or crudités (p. 253). Makes 1 luncheon serving.

CHERRY CHEESECAKE

Cheesecake

⅔ cup cottage cheese
Artificial sweetener to equal 6 tablespoons sugar
1 tablespoon grated lemon rind
½ teaspoon vanilla extract
2 eggs, separated
¼ cup evaporated skimmed milk
⅓ cup instant non-fat dry milk

Cherry Topping

1 cup sweet cherries, pitted
¼ cup cherry-flavored dietetic carbonated beverage
Artificial sweetener to taste
¼ teaspoon cherry extract

Make Cheesecake: Combine cottage cheese, sweetener, lemon rind, vanilla extract, egg yolks, evaporated milk and dry milk in blender and blend for about 1 minute until well mixed. Transfer to bowl. In another bowl beat egg whites until they stand in stiff peaks; fold into cheese mixture. Transfer to springform pan and bake 10 minutes at 450° F., reduce heat to 325° F., bake 40 minutes more.
Make Cherry Topping: In covered saucepan, cook cherries in beverage until they are tender and liquid is evaporated. Sweeten, add extract, spread over baked cheesecake and return to oven 5 minutes more. Makes 2 luncheon servings.

STRAWBERRY-CHEESE BAVARIAN

> 1⅓ cups cottage cheese
> 1 envelope (1 tablespoon) unflavored gelatin
> ¼ cup cold water
> Artificial sweetener to equal 2 tablespoons sugar
> ¼ teaspoon salt
> 2 cups ripe strawberries
> ¼ teaspoon berry extract

Make Sour Cream by pureeing cottage cheese in blender with just enough water (a tablespoon or two) to start the blender. Sprinkle gelatin over ¼ cup water in small saucepan to soften, then place over low heat, stirring constantly to dissolve gelatin. Remove from heat, stir in sweetener and salt. Combine 1 cup of the berries and berry extract, mash lightly and add to gelatin mixture. Fold in the Sour Cream and pour into a wet 3-cup mold or bombe. Chill until firm, 2-3 hours or so. Unmold and garnish with reserved strawberries. Makes 4 luncheon servings; supplement as required.

CHEESE AU GRATIN TOPPING (FOR COOKED VEGETABLES)
Asparagus, green beans, broccoli, cabbage, cauliflower, eggplant or any of our #3B vegetables may be done this way.

> 1½ cups cooked #3B vegetables
> ½ cup fresh or canned, drained mushrooms, sliced
> 2 ounces hard cheese, grated
> 1 slice bread, made into crumbs
> ½ teaspoon mixed dried herbs, or 1 tablespoon any fresh minced herbs (e.g., parsley, chives, basil, etc.)
> Salt and pepper
> ¼ cup tomato juice or other liquid (see note)

In small aluminum foil pan or casserole, layer vegetables, mushrooms, cheese (reserve 2 tablespoons) and herbs; sprinkle with salt and pepper. Stir in tomato juice or other liquid. Mix reserved cheese with the crumbs and spread on top of vegetables. Bake at 350° F. till hot and bubbly. Makes 1 luncheon serving.

DANISH CHEESE TOPPING
To serve over cooked vegetables at lunch.

> 2 radishes
> 1 rib celery
> 1 teaspoon dehydrated pepper flakes, in 1 tablespoon water
> 1 envelope instant onion broth and seasoning mix
> Dash garlic powder
> ⅔ cup cottage or pot cheese

Cut vegetables coarsely, put in blender and blend until finely minced. Add seasonings and cottage cheese, and blend until smooth. Store in refrigerator for 2 hours or more before serving. Makes 2 luncheon servings; supplement as required.

CREAM CHEESE

> 1½ teaspoons unflavored gelatin
> 3 tablespoons cold water or dietetic ginger ale
> ⅔ cup cottage or pot cheese, or 4 ounces farmer cheese
> ⅛ teaspoon vanilla extract
> Dash imitation butter flavoring

Sprinkle gelatin over cold water in small saucepan. Place over low heat, stirring constantly until gelatin dissolves, about 3 minutes. In blender, mash cheese (add a few tablespoons of water if necessary). When mixture is smooth and creamy, add dissolved gelatin, vanilla extract and butter flavoring. Mix well. Transfer mixture to an ice cube tray (divider removed). Chill in refrigerator till set. Divide into 2 equal servings; wrap each serving in wax paper and refrigerate up to 2 days. Makes 2 luncheon servings; supplement as required.

SERVING SUGGESTIONS
1. Use 1 serving Cream Cheese with 2 ounces smoked salmon (lox).
2. You may spread Cream Cheese on bread or mound it over 2 medium pear halves.

VARIATIONS

1. Omit vanilla extract and imitation butter flavoring, and vary the seasonings as you wish. Minced chives, dill or parsley; dehydrated onion flakes reconstituted in water; shredded pimentos; garlic powder or finely shredded garlic; dry or prepared mustard; etc. Or sweeten to taste with artificial sweetener and fruit-flavored extract.

2. *Blueberry Cream Cheese Pie:* Prepare an 8-inch Piecrust (p. 30—count ½ slice bread per serving). Fill with 2 recipes Cream Cheese (count ⅓ cup cottage cheese per serving). Cook 1 cup fresh blueberries in a few tablespoons water, add artificial sweetener to equal 1 tablespoon sugar, zip up the flavor with a few drops of lemon juice, cool, and spread this blueberry topping over Cream Cheese Pie. Makes 4 luncheon servings; supplement as required.

COEUR A LA CREME

> 1 recipe Cream Cheese (p. 51—count ⅓ cup cottage
>   cheese per serving)
> Artificial sweetener to equal 2 tablespoons sugar
> 1 cup fresh strawberries, washed and hulled
> 1 sprig parsley

This glamorous dessert is easy to make. When preparing Cream Cheese, add sweetener, and then before chilling, pour into your heart-shaped mold rather than an ice cube tray. Refrigerate until firm. Unmold on dessert plate and surround with whole strawberries. Garnish with a sprig of parsley, spread out on cheese to form a flower. It's pretty enough to use for a Fourth of July party (red and white against a dark blue glass plate) or for Valentine's Day. Makes 2 luncheon servings; supplement as required.

FROZEN STRAWBERRY CREAM

> 4 cups fresh strawberries
> Artificial sweetener to equal 6 tablespoons sugar
> 1⅓ cups cottage cheese
> 3 tablespoons lemon juice

Puree berries in blender and transfer to mixing bowl. Stir in sweetener. Add cheese and lemon juice to blender and liquefy. Transfer creamed mixture to bowl holding berries and beat smooth with rotary beater. Transfer mixture to shallow container, cover with sheet of wax paper and freeze firm (2-3 hours). Makes 4 luncheon servings; supplement as required.

RICOTTA CONDITA

⅔ cup ricotta cheese
⅓ cup skim milk
Artificial sweetener to equal 6 teaspoons sugar
1 teaspoon rum extract
Instant coffee powder (expresso if available)

Beat ricotta cheese and skim milk in a bowl until creamy. Stir in sweetener and rum extract. Mix well. Spoon into 2 champagne or dessert glasses. Refrigerate until well chilled. Sprinkle lightly with instant coffee. Serve as dessert with fresh fruit. Or use as a sweet main dish for lunch, on mixed salad greens. Makes 2 servings; supplement as required.

DESSERT CHEESE PLATTER

The most popular dessert in France is the platter of cheese, often found in the company of fresh fruit. You could plan a vegetable luncheon, then finish with a cheese display. The recipe which follows is for a single serving.

1 ounce of any of the following hard cheeses: Bleu, Cheddar, Colby, Coon, Edam, Monterey jack, Muenster, Port du Salut, Roquefort, Swiss, Tilsit
⅓ cup cottage, pot or ricotta cheese, or 2 ounces farmer cheese, or 1 serving Cream Cheese (p. 51—count ⅓ cup cottage cheese)
1 medium apple, pear, or other fruit, cored and cut into wedges
1 serving Strawberry Jelly (p. 138—count ¼ cup strawberries)
1 slice toast, cut into fingers

Arrange cheeses, fruit, jelly mound and toast fingers on a dessert plate or small cheese board. Makes 1 luncheon serving.

Daily Choice

Who would have believed, back in 1966 when we published the first *Weight Watchers Cookbook,* that some day we'd be giving recipes for spaghetti and potatoes, beans and rice! We've added a whole new food grouping called Daily Choice and a new chapter to cover it.

What's in it for you? Macaroni and cheese. Spanish Rice, Rice Pilafs, Rice Puddings. Potato pancakes and chips. A succulent bean chowder. Tamale Pie, and dozens of other can't-believe-it's-true dishes.

What's *not* in it for you? Dried peas or beans. Brown rice or wild rice. Potatoes fried in fat. And, on the day you choose from this new group, one slice of bread.

RULES FOR USING DAILY CHOICE GROUP

By omitting 1 slice of bread from your menu, you may substitute one item from the following list, if desired. This option may be exercised only once a day, and you must vary your daily choice from day to day.

Beans, butter: ½ cup cooked
Beans, lima: ½ cup cooked
Cornmeal (enriched), yellow or white: 1 ounce
Cowpeas and/or black-eyed peas: ½ cup cooked
Hominy Grits (enriched): ¾ cup cooked
Pasta (enriched): ½ cup cooked noodles (see note)
⠀⠀⠀⠀⠀⠀⠀⠀⠀½ cup cooked pastina (see note)
⠀⠀⠀⠀⠀⠀⠀⠀⠀⅔ cup cooked macaroni or spaghetti
Potato: 1 medium (about 3 ounces) baked or boiled
Rice (enriched), white: ½ cup cooked

NOTE: Green noodles and green pastina are permitted.

BEAN AND VEGETABLE CHOWDER

> 1½ cups boiling water
> 2 envelopes instant chicken, beef or onion broth and
>   seasoning mix
> ½ cup sliced celery and celery tops
> ½ cup shredded cabbage
> ½ cup chopped mixed vegetables (green beans, spinach,
>   zucchini, etc.)
> 1 medium tomato, diced
> 1 tablespoon fresh minced parsley
> 1 teaspoon dehydrated onion flakes
> 1 clove
> ¼ clove garlic
> ¼ bay leaf
> Dash dried basil or fresh basil leaf
> Salt and pepper
> ½ cup cooked lima beans

In large soup kettle, combine all ingredients except cooked lima beans. Simmer covered about 50 minutes. Add lima beans and heat a few minutes. Remove bay leaf. Serve in large soup bowls. Makes 1 serving.

SPICY LIMA BEAN AND APPLE STEW

Cooked beans are something special baked or simmered with fruit! Try sliced pineapple, pears or—

> 1 tart medium apple, peeled, cored and sliced
> ¼ cup water
> Dash each of salt, pepper, and allspice
> ½ teaspoon dehydrated onion flakes
> ½ cup cooked lima beans
> Dash curry powder

Simmer slices of apple in water seasoned with salt, pepper, allspice and onion flakes. When soft, add cooked lima beans and curry powder. Heat. Serve as main dish accompaniment. Makes 1 serving.

LIMA BEANS AND MUSHROOMS AU GRATIN

½ cup cooked lima beans
½ cup skim milk
½ cup cooked or canned mushrooms, sliced
1 teaspoon dehydrated onion flakes
1 teaspoon margarine
Dash each of cayenne pepper and salt
2 ounces grated Swiss cheese

In small baking dish combine lima beans, milk, mushrooms, onion flakes and margarine with cayenne pepper and salt; toss. Top with grated cheese. Bake 20 minutes at 350° F. Makes 1 luncheon serving.

SWEDISH LIMA BEANS

⅓ cup cottage or 2 ounces farmer cheese
¼ cup skim milk
1 ounce bleu cheese
1 teaspoon minced fresh parsley
1 teaspoon minced fresh chives
1 cup cooked and drained lima beans

In blender container, combine cottage or farmer cheese, milk, bleu cheese, parsley and chives; run blender for 30 seconds. Divide lima beans and pour half of cheese mixture over each serving. Refrigerate and serve cold. Makes 2 luncheon servings; supplement as required.

SPOON BREAD

1 cup boiling water
¼ teaspoon salt
1 ounce enriched cornmeal
1 egg
¼ cup skim milk
Artificial sweetener to equal 2 tablespoons sugar (optional)

Pour boiling water and salt over cornmeal in top of double boiler and cook over hot water for 30 minutes, stirring often. Remove from heat. Beat together egg, milk and sweetener. Mix into cornmeal and stir till free from lumps. Transfer to shallow non-stick baking pan and bake at 400° F. about 20 minutes, to brown top. Serve hot (with spoon) as a filling breakfast dish. Also a delicious luncheon dish; supplement as required. Makes 1 serving.

VARIATION

Cornmeal Muffins: Prepare Spoon Bread batter, transfer to muffin tins lined with paper cups (batter should fill cups about ⅔). Bake for about 20 minutes at 400° F. Makes 1 serving.

"TAMALE" PIE (CORNMEAL)

The amount of chili powder you use depends on how spicy you like your food. Tomatoes may be replaced by ½ cup Tomato Sauce (p. 216), ½ medium green pepper may be added too.

> 1 ounce enriched cornmeal
> 4 tablespoons salted cold water
> ½ cup boiling water
> 1 medium tomato, diced
> 6 ounces cooked ground beef or cooked, finely diced all-beef frankfurters
> Salt and pepper
> Dash each garlic powder and chili powder
> 1 teaspoon dehydrated onion flakes

Mix cornmeal to a paste in salted water. Gradually stir it into boiling water, cover and cook slowly for 20 minutes. Combine tomatoes with cooked meat. Stir in seasonings. In small casserole, arrange layers of cornmeal mush and beef-and-tomato mixture and bake at 350° F. for 30 minutes. Makes 1 dinner serving.

HOMINY GRITS

> 1 egg, yolk and white beaten separately
> Salt
> 1 teaspoon margarine
> ¾ cup hot, cooked enriched hominy grits
> ¼ cup hot Tomato Sauce (½ cup tomato juice reduced by half)

Stir beaten egg yolk into grits, season with salt and add margarine. Fold in stiffly beaten egg white. Transfer to small individual casserole. Set in pan holding hot water which comes about halfway up the dish. Bake at 375° F. about 1 hour. Serve with hot Tomato Sauce. Makes 1 luncheon serving.

HOMINY GRITS AND TURNIP GREENS
Serve with broiled all-beef frankfurters or knockwurst.

> ¾ cup cooked enriched hominy grits
> 1 cup hot cooked turnip greens
> 2 teaspoons vegetable oil

Combine grits, well-drained turnip greens and oil. Blend thoroughly. Makes 1 serving.

PASTAS: MACARONI AND SPAGHETTI

Pastas, in Italian, all have romantic names that roll off the tongue like music — occhi di lupo, spaghettini, fettucini, ravioli — no wonder it is possible to fall in love with the stuff and ruin your waistline. There are many pasta shapes to choose from, but always buy it enriched.

To help you find your way through the many bewildering offerings of pastas at the market, here is a list of varieties and their uses:

For soup: Tiny shells, pastina, noodles, bows, doughnut shapes, circles, seed shapes.

For sauce: Spirals, spaghetti in many thicknesses as well as round or flat (linguini) and curly miniature lasagne.

For baking: Lasagna, any of the hollow tubes like occhi di lupo or macaroni elbows (curved or ribbed), spirals and fancy shapes that look like hats, bows, wagon wheels, etc.

To be stuffed: Large shells, turnover shapes, manicotti, cannelloni or other large tubes (plain or ribbed), ravioli and the round pasta (tortellini) that look like a fortune cookie.

HOW TO COOK MACARONI AND SPAGHETTI

Macaroni and spaghetti usually double in bulk when cooked. Generally, therefore, you will need about ⅓ cup raw enriched spaghetti or macaroni to make your permitted ⅔ cup. Add the uncooked pasta to two quarts boiling salted water and cook it tender, but still chewy (*al dente*) like an Italian would — or soft all through, like an American; cooking time is 8-12 minutes. Drain. Measure. No rinsing necessary, unless it's going into a salad.

MACARONI OR SPAGHETTI PARMESAN

Clove of garlic
⅔ cup hot, cooked enriched macaroni or spaghetti
Dash of salt and pepper
1 teaspoon margarine or vegetable oil
2 ounces grated Parmesan cheese

Rub serving bowl with garlic clove. Stir in pasta, salt, pepper, margarine or oil. Toss. Sprinkle with cheese. Makes 1 luncheon serving.

PASTA CAPERS

⅔ cup cooked enriched elbow macaroni (al dente)
6 ounces cooked, diced chicken, roast beef or lamb
½ envelope instant chicken broth and seasoning mix
½ cup water
½ teaspoon minced capers

Combine macaroni with chicken, roast beef or lamb. Sprinkle with broth mix and water. Let simmer till macaroni has absorbed the stock and meat is very soft. Top with capers and serve hot. Makes 1 dinner serving.

SPINACH AND PASTINA PARMESAN

1 cup cooked spinach, chopped
1 cup cooked enriched baby pastina
2 ounces grated Parmesan cheese
Dash each of red hot sauce, celery salt, pepper and nutmeg

Combine spinach and pastina in small pan. Over low heat, stir in grated cheese, hot sauce, celery salt, pepper and nutmeg. Serve when cheese melts. Makes 2 luncheon servings; supplement as required.

BAKED LASAGNA

½ clove minced garlic
Dash crushed red pepper flakes (optional)
1 teaspoon dried oregano
Artificial sweetener to equal 2 tablespoons sugar (optional)
3 cups Tomato Sauce (6 cups tomato juice reduced by half)
2⅔ cups ricotta cheese
Dash salt and pepper
2⅔ cups (about 8 strips) cooked enriched lasagna macaroni

Add garlic, red pepper, oregano and sweetener (if desired) to
Tomato Sauce. Season ricotta with salt and pepper. Spread some
Tomato Sauce on bottom of a large baking dish. Add 2 strips of
cooked lasagna, top with one quarter of the cheese, cover with 2
more strips of lasagna and top with one quarter of the Tomato
Sauce; repeat with remaining ingredients. Cover dish with foil.
Bake about 1 hour at 325° F. Makes 4 luncheon servings.

LINGUINI WITH CLAM SAUCE

6 ounces canned, minced or whole baby clams
1 cup bottled clam juice
1 garlic clove, minced
1 teaspoon minced parsley
1 tablespoon vegetable oil
⅔ cup cooked enriched linguini

Combine clams in a saucepan with clam juice, garlic clove and
parsley. Bring to a boil and simmer for 15 minutes. Stir in oil, and
pour over linguini. Makes 1 dinner serving; for lunch, use 4 ounces
clams.

MACARONI AND MUSHROOM PILAF

¼ cup fresh mushrooms
1 teaspoon dehydrated onion flakes
1 cup water
⅔ cup cooked enriched elbow macaroni or spaghetti
1 envelope instant chicken broth and seasoning mix

Cook mushrooms and onion flakes in ½ cup of the water in a small uncovered saucepan. When water boils away, let mushrooms brown lightly. Add macaroni, remaining water and broth mix, and continue cooking till most of the liquid evaporates. Or bake the browned mushrooms with all other ingredients at 350° F. for 25 minutes. Makes 1 serving.

MACARONI AND CHEESE AU GRATIN

1⅓ cups cooked enriched elbow macaroni
½ cup canned sliced mushrooms
¼ cup chopped pimentos
3 ounces cubed hard cheese
½ cup evaporated skimmed milk
2 tablespoons dehydrated onion flakes
1 teaspoon dry mustard
½ teaspoon salt
¼ teaspoon Worcestershire
1 ounce hard cheese, grated

In casserole, combine macaroni, mushrooms, pimentos and cubed cheese. Stir with a wooden spoon. Combine milk, onion flakes, mustard, salt, and Worcestershire and pour into casserole. Sprinkle grated cheese on top. Bake uncovered at 350° F. over for ½ hour. Makes 2 luncheon servings.

MACARONI CUSTARD CASSEROLE

1⅓ cups cooked enriched macaroni, drained
1 cup Tomato Sauce (2 cups tomato juice reduced by half)
2 ounces grated Parmesan cheese
1 cup sliced fresh or canned mushrooms
2 tablespoons dehydrated onion flakes
½ teaspoon salt
¼ teaspoon pepper
2 eggs, beaten
1 cup skim milk

In casserole, make layers of half of the macaroni, Tomato Sauce, grated cheese, mushrooms, onion flakes, salt and pepper. Repeat layers, reserving half of the grated cheese. Combine eggs and milk and pour into casserole. Top with reserved cheese and bake at 350° F. for 35 minutes. Serve from casserole. Makes 2 luncheon servings.

BOILED POTATO

Caution: To save the nutrients lying just under the potato skin, it's best to wash the potatoes just before they're cooked; cook them unpeeled in boiling water that covers them; and peel just before serving ... or eat the peel!

Don't peel potatoes in advance; don't soak potatoes in water. Mash potatoes with a little of your skim milk, imitation (or diet) margarrine, or instant non-fat dry milk and a few drops of hot water.

There's a trick to using just enough — but not too much — water for boiling potatoes. The water should be boiled away by the time the potatoes are soft; uncover pan for a minute or two and shake it over the burner till the last of the liquid boils away. Or save the liquid left from cooking potatoes and use it when making vegetable soup or sauce.

Boil tiny new potatoes in salted water (insert knife tip in center to test when done); shake dry in pan. Weigh 3-ounce portion. Serve with salt and pepper.

BAKED POTATOES
Idaho or Russet Burbank varieties are perfect for baking, but don't go overboard on size.

Scrub 1 medium baking potato (3 ounces) with vegetable brush to clean skin. Bake at 400° F. for 50 minutes, or until soft. Serve with 1 teaspoon margarine and chopped chives. If you love potatoes and hate most vegetables (turnips, spinach, etc.), mash the potato with the Hated Vegetable — the potato flavor somehow comes through. Save the skin —

BAKED POTATO SKIN

After you've cut the baked potato in half and removed the inside, put the empty shells back in the hot oven for 5 minutes to brown well. Lightly scrape off any loose pieces of skin and get down to the delectable, crunchy, mineral-rich skin — as delicious as any French-fried vegetable, in my opinion. Season with salt and pepper, if desired. You may serve scooped-out baked potato skin with Onion Spread (p. 224 — count 2 tablespoons imitation — or diet — margarine) and make two daily-choice dishes from one.

HOME "FRIES"

> 4 ounces diced onion
> 1 medium (3-ounce) potato, cooked and diced
> Dash each of salt and pepper

In heavy preheated or non-stick skillet, cook onion in water to cover till soft; let water evaporate and brown onion. Add cooked potatoes and "fry" till brown, turning often. Season with salt and pepper. Makes 1 serving.

O'BRIEN POTATOES

> 1 medium (3-ounce) potato, fine-shredded
> 1 teaspoon dehydrated onion flakes
> 3 tablespoons chopped pimentos
> Salt and pepper (optional)

Using a non-stick or heavy skillet, boil raw shredded potatoes in water to cover. When potatoes are almost tender, let the liquid boil away. Add onion flakes and pimentos; cook and stir 5 minutes longer, then serve hot. Season with salt and pepper, if desired. Makes 1 serving.

CHIPS FOR YOUR FISH AND . . .

Peel and cut in julienne strips (matchstick pieces) one medium (3-ounce) potato. Sprinkle with onion salt and bake at 400° F. in individual baking dish for 15 minutes, turning to brown all sides. Dot with 1 tablespoon softened margarine, and run under broiler to crisp.

PETITE POTATO PANCAKES WITH CHEESE DRESSING

> 1 medium (3-ounce) potato, scrubbed clean and cut up
> 1 egg
> 1 slice bread, cut up
> 1 teaspoon dehydrated onion flakes, reconstituted in 1
>   tablespoon water
> Salt and pepper
> ⅓ cup cottage cheese
> ½ teaspoon minced dill (optional)
> 2 tablespoons water (optional)

Combine potato, egg, bread, onion flakes, salt, pepper; mix well, drop by tablespoonfuls onto a non-stick griddle or preheated heavy pan. Brown on both sides. Sprinkle cottage cheese with dill and use as spread for pancakes, or whip in blender with water. Makes 1 luncheon serving.

VARIATION
Potato Kugel (Pudding): Transfer potato batter to small casserole. Set in a shallow pan holding ½-inch water. Bake at 350° F. for about 45 minutes, or until mixture is firm and top is browned.

POTATO SALAD

Two unusual variations: add ½ medium sour dill pickle, finely diced; or 2 ounces cooked, diced okra (yes, okra).

> 1 medium (3-ounce) potato, boiled or baked
> 1 tablespoon mayonnaise
> 1 tablespoon vinegar
> 1 teaspoon dehydrated onion flakes, reconstituted in 1 table-
>   spoon water
> 1 teaspoon dehydrated pepper flakes, reconstituted in 1 table-
>   spoon water
> ½ teaspoon prepared mustard
> Salt and cayenne pepper
> Chopped pimento and chives for garnish

Boil or bake the potato with its skin on, and peel while it's warm. Dice evenly. Combine remaining ingredients (except pimento

ınd chives) and stir gently into diced potatoes. Garnish. Let stand
ın refrigerator half an hour or more. Makes 1 serving.

VARIATION

Pour a thin film of partly set Tomato Aspic (p. 240 — count tomato
juice) into the bottom of a coffee cup rinsed in cold water, and
let set till firm. Transfer potato salad (above) to cup, leaving
space at the sides for more aspic. Pour in the aspic to cover sides
and top of the potato salad. Chill in refrigerator until firm. Unmold on bed of watercress or lettuce. A border of shredded carrots
is pretty, nutritious and permitted — but it's a #4 vegetable, be
sure to count it.

QUICK VICHYSSOISE (COLD POTATO SOUP)

> 1 medium (3-ounce) potato, peeled or scrubbed and quartered
> 2 tablespoons dehydrated onion flakes
> 1 cup water
> ¼ cup skim milk
> 1 sprig parsley
> ½ teaspoon celery seed
> Dash Worcestershire
> Dash nutmeg
> Dash imitation butter flavoring
> Chopped chives (for garnish)

Cook quartered potato in boiling water with onion flakes until
potato is soft. Transfer to blender. Add other ingredients (except
chives) and blend until potatoes are pureed. Chill (or serve hot —
but then, of course, it's hot potato soup). Garnish with chives.
Makes 1 serving.

POTATO SOUFFLE

> 1 medium (3-ounce) potato, cooked and peeled
> 2 tablespoons skim milk
> Dash salt and nutmeg
> 1 ounce grated cheese
> 1 egg, separated

Mash the hot potato in the pan, and stir in milk, salt and nutmeg. Add grated cheese and beaten egg yolk, a little at a time. Beat egg whites till stiff but not dry. Fold in the egg white and bake at 375° F. for 25-30 minutes. Makes 1 luncheon serving.

NOODLES

Program allows ½ cup cooked enriched noodles. Noodles do not swell much when cooked, so if you are making only one serving we suggest that you start with about 6 tablespoons. Use plenty of boiling salted water.

> About 6 tablespoons enriched noodles
> 3 cups boiling salted water

Add noodles to boiling water and cook until they are tender. Drain, rinse, measure, and serve at once. To store noodles, sprinkle them lightly with water so they don't dry out; heat before serving. Any of the Margarine Spreads (p. 223) may be stirred into the cooked noodles. Makes 1 serving.

NOODLES WITH CHEESE AND BROCCOLI

> 1 cup cooked broccoli
> ½ cup firm-cooked enriched noodles
> ⅓ cup cottage or pot cheese
> 1 ounce grated hard cheese
> Dash of paprika
> 1 teaspoon chopped pimento

Spread broccoli in a small baking pan. Combine cooked noodles with cottage or pot cheese. Spread on broccoli. Sprinkle top with cheese (e.g., Parmesan, or other hard cheese) and paprika, and put under broiler, in warming well, or oven to melt cheese. Sprinkle with chopped pimentos. Makes 1 luncheon serving.

CHINESE "FRIED" NOODLES

Planning a Chinese dinner? That's the time to spread your ½ cup cooked enriched noodles in a shallow pan and bake at 350° F. till crisp and brown. Makes 1 serving.

JAMBALAYA OF NOODLES AND VEGETABLES

1 cup chicken bouillon
½ cup firm-cooked enriched noodles
½ cup cooked sliced celery
1 medium tomato, diced
2 ounces canned sliced okra
1 teaspoon minced parsley
1 teaspoon dehydrated onion flakes
Dash of salt, pepper, garlic powder and thyme

Heat chicken bouillon in saucepan. Add remaining ingredients (except noodles). Continue cooking till liquid is almost all evaporated. Stir in noodles and reheat. Makes 1 serving.

COTTAGE NOODLES

⅔ cup cottage cheese
3 tablespoons skim milk
¼ teaspoon lemon juice
1 cup cooked enriched wide egg noodles
¼ cup diced pimento
2 hard-cooked eggs, sliced
Dash each of salt and white pepper
¼ teaspoon caraway seeds
¼ teaspoon Worcestershire

Combine first 3 ingredients in blender and whiz smooth. Layer remaining ingredients in a small baking dish and cover with blended mixture. Bake at 350° F. for about 15 minutes or till bubbly hot. Makes 2 luncheon servings.

NOODLE-KRAUT CASSEROLE

1 cup sauerkraut, rinsed and drained
½ teaspoon caraway seeds
⅛ teaspoon celery salt
1 cup cooked enriched noodles
1 tablespoon imitation (or diet) margarine
Dash each of salt, pepper and nutmeg
4 ounces sliced or shredded cheddar cheese

Combine sauerkraut, caraway seeds and celery salt. Set aside Combine noodles, margarine, salt, pepper and nutmeg. Mix thoroughly. Place ¾ of the sauerkraut in a small casserole. Cover with noodles. Arrange cheese over noodles and top with remaining sauerkraut. Bake at 375° F. for approximately 15 minutes or until cheese is melted. Makes 2 servings.

FETTUCINI AND SPROUTS ALFREDO

Alfredo never made his famous noodle dish with bean sprouts, but we've stretched the original to produce a hearty luncheon dish.

> ½ cup firm-cooked enriched noodles
> ½ cup cooked or canned bean sprouts, drained and rinsed
> 2 ounces grated Parmesan cheese
> 2 tablespoons instant non-fat dry milk (equals 1 fluid ounce skim milk)
> Dash of imitation butter flavoring
> Dash of salt and freshly-milled black pepper

Combine noodles and bean sprouts (containing some moisture) in small saucepan, and set over low heat in a larger saucepan holding water. Toss in half of the cheese, dry milk and butter flavoring. Stir well; add remaining cheese and toss till cheese is melted. Serve with salt and pepper mill. Makes 1 luncheon serving.

HOW TO COOK RICE

Rice may be cooked on top of the stove or in the oven, in a wide choice of liquids (water, clam juice, tomato juice, or stock made from a bouillon cube or an envelope of instant broth and seasoning mix). Cooking time and amounts will vary according to the kind of rice you buy: follow package directions. In general, raw enriched rice will usually triple in bulk when cooked, so to make 1 serving, you should use about 3 tablespoons raw enriched rice. Measure again when cooked to be sure it makes the allowed ½ cup. A family-size recipe follows:

> 1 cup raw enriched rice
> 3 cups cold water or other liquid
> 1 teaspoon salt
> 1 teaspoon lemon juice or vinegar (to keep rice white)

Combine ingredients in saucepan, bring to boil, cover and simmer 20-30 minutes. Timing varies according to the size of the rice grains and whether or not they have been converted (parboiled) or precooked before they are packaged. Makes 3 or more cups cooked rice. Measure your allowed ½ cup for each serving.

Reheating Rice: After rice is cooked firm, drain and wash in strainer. Set aside till mealtime. Fifteen to twenty minutes before serving, set strainer holding ½ cup cooked rice over a pan of boiling water, cover pan (aluminum foil will do) and let steam till rice is hot. Or reheat cooked rice in a saucepan holding a few tablespoons hot chicken bouillon. Or add liquid from can and ½ cup canned button mushrooms.

GREEN RICE LUNCHEON CUSTARD
Ratatouille (p. 270) may replace the green beans or broccoli.

> ½ cup cooked enriched rice
> 1 tablespoon minced parsley
> ½ medium green pepper, chopped
> ½ cup cooked, canned or frozen green beans or broccoli, chopped
> ½ cup evaporated skimmed milk
> Salt and chili powder
> 1 egg
> 1 ounce grated hard cheese
> ¼ clove garlic (optional)

Combine ingredients, mix well and transfer to small oven-to-table baking dish. Set dish in pan half-filled with hot water. Bake at 350° F. for 30-40 minutes or until firm. Makes 1 serving.

CHINESE "FRIED" RICE

> 2 ounces diced, cooked chicken, veal or shrimp
> ¼ cup canned drained bean sprouts or braised celery
> Salt and pepper
> ½ cup cooked enriched rice
> 1 egg, beaten
> 2 ounces diced scallion
> 2 teaspoons soy sauce

In non-stick skillet, combine meat, bean sprouts, salt and pepper, and heat for 5 minutes. Add rice and beaten egg, and cook 5 minutes more, stirring constantly. Add scallions and soy sauce and heat an additional 2 minutes. Serve hot. Makes 1 luncheon serving.

RICE SALAD BOWL

> 1 cup cooked enriched rice
> 4 ounces cooked artichoke hearts, sliced
> 4 ounces chopped scallions
> 2 medium tomatoes, diced
> 2 teaspoons drained capers
> 1 recipe Mock Hollandaise Sauce (p. 225 — count 1 tablespoon daily fat allowance per serving)

In separate salad bowls, divide equally rice, artichoke hearts, scallions, tomato and capers. Chill. Serve with Mock Hollandaise Sauce also divided equally. Makes 2 servings.

RISI E BISI (ITALIAN RICE AND PEAS)

> ½ cup hot, firm-cooked enriched rice
> ¼ cup boiling water
> 1 envelope instant chicken broth and seasoning mix
> ½ teaspoon dehydrated onion flakes
> 1 teaspoon minced parsley
> Salt and pepper
> Few drops sherry extract
> 1 teaspoon margarine
> 4 ounces uncooked green peas

Combine all ingredients in small saucepan. Bring to a boil, reduce heat and simmer covered for 15 minutes, or until peas are soft. Remove cover and continue cooking if rice and peas are too moist. Makes 1 serving.

VARIATION

Spanish Rice: In saucepan combine ¾ cup tomato juice, ½ cup diced celery, ½ diced medium green pepper, ½ shredded pimento, ½ teaspoon Worcestershire and a dash cayenne pepper. Cook till vegetables are soft, add rice and heat. Makes 1 serving.

FRUITED RICE

1 cup shredded lettuce
2 small slices pineapple (canned in its own juice), cut in
    pieces, plus 2 tablespoons juice
Artificial sweetener to equal 1 teaspoon sugar
1 teaspoon soy sauce
Dash cinnamon
½ cup cooked enriched rice

In saucepan, cook lettuce in water to cover. When lettuce is soft, drain, stir in remaining ingredients except rice. When hot, stir in rice and mix well. Makes 1 serving.

INDIAN CURRY OF RICE

1 medium apple, peeled, cored and chopped
1 medium green pepper, diced
½ cup celery, diced
1 cup chicken bouillon
2 tablespoons Chili Sauce (p. 216—count ½ cup tomato juice)
Dash each of garlic powder, ginger and turmeric
¼ teaspoon coconut extract (optional)

In small saucepan, combine apple, green pepper and celery and cook until apples are soft and liquid almost evaporated. Stir in remaining ingredients (except coconut extract); heat well. Just before serving, add extract, if desired. Makes 1 serving.

TOASTED RICE PILAF

To toast rice, spread a cup or two of enriched white rice on a shallow baking sheet, one layer deep. Bake at 325° to 425° F. for 10 to 25 minutes, turning to brown all sides. Let rice cool, store in canister or jar and cook just as you would plain white rice. Measure cooked rice so you do not exceed your allowed ½ cup.

1 cup cooked enriched rice (made from toasted rice, see above)
1 cup sliced mushrooms
1½ cups boiling beef bouillon
2 teaspoons dehydrated onion flakes
Pinch saffron
2 teaspoons minced parsley

Combine ingredients in casserole, mix well, and bake uncovered at 375° F. for 25-35 minutes until piping hot. Makes 2 servings.

RICE AND APPLE MERINGUE PUDDING

½ cup cooked enriched rice
½ cup skim milk
1 egg, separated
Artificial sweetener to equal 2 tablespoons sugar
¼ teaspoon vanilla extract
Dash cinnamon
1 medium apple, cored and cut in slices
Dash lemon juice
Dash cream of tartar and salt

Combine rice, milk, egg yolk, half of the egg white (reserving remaining half), sweetener, vanilla extract and cinnamon. Transfer to small ovenproof serving dish. In small saucepan poach apple slices in a few tablespoons water and lemon juice. Add to rice mixture. Beat reserved half of egg white with cream of tartar and salt until stiff. Heap egg white over apples. Bake at 375° F. until golden brown, about 20 minutes. Makes 1 luncheon serving; supplement as required.

RASPBERRY-RICE PARFAIT

½ cup cooked enriched rice
½ cup ripe raspberries or other berry
Artificial sweetener to equal 2 teaspoons sugar or to taste
1 serving Best Whipped Topping (p. 198 — count 1 fluid
    ounce evaporated skimmed milk)

Refrigerate all ingredients until mealtime. Just before serving, lightly mix rice, fruit and topping (save a handsome berry and a dollop of topping for garnish). Spoon into large parfait glass, add the reserved topping and pretty berry. Makes 1 serving.

VARIATION

Omit raspberries. Cook 2 medium pitted plums in water to cover, sweeten artificially, puree in blender and freeze to consistency of mushy ices, about 40 minutes. Just before serving, combine rice and plum sherbet in pretty glass bowl. Makes 1 serving.

Eggs

You can do wonderful things with eggs if you follow the recipes in this chapter. Airy light soufflés, filled and rolled crepes or pancakes, fritters (and their cousins the frittatas and foo yungs) are included. We show you how to fill an omelet with everything from spinach or mushrooms to strawberries or cheese. And best of all, we show you how to make a two-part meal or desserts like custards and meringues from one egg!

RULES FOR USING EGGS

1. Use 4 eggs a week, for breakfast or lunch only, never for dinner.
2. Eggs may be cooked in shell, or poached or scrambled without added fat. Do not eat raw eggs.
3. Egg whites and egg yolks may be prepared in separate recipes, provided that both white and yolk are consumed as part of the same meal.

FRENCH TOAST

> 1 egg, beaten
> Artificial sweetener to equal 2 teaspoons sugar (optional)
> ½ teaspoon cinnamon (optional)
> ⅛ teaspoon nutmeg (optional)
> 1 slice enriched white bread

Combine beaten egg with half of the sweetener, cinnamon and nutmeg, if desired. Soak bread in this mixture until egg is thoroughly absorbed. Cook in a non-stick pan or heated heavy iron skillet. Or bake or broil on aluminum foil, turning to brown both sides. Remove from skillet or oven. Sprinkle with remaining sweetener and cinnamon, if desired. Makes 1 serving.

VARIATIONS

1. Follow directions above but let bread stand in batter overnight (or for several hours) in refrigerator. In the morning, slip the soaked bread onto a non-stick baking sheet and bake at 400° F. for 12 minutes or until top is puffy and brown. This is an easy way to get a lot of puffy toast for a big family, company, etc. without last-minute fuss.

2. For a company treat, you can make two elegant dishes from your breakfast egg. For each serving, separate the yolk from the white. Beat yolk with one teaspoon water and use as a batter for French toast, following recipe above. Beat the egg white with ⅛ teaspoon cream of tartar and a dash of salt until it stands in stiff peaks. With a knife, loosen the pulp of ½ medium grapefruit; remove seeds and tough center membrane. Pile meringue topping on grapefruit and bake in small foil pan at 400° F. along with French toast. If you wish, artificial sweetener to equal 1 teaspoon sugar may be beaten with egg white; cream of tartar (which gives added height to the meringue) may be omitted. Makes 1 serving.

3. Optional seasonings for French toast: extracts (vanilla, orange, maple, rum, brandy, etc.), spices, herbs.

SUNNYSIDE UP

Use a non-stick or heated heavy iron skillet. Break an egg into a cup, slip it into the skillet and cook to your taste. To firm the top without turning egg, cover skillet. Makes 1 serving.

SOUFFLE WITH PINEAPPLE TOPPING

> 4 eggs, separated
> Artificial sweetener to equal 4 tablespoons sugar
> 2 teaspoons water
> Salt
> Pineapple Topping (see recipe below)

Beat egg yolks with sweetener to equal 3 tablespoons sugar until very thick. Add water and salt to egg whites; beat until stiff. Fold whites into yolks. Pour into hot 10½-inch non-stick pan, and cook over medium heat without stirring, until it is lightly brown on the bottom and sides, and top is firm. With a spatula, fold in half and place on hot dish. Sprinkle lightly with remaining sweetener and serve with Pineapple Topping. Makes 2 luncheon servings.

Pineapple Topping

> 2 small slices pineapple (canned in its own juice) plus
> 2 tablespoons juice
> 1 tablespoon water
> Artificial sweetener to equal 4 teaspoons sugar
> ¼ teaspoon vanilla extract

Crush pineapple in blender with juice and water. Transfer to saucepan and simmer until pineapple is soft and tender. Add sweetener and vanilla. Divide evenly into 2 servings and pour over soufflé.

OEUFS POCHE DIVAN (POACHED EGGS AND BROCCOLI)
There's an ace up your sleeve when you serve this at your bridge luncheon—you can have everything prepared ahead, including the eggs.

> 1 cup cooked broccoli florets, drained
> 2 teaspoons salt
> 2 teaspoons pepper
> Dash nutmeg
> 4 soft-set poached eggs, drained on paper towels
> 4 slices bread, made into crumbs
> 2 cups skim milk
> 4 slices hard cheese, 1 ounce each

Arrange florets in 4 individual ramekins. Season with salt, pepper and nutmeg. Add a poached egg to each one. Top with crumbs, pour in milk and cover with cheese. Bake at 375° F. until piping hot; cheese should be fully melted. Makes 4 luncheon servings.

How to poach an egg: Break 1 egg into a cup and slip into saucepan containing boiling water, a teaspoon of vinegar, and salt. Reduce to simmer and poach gently about 3 minutes for soft-set egg; 5 minutes for firm. Remove with slotted spoon and let water drain off.

POACHED EGG IN BOUILLON

Serve this on a wintry day, before you all go off to the ski slopes, or on any day when appetites are huge. It is easily made in individual servings on top of the stove using flameproof glass pans that have their own lids, or baked in a casserole.

¾ cup water
1 envelope instant chicken or beef broth and seasoning mix
1 slice toast
¼ teaspoon dehydrated onion flakes
1 egg
Salt and pepper (optional)
½ teaspoon fresh or dried herbs to taste, or minced capers

Bring to boiling point water and broth mix in small oven-to-table pan. Stir, top with a slice of toast, add onion flakes, and open an egg onto the toast. Sprinkle with salt and pepper, if desired, and with your choice of herbs. Cover pan and poach egg for a few minutes over low heat (or bake at 375° F. in covered casserole) until done to taste. Serve with spoon. Makes 1 luncheon serving; supplement as required.

EGGS IN CELERY NESTS

Great Easter Sunday breakfast to delight overweight children. Add food coloring to the drained, cooled celery (or bean sprouts) to make the nest more decorative. A few drops red and green will make brown.

4 cups finely chopped celery or 2 cups drained bean sprouts
¼ cup chopped parsley
1 teaspoon dehydrated onion flakes, soaked in 2 tablespoons water
1 teaspoon salt
4 eggs

Cover celery with water, bring to boil and simmer 5 minutes. Drain and cool. (If using canned bean sprouts, rinse and drain.) Combine celery, parsley, onion flakes and water in which it soaked, and salt; mix well. Shape into four even nests on a non-stick baking sheet (or use custard cups). Break one egg into each nest. Bake at 350° F. (moderate oven) for 20 minutes or to taste. Makes 4 luncheon servings; supplement as required.

AVGOLEMONO SOUP (GREEK EGG AND LEMON SOUP)

A savory peasant-style breakfast for people who don't like breakfast. Or serve as a soup-and-salad luncheon dish and supplement as required.

¾ cup water
1 envelope instant chicken broth and seasoning mix
1 egg
2 teaspoons cold water
2 teaspoons lemon juice (more if desired; there should be a decided lemony taste)

Combine water and broth mix in small saucepan, and bring to light boil. In small bowl, beat egg and 2 teaspoons cold water. Gradually stir in a few teaspoons of the hot bouillon and the lemon juice. Pour egg mixture back into the hot chicken bouillon and heat, stirring until thickened. Serve at once. Makes 1 serving.

VARIATION
1. Follow recipe above but use egg yolk only. Bake tiny Meringue Kisses (p. 89) from egg white, omitting sweetener; serve in soup. Makes 1 serving.
2. *Avgolemono Sauce:* Follow recipe above but use only ½ cup chicken bouillon made from ½ cup water and 1 envelope instant chicken broth and seasoning mix. Add 1 teaspoon dehydrated onion flakes. Serve hot over 1 cup cooked zucchini or other cooked green vegetable for luncheon. Makes 1 serving.

SCRAMBLED EGGS

Just beat an egg in a bowl with a few teaspoons water to fluff it up, and pour into a non-stick or preheated iron skillet. Stir until egg is as you like it. Or drop the open egg into a preheated pan and scramble it in the pan, using a fork. Makes 1 breakfast serving; for luncheon, supplement as required.

VARIATIONS
1. For *Oeufs aux fines herbes,* add a teaspoon each of minced fresh parsley, chives and chervil to 2 eggs.
2. One nice way to serve scrambled eggs is over 1 cup cooked, diced asparagus tips, seasoned with savory.

EGGS AU GRATIN

2 ounces American cheese, diced
2 tablespoons skim milk
½ teaspoon dehydrated onion flakes
2 hard-cooked eggs, chopped
1 tablespoon chopped celery
½ teaspoon prepared mustard
½ teaspoon Worcestershire
Salt and white pepper
2 slices toast

In small saucepan, combine cheese, skim milk, and onion flakes. Heat until cheese is melted. Remove from heat. Add remaining ingredients (except toast). Serve hot over toast. Makes 2 luncheon servings.

EGGS PIPERADE

2 tablespoons dehydrated onion flakes
1 medium tomato, cut up
½ medium green pepper, diced
4 eggs, beaten
Salt and pepper
Pinch basil

Soak onion flakes in tomato; if tomato is not ripe and succulent, add a tablespoon or two of water. Combine with green pepper. Soften vegetable-tomato mixture by cooking for a few minutes in a hot non-stick pan. Combine beaten eggs with salt, pepper and basil. Add egg mixture to vegetable mixture in pan. Scramble. Makes 2 luncheon servings.

DEVILED EGGS

2 hard-cooked eggs
1 tablespoon mayonnaise
½ teaspoon dry mustard
Dash each of Worcestershire and curry
Salt and pepper

Slice eggs in half lengthwise, transfer yolks to small bowl and mash lightly. Stir in remaining ingredients and put yolk mixture back into whites. Serve on shredded lettuce. Makes 1 luncheon serving.

VARIATION
One tablespoon finely minced celery may be added to the egg yolks before they are put back into egg white halves. Cumin seeds, celery seeds or dill are also optional additions.

MAKING A BASIC FAT-FREE OMELET

Even a one-egg omelet can be made without fat and without a special omelet pan. I use a 5-inch heavy iron skillet (a non-stick pan is fine too). Preheat the pan. Beat up one egg (two at luncheon), add a few drops of water (turn on the tap in the kitchen sink, turn it off, and catch the few drops that drip out). When the pan is almost smoking hot, add egg, turn down heat to moderate and let the egg cook on the bottom, lifting the edges so that the uncooked portion runs to the bottom. Shake pan back and forth to keep omelet free. When the bottom is brown, you can add filling, or turn the omelet onto your plate, or let it continue to cook until the top is dry (as I do; I have a prejudice against runny eggs). Serve the egg flipped over in half, to show off your well-turned omelet. Makes 1 serving.

VARIATIONS
1. When egg is almost set, before you turn the omelet, sprinkle it with 1 ounce grated hard cheese and let cheese melt.

2. Or spread omelet (just before it sets) with ⅓ cup cottage or ricotta cheese. Flip omelet over and serve. The combination of hot egg and cool cheese appeals!

3. *Spicy Spanish Omelet:* Add a tablespoon of the following mixture when it is set on one side: 1 tablespoon tomato juice combined with a dash each of dehydrated onion flakes, dehydrated pepper flakes, salt and cayenne pepper. Turn omelet, cook until second side is set, fold in half and serve.

4. *Filled Omelet:* For every 2 eggs, add ½ cup cooked spinach, diced zucchini, eggplant or other cooked vegetable. Season with

salt, pepper and ½ teaspoon basil. Add vegetable mixture to eggs before pouring them into pan. A *Mushroom Omelet* with ½ cup cooked or canned mushrooms is a special treat.

STRAWBERRY OMELET SURPRISE
Only the cook knows for sure what's tucked inside . . . but after one forkful the luscious secret is out.

> 2 eggs
> ¼ recipe Strawberry Jelly (p. 138 — count as ¼ fruit)
> Artificial sweetener to equal 2 teaspoons sugar

Beat eggs until light. In heated non-stick pan or heavy iron skillet, add eggs. Stir once, then quickly lift the edges as the eggs begin to cook and let the liquid part run under. When cooked but still soft on top, spoon Strawberry Jelly on one side and fold other side over filling. Sprinkle with sweetener. Makes 1 luncheon serving.

BAKED FRITTATA

> 1 cup cooked, chopped green beans, wax beans or snow peas
> 2 eggs, separated
> Salt and pepper
> Dash garlic powder
> 1 tablespoon minced, fresh herbs (e.g. chives, parsley or
>   rosemary), or 1 teaspoon dried herbs
> ¼ teaspoon fresh chopped chives for garnish

Combine beans with beaten egg yolks. Add seasonings and minced herbs except the chives for garnish. Beat egg whites until stiff and fold, ⅓ at a time, into vegetable mixture. Pour batter into a heated heavy iron skillet (be sure the handle is neither flammable nor meltable) and bake at 350° F. for 20 minutes. Cut in wedges and serve from skillet with a sprinkling of fresh chives. Makes 1 luncheon serving.

VARIATIONS
You may replace green beans with ½ cup cooked broccoli, plus ½ cup cooked mushrooms and 1 medium canned tomato, all

chopped fine. This will make your daily allowance of #3B vegetables. Or, use 1 cup braised celery, or 1 cup cooked bean sprouts.

EGGS FOO YUNG

Option: Make with 2 egg yolks and 1 egg white. Use second white for Grapefruit Alaska, p. 199.

2 tablespoons diced celery
1 tablespoon dehydrated onion flakes
1 tablespoon dehydrated pepper flakes
¼ cup rinsed and drained bean sprouts
2 eggs
Salt and pepper
Soy sauce

Combine diced celery, onion and pepper flakes in saucepan. Cover with ½ cup water. Cook about 15 minutes until celery is tender; add bean sprouts. Beat eggs until light, season with salt and pepper, and add vegetable mixture. Drop tablespoonfuls of egg batter onto hot non-stick or heavy iron skillet. Brown both sides. Serve immediately with soy sauce. Makes 1 luncheon serving.

ZUCCHINI AND POTATO FRITTATA

½ cup zucchini, peeled and coarsely grated
¼ teaspoon salt
1 egg, separated
1 medium (3-ounce) potato, cooked, peeled and mashed
1 teaspoon dehydrated onion flakes
1 ounce freshly grated Parmesan cheese
Dash garlic powder
Salt and pepper

Sprinkle grated zucchini with salt and let stand to draw moisture (about 15 minutes). Drain. Combine zucchini in bowl with egg yolk, lightly beaten. Add mashed potato, dehydrated onion flakes, half of the freshly grated Parmesan cheese, garlic powder, salt and pepper. Beat the egg white with a pinch of salt until stiff; fold into zucchini mixture. Pour into individual casserole, sprinkle with remaining grated cheese and bake at 350° F. for 30-40 minutes, or till browned. Serve piping hot. Makes 1 luncheon serving.

SPINACH SOUFFLE
A grand luncheon for two.

> 2 eggs, separated
> 1 recipe Florentine Sauce (p. 222 — count ½ slice bread,
>   ½ cup milk, ¼ cup #3B vegetable, per serving)
> 2 ounces grated Parmesan cheese

Beat egg yolks; combine with Florentine Sauce and mix well. Beat egg whites till stiff, then fold gently into yolk mixture. Divide mixture equally into 2 individual casseroles. Sprinkle half of grated cheese into each casserole; bake at 350° F. for 30 minutes, till puffed and brown. Makes 2 luncheon servings.

CREPES WITH APPLE FILLING

> 1 slice enriched white bread
> 1 tablespoon water, or flavored dietetic carbonated beverage
> 1 egg
> ⅛ teaspoon almond extract
> ⅛ teaspoon rum extract
> Artificial sweetener to equal 2 teaspoons sugar
> Apple Filling or Topping (below)

Combine bread, liquid, egg, extracts and sweetener in blender. Blend until mixture is smooth. Pour into hot non-stick pan, cook until bubbles appear on surface, turn and brown second side. Keep warm. Spread with hot apple filling and roll up, or use fruit as topping. Makes 1 serving.

Apple Filling or Topping

> 1 medium apple, peeled and diced
> 1 tablespoon water
> Artificial sweetener to equal 4 teaspoons sugar
> ¼ teaspoon apple pie spice, or cinnamon

Combine ingredients in saucepan. Cover and simmer slowly until apples are soft. Use to fill or top crepes above.

COFFEE GELATIN CREME

    ¾ tablespoon unflavored gelatin
    ¼ cup cold water or cold coffee
    1 teaspoon instant or freeze-dried coffee powder
    ½ cup water
    ½ cup skim milk
    1 egg, beaten
    Artificial sweetener to equal 4 tablespoons sugar
    ¼ teaspoon vanilla extract

In top of double boiler, sprinkle gelatin over water; let soften 3 minutes. Add instant coffee powder, water, skim milk and beaten egg; mix well. Cook over boiling water till gelatin dissolves and mixture thickens, stirring well. Remove from heat, stir in sweetener and vanilla. Transfer to custard cups; chill until firm. Makes 1 breakfast or luncheon serving; for luncheon, supplement as required.

APPLE BREAKFAST FRITTERS

    1 medium apple, peeled and cored
    1 egg
    1 slice bread, cut in pieces
    ⅛ teaspoon vanilla extract
    1 tablespoon water
    Artificial sweetener to equal 4 teaspoons sugar
    Dash cinnamon

Grate apple and set aside. Combine all ingredients, except apple, in blender or mixing bowl. Blend or beat with electric mixer until mixture is smooth. Fold in grated apple; mix well. Drop by tablespoons onto a hot non-stick skillet. Cook on both sides to a golden brown. Makes 1 serving.

VARIATION
Blueberry Pancakes: Omit apple. Fold ½ cup crushed blueberries into blended or beaten egg-and-bread mixture. Bake as above.

APPLE CUSTARD MERINGUE PIE

Fruit Filling

> 2 firm medium baking apples, peeled, cored and cut into
>   wedges
> 3 tablespoons boiling water
> Artificial sweetener to equal 2 tablespoons sugar
> ¼ teaspoon cinnamon
> Dash each of nutmeg, cloves and ginger
> Few drops lemon extract

Bread Layer (optional)

> 2 slices day-old bread, cut horizontally to make 4 slices

Custard

> 1 cup skim milk, scalded
> 2 egg yolks, beaten
> Artificial sweetener to equal 2 tablespoons sugar
> ¼ teaspoon vanilla extract
> ¼ teaspoon imitation butter flavoring
> Dash salt

Meringue

> 2 egg whites
> ⅛ teaspoon cream of tartar (to help stabilize the meringue)
> Artificial sweetener to equal 2 teaspoons sugar
> Pinch salt

Cut apples into quarters and cut each quarter into 4 wedges. Combine apples and water in shallow pan and cook briefly until they are just tender, not soft. Arrange in 8-inch or 9-inch pie plate. Sprinkle with mixture of remaining fruit filling ingredients. Spread bread slices on top of apples, if desired. Preheat oven to 300° F.

To make custard: Combine scalded milk, egg yolks and remaining custard ingredients. Pour over bread in pie plate. Set pie plate in a pan of hot water. Bake in preheated oven for 35-40 minutes.

Meanwhile prepare meringue topping: Beat egg whites, cream of tartar, sweetener and salt until mixture stands in stiff, glossy peaks.

When custard is firm on the outer edges, add a little cold water to pan holding pie plate, and carefully remove from oven. Spread meringue on top of custard, piling it high in center. Put back in oven (in pan with water), and bake about 15 minutes, or until meringue is golden. Remove and let cool, then chill. Makes 2 luncheon servings; supplement as required.

COCONUT-FLAVORED CUSTARD IN MERINGUE PIECRUST

Meringue Piecrust

> 2 egg whites
> ⅛ teaspoon cream of tartar
> Dash salt
> ⅓ cup instant non-fat dry milk
> Artificial sweetener to equal 3 tablespoons sugar
> ½ teaspoon coconut extract

Custard Gelatin

> 1 cup skim milk
> 1 small piece of vanilla bean or ¼ teaspoon vanilla extract
> 2 egg yolks
> Pinch salt
> Artificial sweetener to equal 2 teaspoons sugar
> ¼ teaspoon coconut extract
> 2 teaspoons unflavored gelatin
> ¼ cup water

Make Meringue Piecrust: Combine egg whites, cream of tartar and salt, and beat till soft peaks form. Add dry milk, sweetener and coconut extract, beating until stiff. Spread over the bottom and sides of a deep 9-inch pie plate. Bake at 250° F. for 1 hour, or until meringue is set. Let stand for several hours before using.

Make Custard Gelatin: Scald milk with small piece of vanilla bean, and let stand 10 minutes; remove bean. (If vanilla bean is not available, simply scald milk, and add extract). Beat egg yolk with salt, sweetener and coconut extract, and add to hot milk, a little at a time, stirring constantly, until mixture coats the spoon. In a small cup, sprinkle gelatin over cold water and let stand a few minutes. Add to hot custard and stir well. Let cool. Transfer to dry crust and chill until filling is firm. Makes 2 luncheon servings; supplement as required.

MENU FOR A FESTIVE BREAKFAST (FOR ONE)

It's Christmas or New Year's morning, and everyone is partying. You don't have to drop out of the festivities just because you're on Program. Here's an irresistible holiday menu (no substitutions, please):

Frosty Rum-Flavored Sherbet
Poached Egg Yolk in Bouillon
(On Toast)
Pineapple Ambrosia Meringue Crown
Hot Coffee

1. Frosty Rum-Flavored Sherbet

Combine 2 tablespoons pineapple juice from pineapple canned in its own juice (set aside pineapple for Pineapple Ambrosia Meringue Crown below), ½ cup orange-flavored dietetic carbonated beverage and ¼ teaspoon orange extract. Freeze 40-50 minutes to sherbet consistency. If mixture is frozen solid, let it stand in the refrigerator about 20 minutes, or until it can be spooned into a champagne or juice glass with ¼ teaspoon rum extract stirred in. You'll want a short straw to sip it from.

2. Poached Egg Yolk in Bouillon (On Toast)

Using small, flameproof casserole, prepare Poached Egg in Bouillon (p. 76), but use only the egg yolk, not the whole egg.

3. Pineapple Ambrosia Meringue Crown

2 small slices pineapple (canned in its own juice)
Few drops each orange and coconut extracts
1 egg white
⅛ teaspoon cream of tartar
Dash salt
Artificial sweetener to equal 2 teaspoons sugar
Few drops red food coloring

Cut pineapple into wedges and arrange them in an attractive individual casserole. With fingers dot pineapple with coconut and orange extracts. Beat egg white, cream of tartar, salt, sweetener and red coloring until whites are stiff and stand in glossy peaks. Pile mixture onto the pineapple to form crown. Bake at 250° F. for 40 minutes, or until top is well browned. Serve immediately.

OEUFS A LA NEIGE (SNOW EGGS)
Sometimes called Floating Island.

Custard Sauce

    2 cups skim milk
    Artificial sweetener to equal ¼ cup sugar
    4 egg yolks
    ½ teaspoon vanilla extract

Scald milk over low heat, or in double boiler. Beat yolks and sweetener until light. Stir a few spoonfuls of scalded milk into the yolks, then gradually add the yolk mixture to remaining hot milk, stirring constantly. Return pan to low heat (or use a double boiler) and cook, stirring constantly, until mixture coats spoon. Stir vigorously to smooth out lumps. Transfer to serving dish, then chill until set, stirring once or twice to prevent skin from forming.

Snow Eggs

    4 egg whites
    Artificial sweetener to equal ½ cup sugar

Half fill saucepan with water, heat to simmering. Beat egg whites and sweetener until stiff. Using a wet tablespoon, form the meringue into oval shapes the size of eggs. Slip them off the spoon into the simmering water and poach, one layer at a time, on both sides, turning them after 2 minutes. Remove from saucepan with slotted spoon, and dry on paper towels. Serve over chilled Custard Sauce. Makes 2 luncheon servings.

PINEAPPLE UPSIDE-DOWN CUSTARD

1 egg, separated
1 teaspoon lemon juice
¼ teaspoon almond extract
Dash nutmeg
3 tablespoons instant non-fat dry milk
⅛ medium fresh pineapple, diced
Dash artificial sweetener

Beat egg with fork until light and lemon-colored. Stir in lemon juice, extract and nutmeg. Add dry milk and blend till it makes a thick paste. In a small bowl beat egg white till stiff. Fold egg white gently into yolk mixture. Arrange pineapple on bottom of pie plate and sprinkle with sweetener. Spread egg mixture over pineapple and bake on bottom shelf of oven at 350° F. for 30 minutes, or until puffed up and brown. Makes 1 breakfast or luncheon serving; for luncheon, supplement as required.

LUNCHEON FEATURING A MUG OF SOUP, HOT CROUTONS AND A LOT OF "KISSES"

Here's a hearty luncheon to serve on a blustery day when puttering in the kitchen is exactly what you feel like doing. A tossed salad is all you need to complete the meal.

Soup

¾ cup tomato juice
¼ cup clam juice
Dash garlic powder (optional)
Dash minced parsley
Slice gherkin (optional)

Combine all ingredients except gherkin in saucepan. Bring to boil and serve hot in a colorful mug. Float slice of pickled gherkin on top, if desired. Makes 1 serving.

Croutons

    1 egg yolk
    1 ounce grated Parmesan or Romano cheese
    Salt and pepper
    Dash dry mustard
    1 slice day-old bread, cut horizontally to make 2 slices

Beat egg yolk with a fork, stir in grated cheese, salt, pepper and mustard to make a paste. Cut bread into quarters. Heap paste on each quarter. Bake on non-stick baking sheet at 250° F. until cheese melts, about 25 minutes. These must be served with Meringue Kisses which follow. Makes 1 luncheon serving.

Meringue Kisses

    1 egg white
    ⅛ teaspoon cream of tartar
    Dash salt
    Artificial sweetener to equal 4 teaspoons sugar
    ¼ teaspoon flavor extract (vanilla, almond, etc.)

Line a baking sheet with parchment paper, aluminum foil or brown paper. Beat egg white, salt and cream of tartar until foamy, then add sweetener and flavor extract. Continue to beat at low speed until very stiff (stands in glossy peaks). Drop mixture from spoon onto lined baking sheet. Bake at 250° F. for 40 minutes, turn off heat, and let stand about 10 minutes more. Remove meringues from paper, using a spatula or pancake turner. Makes 1 luncheon serving.

6. Fats (see p. 213) may be added by any of the following methods:

a) After fish has been cooked and served on your individual platter, you may add fat.

b) After fish has been broiled, transfer it to an individual broiling pan, spread it with "legal" fat, and return it to the broiler for no longer than one minute.

c) For luncheon, combine "legal" bread crumbs with fat, and spread on cooked fish in an individual pan, then put under broiler just long enough to melt fat (not more than one minute).

7. *Approved fish (select 5 meals weekly from this list):*

Abalone
Angel
Bass
Blackfish
Bluefish
Bonita
Bullhead
Butterfish
Carp
Catfish
Chicken haddie
Cod
Crappie
Dolphin
Drum fish
Eel
Finnan haddie
Flounder
Frog's legs

Grouper Fish
Haddock
Halibut
Leopard shark
Mackerel
Mullet
Octopus
Perch
Pike
Pompano
Porgy
Porpoise
Red snapper
Roe (from any fish in this group)
Salmon
Scrod

Sculpin
Scup
Shad
Smelts
Snook
Sole
Speering
Squid (cuttlefish)
Sturgeon
Sucker
Swordfish
Tile fish
Trout
Tuna
Turbot
Weakfish
Whitefish
Whiting

8. *Choose only once a week, if desired:*

Clams
Crab
Crayfish
Lobster

Lobster roe
Mussels
Oysters

Scallops
Scungilli
Shrimp

HOW TO BUY FISH

Select fillets or steaks freshly cut if possible. If precut, be sure edges do not look dry or discolored. Flesh should be firm, not mushy. Keep fish in refrigerated airtight package until used; use within 24 hours. Fresh fish have clear eyes (sunken eyes are a sign of poor quality). Flesh is springy (springs back when pressed lightly with fingers). It should not have strong or unpleasant odor. The cooking method you use for fish depends on its size and cut, rather than on the kind you buy. Market forms and suggested cooking methods are:

Whole dressed: Entrails, scales and fins removed. Head and tail may be removed or left on for decorative effect. Use for baking, poaching, or broiling.

Cut in steaks: Slices cut crosswise (across the grain) from large fish. Use for baking, broiling or poaching. For broiling, cut no more than 1 or 1½ inches thick. For stuffing, a pocket may be cut into the steak.

Fillets: Slices of cleaned fish cut lengthwise, from backbone. Order them skinless and boneless. Use for broiling.

Butterfly Fillets: Two matching pieces of fillet.

Sticks: Pieces of fish fillets or steaks, cut lengthwise or crosswise into pieces about 1 x 3 inches. Use for chowders.

Frozen: Be sure package is firm, frozen solid and whole, not caved in or iced on any side.

HOW TO PREPARE FISH

Fresh or frozen fish: Keep fresh fish refrigerated, in an airtight wrapping (on ice cubes, if you wish), until just before use. Then unwrap and dip quickly in warm salted water to clean. Dry immediately, inside and out, with lemon juice, salt and pepper, if desired. For rich brown color, sprinkle exposed surface heavily with paprika.

Use frozen fish as quickly as possible after you buy it. Defrost it before use, following package directions. For maximum flavor slow-defrost fish at refrigerator temperature. It is best to use fully defrosted fish; partially defrosted fish may be used in a pinch too.

To remove fishy odor from hands, rub them with salt, vinegar or lemon juice before washing them.

Tests for doneness:

1. Make a tiny slice where flesh and backbone meet in center of fish; fish is done if flesh is creamy white and no longer transparent. For thin fillets, both sides should be creamy white. Overdone fish becomes yellowish and tough.

2. Press thick part of fish with finger. If imprint remains, fish should be done. Or test with fork; fish is done when it flakes easily.

3. Insert a thermometer at the thickest part of the fish, in the center below the gills. Fish is done when thermometer reaches 140 to 145 degrees.

Waiting for company: It may be necessary to keep fish waiting through a first course or for company after it is baked or roasted. If so, cook it slightly underdone (it will look slightly transparent only at the thickest part), or to a temperature of 140° F. Turn off heat and leave fish in oven with door open. Use wide pancake turner, or 2 pancake turners, to transfer fish to serving platter.

Serving and weighing large whole fish: There's an art to serving large whole cooked fish. Strip off skin and remove any inedible parts which in some fish may be just under the skin. With knife parallel to serving plate, cut through top half of fish to the backbone (for very large fish, do one side at a time). When top half of fish has been picked, the backbone will be exposed. Lift off backbone and head and tail, if any, and set aside. Now weigh your own boneless and skinless serving.

HOW TO BROIL FISH
For most kinds of fish, prepared in these forms: fillets, steaks, and whole dressed fish ¾ to 1½ inches in thickness.

Preheat broiling pan and rack (if you are using one); the bottom of the fish will cook in the heat of the pan. If desired, you may line baking sheets with aluminum foil to make clean-up easier, but aluminum foil does retard the cooking process. Add seasoned fish and sprinkle heavily with paprika. Baste once or twice with tomato juice or clam juice if desired. Remove from broiling pan to serving plate as soon as fish is done. Serve plain or with one of our toppings (p. 98).

Fillets: Baste them with tomato or clam juice to prevent drying out. Do not turn them unless they are thick. Set them close to broiling unit. Allow 3-5 minutes.

Fish steaks: Order them cut about ¾ to 1 inch thick. Turn with pancake turner to broil both sides. Allow 3-6 minutes in all.

Small dressed fish: Usually broiled with head and tail left on, but make several diagonal slashes 2 inches apart on each side, to prevent fish from curling. Turn with pancake turner. Allow 3-10 minutes in all. Please note that the smaller the fish, the closer to the broiling unit it should be — right up under the source of heat for the little trout or smelts.

HOW TO BAKE FISH
For rolled fillets, steaks and whole dressed fish (head and tail usually left on for baking). Good method for bluefish, mackerel, shad, etc.

During the baking process, fish rests directly on pan, creating a warm, moist heat, so that it cooks partly by its own steam and partly by dry oven heat. Line baking pan with aluminum foil if desired. Set in oven to preheat for 10 minutes. Add fish to heated baking pan. For rich brown color, sprinkle fish generously with paprika before baking. Fish may be baked dry and served with a sauce, or it may be basted several times during baking. When fish is done, lift it out of pan using one or two pancake turners.

Thin fillets: Bake at 450° F. until fish loses its transparency, about 5-15 minutes, depending on size of fish. Turning is not necessary unless you wish to brown second side.

Thick fillets, steaks or whole fish: Bake at 375° F. for 15-45 minutes, or until fish tests done. Time varies according to thickness of fish. Again, turning is not necessary unless you wish to brown second side.

Some chefs prefer to bake fish at moderately hot temperature (400° F.) to produce a crisp, rather than a moist texture. This reduces cooking time by almost 20 per cent. However, I'd like to stress that there can be no exact timetable for fish cooking. You'll have to learn by experience and testing.

How to Braise

Braising is a variation of baking. Make a mirepoix (p. 99), and place it in the bottom of a shallow casserole or baking dish. Pour in ½ cup water (or tomato or clam juice). Add fish. Cover fish lightly with a sheet of parchment paper or heavy brown paper, with hole cut in middle so steam escapes. Bake at 375° F. following timetable above, or until fish flakes easily. Remove fish to plate and discard mirepoix.

HOW TO ROAST OR BARBECUE FISH
For large fish or steaks, for mackerel, salmon, shad, etc.

Fish may be roasted on a rack above a baking pan or open fire so that it cooks by dry heat alone. Preheat oven and baking rack (or barbecue rack). Place fish on hot rack and roast on one side until thickest part of fish tests done halfway through (to the backbone). Then turn fish and roast second side. Baste several times if desired. Remove to serving platter as soon as fish is done.

HOW TO POACH FISH
Recommended for whole dressed fish, thick steaks and thick fillets: striped bass, cod, haddock, halibut, salmon, turbot, etc. Not for strong-flavored fish like mackerel.

Poaching Liquid (Court Bouillon)
    1½ quarts water
    ⅓ cup vinegar
    2 tablespoons dehydrated onion flakes
    2 sprigs parsley
    2 ribs celery with leaves
    2 small bay leaves
    4 peppercorns
    2 teaspoons salt
    Dash allspice

Bring proaching liquid to boil and cook uncovered for 1 hour. This may be done ahead, and refrigerated until needed. Heat to boiling for poaching small fish and steaks; start large fish in cold court bouillon, following directions below.

Poaching Large Fish: Season large fish inside and out with salt and pepper, and place on perforated tray or rack of long, narrow fish steamer, or tie fish in several thicknesses of cheesecloth (see note). Place rack with fish in pan of approximate size (roasting pan, wide skillet, etc.). Pour cold poaching liquid over the fish, just enough to cover it fully. Bring liquid to simmering heat and continue cooking at a very low simmer (shiver). Be sure fish is always covered with poaching liquid. Time after liquid simmers.

> Whole fish up to 3 pounds: 10-12 minutes a pound
> Whole fish 3 or more pounds: 7-9 minutes a pound

When fish tests done, remove it from poaching liquid to plate, sliding it off the tray with a wide pancake turner (use 2 pancake turners if necessary). If it is wrapped in cheesecloth, unfold it and gently roll onto plate.

Poaching Small Fish, Steaks and Thick Fillets: Season boned fish steaks cut to individual portions with salt and pepper. Lay side by side in a shallow saucepan or skillet. Pour in just enough hot poaching liquid to cover fish; keep it moist during poaching, but don't drown it. Cook at simmering temperature until fish is done, then carefully remove from saucepan to platter, using pancake turner. Fish steaks 1-inch thick should be done in 8-12 minutes.

NOTE: Tie cheesecloth, leaving long handles of cloth to make it easier to lift fish out of water; otherwise it tends to fall apart when cooked. If you buy a good hemmed cheesecloth, it will last through many launderings in your washing machine.

In recipes for more than one serving, divide mixture evenly so every portion has an equal amount of each ingredient. For soups and stews:

1. Drain the liquid and set aside
2. Divide solid ingredients evenly, and
3. Add equal amounts of the liquid to each portion

HOW TO STEAM FISH
For clams, crayfish, shrimps, lobster and any delicate fish.

Place fish on steamer, colander, or any perforated rack. Set it in a skillet or saucepan of appropriate size and pour in boiling salted water. Use just enough water to create steam in bottom of skillet, but not enough to touch the fish. (You can raise the level of the steamer or rack, if necessary, by setting it on 2 coffee cups.) Place cover atilt on pan so steam can escape. Cook fish until it is just done — it continues to cook in its own steam after it is removed to the serving platter, so do not overcook it. Serve hot or cold, with or without one of our sauces. Flake for use in salads.

Fish 1 inch thick, 3-5 minutes
Fish 2 inches thick, 7-9 minutes

BASTES, MARINADES AND TOPPINGS FOR UNCOOKED FISH
See chapter on Sauces and Salad Dressings (p. 213-231) for other possibilities.

All-Purpose Barbecue Sauce,
  p. 214
Clam juice, lemon or lime
  juice, or tomato juice

Mirepoix, p. 99
Tangy French Dressing, p. 220
Teriyaki Sauce, p. 221

SAUCES AND TOPPINGS FOR COOKED FISH
Serve sauces well-heated; allow about ¼-½ cup for each serving, and be sure to note food count.

Buttery Sauce, p. 224
Creole Sauce, p. 217
Cucumber Sauce, p. 231
Herb Horseradish Sauce, p. 221
Lemon juice — Soy Sauce combined
Margarine Spreads, p. 223
  (Maitre d'Hotel, especially)
Mayonnaise Dressings, p. 225
Mushroom Sauce, p. 222

Newburg Sauce, p. 231
Prepared horseradish
Ravigote Sauce, p. 223
Cocktail Sauce for Seafood,
  p. 216
Soubise Sauce, p. 218
Tartar Sauce, p. 226
Tomato Sauce, p. 216

GARNISHES FOR FISH
Decorative garnishes add appetizing colors to cooked fish. They're meant to be eaten too, so don't exceed vegetable allowances.

BEAN SPROUTS: Washed and drained. BEETS: Cooked whole, sliced or shredded. BROCCOLI: Cooked or raw florets. CARROTS: Shredded, in sticks, curls or rounds; raw or cooked. CELERY: Tops, hearts, sticks, curls. CUCUMBER: Sliced in rounds or sticks; diced and combined with mayonnaise. GREENS: Lettuce; mustard and beet greens, etc. GREEN PEPPER: Sticks, rings, squares. LEMON: Slices or wedges. LETTUCE: Leaves, shreds, cups. MINT: Leaf or sprigs. ORANGES: Slices. PAPRIKA: Sprinkle on lightly. PARSLEY: Sprigs or chopped. PICKLE: Whole, sliced, minced, chopped. RADISH: Roses, whole, sliced. RED PEPPER: Sticks, rings, squares. TOMATOES: Quarters, slices, home-stewed (p. 280). WATERCRESS: Sprigs or chopped.

MIREPOIX (SKINNY VERSION)
For added flavor, French chefs often bake fish on a bed of vegetables called "mirepoix" (meer-pwa). We have adapted this professional cooking technique to Program, using only #3A vegetables.

1 cup celery, cut into small even dice
¼ cup liquid (clam or tomato juice, or bouillon)
1 tablespoon dehydrated pepper flakes
2 teaspoons minced parsley
½ envelope instant chicken broth and seasoning mix
1 teaspoon dehydrated onion flakes
Dash poultry seasoning
Other seasonings ad lib (thyme, parsley, dill)

Cook celery covered in small saucepan for 10-15 minutes in liquid. When liquid is evaporated, turn off heat, add remaining ingredients and let stand 10 minutes before using, or store in refrigerator and use as needed. Spoon strained vegetables onto fish before baking, or onto broiled fish after it has been browned on one side, or use as stuffing for cooked fish.

BOUILLABAISSE

Saffron, garlic and tomatoes are essential flavorings here. To approximate a French fish stew known as "matelote", add ¼ cup mushrooms and ¼ teaspoon brandy extract. For fish stew Indo-Chinese style, add pineapple dice cut from ½ fresh medium pineapple and a dash of soy sauce.

> 2 pounds assorted fresh fish (sea bass, striped bass, cod, haddock, halibut, mackerel, pike, red snapper, even sliced eels)
> 2 teaspoons lemon juice
> 2 medium tomatoes, cut up
> 2 cups tomato juice
> 2 cups water
> 3 tablespoons dehydrated onion flakes
> 1 clove garlic, minced
> 1 bay leaf
> Pinch each of saffron, thyme, and fennel tips (if available)
> Salt and pepper

Cut fish into slices or sticks about 1½ inches wide, brush with lemon juice, and set aside. Combine remaining ingredients in a saucepan, bring to boil and continue boiling until liquid is reduced by almost half. Broil fish lightly under broiler (or poach gently in water), transfer to saucepan, lower heat to simmering, and cook 5 minutes longer. Bouillabaisse is usually served with broth in one bowl and fish on a separate platter — so you'll have no trouble checking fish weight. For a mid-Sunday meal, use 1½ pounds fish. Rub bread lightly with garlic, toast and cut it into croutons, to be enjoyed with the broth. Makes 4 dinner servings.

SCANDINAVIAN FISH CHOWDER

Do become acquainted with the many different kinds of fish allowed on Program. Not all will be available to you, but try to order at least one of the unfamiliar kinds each week. Include it with your favorite fish the next time you prepare a chowder. Buy a variety of fresh fillets, make up your own assortment, and weigh and freeze in serving-size amounts.

1 medium (3-ounce) potato, peeled and cut in chunks
½ cup skim milk
Salt and pepper
1 teaspoon dehydrated onion flakes
8 ounces assorted fish fillets or sticks (whiting, cod, flounder, or less familiar kinds)
2 teaspoons salt
½ bay leaf
1 teaspoon margarine
½ teaspoon fresh chopped dill

Using very low heat, simmer potato in skim milk with salt, pepper and onion flakes. In separate saucepan, immerse fish in 3 cups boiling water with salt and bay leaf. Cook gently at low simmer for 5 minutes, and drain. Combine fish and potato mixture in serving bowl. Add margarine and dill. Serve hot; for dessert, cooked cranberries would be an authentic Norse touch. Makes 1 dinner serving.

CIOPPINO

16 ounces assorted fish and shellfish (grouper, cod, clams, halibut, etc.) cut in 1-inch pieces
2 cups tomato juice
¼ teaspoon garlic powder
2 tablespoons dehydrated onion flakes
2 tablespoons dehydrated pepper flakes
1 tablespoon chopped parsley
1 tablespoon vinegar-packed capers, drained
2 teaspoons basil
1 teaspoon rosemary
3 tablespoons wine vinegar
2 teaspoons lemon juice
Artificial sweetener to equal 2 teaspoons sugar

Precook fish in water to cover for a few minutes. Drain and transfer fish to medium-size saucepan with remaining ingredients. Simmer uncovered approximately 20 minutes. Remove fish to serving bowls. Boil down liquid remaining in pan to make a thick sauce. Pour over fish in bowls. Makes 2 servings.

BLUEFISH AND OKRA STEW, PORT-AU-PRINCE

8 ounces fresh or frozen okra
3 cups washed spinach or turnip greens, chopped coarsely
2 fillets bluefish, or other fish, 8 ounces each
Salt and pepper
½ bay leaf
1 teaspoon thyme
½ teaspoon chili powder or cayenne pepper
1 cup cooked enriched rice (optional)

If okra is fresh, cut into slices ½-inch thick (ends should be trimmed off first) and cook in boiling salted water. For frozen okra, cook according to package directions. Add spinach or turnip greens and continue cooking for 10 minutes. Meanwhile, broil fish fillets until fish loses its translucence. Add to vegetables. Sprinkle with salt, pepper, bay leaf, thyme and chili or cayenne pepper. Heat well. Serve each portion over ½ cup rice, if desired. Makes 2 dinner servings.

FIVE EASY ONE-DISH FISH DINNERS

1. HALIBUT MONGOLE

1 cup tomato juice
1 medium tomato, diced
8 ounces cooked peas, mashed
¾ cup evaporated skimmed milk
12 ounces cooked, flaked halibut (or other fish)
1 cup cooked enriched rice

In saucepan cook tomato juice till reduced by half. Stir in tomato, peas, skimmed milk and fish; heat over very low heat. Put ½ cup rice into each of two soup bowls, and top with hot fish mixture, evenly divided. Makes 2 servings.

2. FISH SOUFFLE OLE

4 ounces cooked fish
2 cups cooked asparagus, green beans, cauliflower, or spinach, etc.
1 cup water, chicken bouillon or skim milk
2 slices bread, cut in pieces
2 eggs, separated
1 teaspoon chili powder
Salt

Combine fish, vegetable, water, bread, egg yolks, chili powder and salt in blender, and whip until smooth. Remove mixture to bowl. Beat egg whites stiff and fold into fish mixture, ⅓ at a time. Bake in 2 individual casseroles at 350° F. for 25-30 minutes, or until puffy and brown. Makes 2 luncheon servings.

3. MARINE DIVAN

1 cup frozen broccoli or chopped spinach
½ cup boiling water
1 tablespoon dehydrated onion flakes
8 ounces frozen, defrosted or fresh fish fillets
Salt and pepper
½ cup evaporated skimmed milk
¼ teaspoon oregano
Dash paprika

In saucepan, combine broccoli, water and onion flakes and cook until just tender; drain and transfer to shallow casserole. Broil fish for about 5 minutes in foil-lined broiling pan, then put over vegetables in casserole. Sprinkle with salt and pepper. Pour in milk. Add oregano and sprinkle generously with paprika. Bake uncovered at 400° F. until bubbly hot and brown on top. Makes 1 serving.

4. TWO-BEAN FISH BAKE

1½ cups canned, cut, drained green beans
1½ cups canned, drained wax beans
1 cup canned, drained mushrooms
1 cup evaporated skimmed milk
1 teaspoon lemon juice
¼ teaspoon celery seed
¼ teaspoon tarragon
12 ounces gently poached fish fillets, cut in sticks

Combine all ingredients in 1½-quart shallow casserole. Bake uncovered at 375° F. until piping hot. Makes 2 dinner servings.

5. TUNA AND MACARONI CASSEROLE

6 ounces canned tuna or salmon, drained and flaked
⅔ cup cooked enriched elbow macaroni
4 ounces peas (or frozen defrosted peas and carrots)
½ cup cooked or canned mushrooms, drained
Salt
½ cup evaporated skimmed milk
½ teaspoon Worcestershire, red hot sauce, or curry powder
Dash paprika

In attractive casserole, arrange 2 layers each of fish, macaroni, peas, and mushrooms. Sprinkle each layer with salt. Combine milk with Worcestershire or other seasoning and pour into casserole. Sprinkle generously with paprika and bake at 375° F. until piping hot and brown. This dish may easily be extended to include other #3B vegetables — drained, rinsed bean sprouts; cooked or canned wax beans, sliced tomatoes, etc. Makes 1 serving.

CLAM-STUFFED ROULADES (FILLET ROLL-UPS)

4 flounder, sole or mackerel fillets, 6 ounces each
1 teaspoon salt
Freshly ground pepper
8 ounces canned minced clams, well drained
¼ cup lemon juice
Dash paprika

Season fillets with salt and pepper. Spread clams evenly over the center of each fillet. Roll up and secure with toothpicks. Brush tops with lemon juice and, for rich brown color, sprinkle generously with paprika. Bake at 375° F. in foil-lined pan, for 25-30 minutes, or until fish flakes easily when tested. Makes 4 dinner servings.

FISH TURNOVERS MONTE CRISTO

1 egg
2 ounces cooked fish
Salt and pepper
Dash oregano
1 slice bread

Beat egg; reserve half. Combine remaining half with fish, salt, pepper and oregano; mash to a paste. Cut bread horizontally into twofers. Flatten with rolling pin. Place half of fish mixture in center of each, fold bread over to form triangle, and fasten edges with toothpicks. Dip both sides of turnovers in reserved half egg. Transfer to non-stick baking sheet (or sheet lined with aluminum foil); bake at 375° F., turning once to brown both sides. Makes 1 luncheon serving.

COD KABOBS

1 tablespoon lemon juice
1 tablespoon soy sauce
¼ teaspoon garlic powder
Artificial sweetener to equal 1 teaspoon sugar
8 ounces cod or any firm-fleshed fish (halibut, haddock, etc.),
    cut in 1-inch cubes
6 cherry tomatoes
1 medium cucumber, cut in thick slices
½ cup cooked enriched rice

Make marinade by combining lemon juice, soy sauce, garlic powder and sweetener, and pour over fish in mixing bowl. Let stand 30 minutes. Drain, reserving marinade. Thread fish, tomatoes and cucumbers alternately on skewers. Broil indoors or over outdoors barbecue until fish is done, basting with marinade. Serve on ½ cup rice. A salad of tossed greens completes the meal. Makes 1 dinner serving.

FISH CAKES

> 1 slice bread, made into crumbs
> ½ cup skim milk
> Salt and pepper
> Dash dill
> 4 ounces cooked fish, ground, minced or chopped
> ½ cup tomato juice, reduced by half

Reserve 3 tablespoons bread crumbs and 2 tablespoons skim milk. Combine remaining crumbs and milk in saucepan and heat for 10 minutes to make thick white sauce. Add salt, pepper and dill. Stir in fish. Refrigerate mixture on flat plate for about 30 minutes, to make shaping easier. Make into flat cakes. Dip cakes in reserved bread crumbs seasoned with salt and pepper. Bake at 375° F., about 30 minutes, on non-stick baking sheet. Combine tomato juice with reserved milk and any remaining crumbs, heat and serve over fish with more dill. Makes 1 luncheon serving.

EASY FISH HASH

> 12 ounces cooked fish
> 2 medium (3-ounce) potatoes, boiled
> 2 ounces onion
> ½ medium green pepper, sliced
> 1 teaspoon salt
> 1 tablespoon vegetable oil
> ¼ cup Chili Sauce (p. 216 — count ½ cup tomato juice per
>   serving)
> Parsley for garnish

Put fish, potatoes, onion and green pepper through food grinder, or chop in blender. Sprinkle with salt and stir in oil. Mix well. Transfer to aluminum foil pie plate and bake at 400° F. for 25-30 minutes or until lightly brown on top. Divide equally and serve with Chili Sauce. Garnish with parsley sprigs. Makes 2 dinner servings.

FLOUNDER AND SALMON BLANKETS

4 flounder fillets, 4 ounces each
Salt and pepper
1 pound boned salmon steak, cut in lengthwise pieces, 4
ounces each
Dash paprika
1 cup tomato juice
16 ounces fresh, frozen or canned peas and carrots
½ cup evaporated skimmed milk

Season fillets with salt and pepper, and roll each one around a piece of salmon. Secure with toothpicks. Sprinkle with paprika. Bake in shallow pan at 375° F. for 40 minutes. Heat tomato juice in saucepan, add peas and carrots, and cook until tender (do not overcook). Stir in milk and heat gently (evaporated milk curdles if boiled). Serve equally divided over each portion of fish. Makes 4 dinner servings.

GEFILTE FISH

12 ounces whitefish
12 ounces pike
4 ounces onion
¼ cup celery
¼ teaspoon garlic powder
2 teaspoons salt
¼ teaspoon pepper
¼ cup skim milk
4 ounces cooked, sliced carrots
1 envelope (1 tablespoon) unflavored gelatin
2 cups water
1 chicken bouillon cube

Cut fish, onion and celery into dice. Put through meat grinder twice into mixing bowl. Add garlic powder, salt and pepper; pour in milk and mix thoroughly. Shape into 4 equal portions. Poach for 15 minutes. With slotted spoon, transfer fish to platter; arrange 1 ounce of carrots on each portion. Refrigerate. In saucepan, sprinkle gelatin over water, add bouillon cube and heat, stirring until dissolved. Remove and place in refrigerator until loosely set. Arrange around fish. Makes 4 servings.

FISH-STUFFED POTATO BOATS

    4 medium (3-ounce) potatoes
    16 ounces cooked fish
    4 tablespoons hot skim milk
    1 teaspoon onion salt
    Paprika

Bake scrubbed, mature potatoes at 425° F. for 40-50 minutes. When they are soft, cut in half lengthwise, remove insides, leaving skin intact. Mash potato pulp with fish, hot milk and onion salt. Divide mixture equally into 8 potato halves, piling high in center. Sprinkle paprika on top. Set aside till ready to use, then bake on shallow pan at 400° F. until hot and brown on top. Allow 2 "boats" per serving. Makes 4 luncheon servings.

GESMOORDE SNOEK
This South African dish could also be made with pike.

    1 pound fresh or frozen snoek (snook)
    4 ounces onion, sliced
    1 medium tomato
    2 chili peppers, sliced
    Salt and pepper
    Dash cayenne pepper
    2 cups cooked cauliflower (optional)

Boil and flake the snoek. Chop onions and brown in non-stick skillet. Add the tomato and sliced chili peppers. Season with salt and pepper. Simmer for ½ hour, add flaked fish, cover and heat. Sprinkle with cayenne. Serve on cauliflower florets if desired. Makes 2 dinner servings.

FISH CHEESEBURGERS

    2 ounces cooked fish (tuna, etc.)
    1 slice bread
    ½ cup cooked asparagus, broccoli, or leftover vegetable
    1-ounce slice cheddar or American cheese

Mash well-seasoned fish to a paste and spread on 1 slice bread, cover with vegetable, top with cheese and broil until cheese melts. Makes 1 luncheon serving.

DANISH LUNCHEON SALAD
You don't really need a recipe for fish salad. Almost anything goes with it—cooked, diced vegetables; raw carrots or cauliflower florets; fresh salad greens; foods from your daily choice group; fruits too.

4 ounces cooked flaked fish (salmon or other fish)
1 cup diced celery
1 medium cucumber, diced
1 medium dill pickle, diced
2 hard-cooked eggs, diced
¼ cup buttermilk
2 teaspoons minced dill
2 tablespoons mayonnaise

Combine fish with all other ingredients, mixing very thoroughly. Divide salad into 2 even portions and serve in individual lettuce cups. Makes 2 luncheon servings.

MARINATED FISH A LA PORTUGUESE

¾ cup water
½ cup white vinegar
2 tablespoons red wine vinegar
½ bay leaf
½ teaspoon salt
¼ teaspoon cinnamon
½ teaspoon garlic powder
½ teaspoon crushed red pepper
1 pound cod, haddock or flounder fillets
Paprika

Combine all ingredients except fish and paprika in a bowl. Place fish in mixture and refrigerate 2 to 4 hours. Remove fish and reserve marinade. Sprinkle fish with paprika and broil until it is tender and flakes easily when tested with a fork; baste with reserved marinade. Makes 2 dinner servings.

HALIBUT (OR SALMON) LOAF WITH LOBSTER SAUCE

If you've already used your once-a-week fish, you could replace the lobster with cooked turbot, haddock, flounder, etc.

Loaf

    2 slices bread, made into crumbs
    ½ cup evaporated skimmed milk
    18 ounces poached, flaked halibut or salmon
    ¼ cup chicken bouillon
    ¼ cup cooked pureed celery (optional)
    ½ teaspoon onion salt
    Dash paprika or cayenne pepper

Lobster Sauce

    1 slice bread, made into crumbs
    1 cup evaporated skimmed milk
    ¼ cup clam juice or chicken bouillon
    6 ounces cooked lobster, cut into small dice
    Dash paprika

In mixing bowl, soak crumbs in milk, add remaining ingredients for loaf and mix well. Pack lightly into non-stick loaf pan. Set pan into another pan holding hot water and bake at 350° F. for 1 hour. Let cool slightly. To prepare sauce, combine ingredients for sauce and heat gently in double boiler, or use very low heat (evaporated skimmed milk will curdle if it boils). Serve loaf in 6 slices with Lobster Sauce divided equally over each slice. Makes 6 luncheon servings.

PINK LADY SALAD (FISH, POTATO AND BEETS)

    1 medium apple, peeled, cored and sliced
    6 ounces poached firm fish, boned and flaked
    1 medium (3-ounce) potato, boiled and diced
    2 ounces cooked beets, diced
    2 ounces raw onions, diced
    ½ tablespoon diced gherkins
    ½ tablespoon drained capers, diced
    Salt and pepper
    Dash paprika
    1 recipe Basic French Dressing (p. 227 — count 1 tablespoon
      vegetable oil)

Combine all ingredients, except French Dressing. Add dressing last and mix gently. Shape in large coffee cup and refrigerate until ready to serve. Unmold on lettuce leaves when well chilled. Makes 1 dinner serving.

BROILED FINNAN HADDIE
Smoked haddock is generally marketed as "finnan haddie" — and yes, it's on Program.

> ½ cup boiling water
> ½ cup instant chicken broth and seasoning mix
> 2 tablespoons lemon juice
> ⅛ teaspoon cayenne pepper
> ⅛ teaspoon paprika
> ¼ teaspoon nutmeg
> 1 pound finnan haddie

Combine all ingredients except fish. Brush mixture over fish. Broil about 4 inches from source of heat for 10 minutes or until fish flakes easily with fork. Baste with broth mixture during broiling. Makes 2 dinner servings.

IA HALAKAHIKI
Abalone, dolphin (mahimahi) and hundreds of other species of marine life swim in the seas around Hawaii, but if you can't find these exotic kinds, even in the frozen-food department, use sea bass, bluefish, cod, flounder, mackerel, red snapper or trout. The fish of the islands, like the king of Hawaiian fruits, deserve a chapter by themselves, but they are put together here in one delicious recipe named for Hawaiian words meaning, in order, fish and pineapple.

> 2 pounds fish fillets or boned steaks
> 1 recipe Teriyaki Sauce (p. 221)
> 8 small slices pineapple (canned in its own juice) plus 8
>   tablespoons pineapple juice

Marinate fish in Teriyaki Sauce for 1 hour. Drain; transfer sauce to pan with half of pineapple slices, cut into pieces, and pineapple juice. Heat gently. Arrange fish with remaining slices of pineapple alongside each other on foil-lined plan. Sprinkle with paprika, broil until fish flakes easily when tested with fork. Serve with pineapple sauce equally divided over fillets. Makes 4 dinner servings.

POMPANO FLORIDA STYLE

4 pompano fillets or boned steaks, 8 ounces each (or sea bass, mullet, red snapper, etc.)
1 lemon or lime, sliced
½ cup lemon or lime juice
4 small oranges, sliced
8 ounces Bermuda onion, sliced
Dash paprika

Rinse and dry fillets and sprinkle with salt and pepper. Line center of baking pan with slices of lemon or lime and lay fish on top. Sprinkle with juice. Bake at 350° F., basting with the juice, until fish flakes easily when tested, 25-30 minutes, depending on the size of the fillets or steaks. Arrange overlapping slices of orange and onion on 4 individual serving plates, each holding a cooked fillet. Dust with paprika. Serve at once. Makes 4 dinner servings.

KAMANO LOMI

Lox, New York's affectionate name for smoked salmon, sure gets around; it's a Honolulu favorite too. Hawaiians prefer only scallions with their kamano (*salmon*); *they* lomi (*crush*) *the sliced green onions with ice-cream salt, using fingers or a wooden potato masher.*

12 ounces smoked salmon, boned and skinned
4 medium tomatoes, peeled and sliced
4 ounces scallions or white onions, chopped fine
¼ to ½ cup ice water
1 teaspoon ice-cream salt (coarse rock salt)
Cracked ice

Soak salmon 3-4 hours or overnight in cold water. Drain; shred into ¼-inch pieces. Combine tomatoes and shredded salmon, and mash with fork. Stir in ice water. *Lomi* (crush) onions with ice-cream salt, add to fish and tomatoes, mix thoroughly, divide evenly into 2 shells, and serve over cracked ice. Makes 2 dinner servings.

SMOKED SALMON CANAPES

> 1 recipe Cream Cheese (p. 51 — count ⅓ cup cottage cheese
> per serving)
> 1 teaspoon dehydrated onion flakes, reconstituted in 1
> tablespoon water
> ½ teaspoon curry powder
> 4 ounces smoked salmon, cut into 4 thin slices
> 1 medium cucumber, scored with fork and cut into 12 slices
> 12 thin strips pimento, rolled up (optional)

Mash Cream Cheese with onion flakes and curry; spread on salmon
slices and roll up each, jelly-roll fashion. Chill overnight or for
several hours. Cut each salmon roll into 3 slices and place on
cucumber slices. Garnish with pimento, if desired. Makes 12
canapés; 2 luncheon servings.

QUICK-SET SALMON MOUSSE
A fine summer dish.

> 2 envelopes (2 tablespoons) unflavored gelatin
> 1 cup evaporated skimmed milk
> ¾ cup hot chicken bouillon
> 16 ounces canned salmon, drained and flaked
> 4 tablespoons mayonnaise
> 2 tablespoons lemon juice
> ½ cup finely chopped celery
> 1 cup crushed ice
> 1 teaspoon Worcestershire

Sprinkle gelatin over milk in blender. Let soften for 2 minutes,
then add hot chicken bouillon and blend for 30 seconds at high
speed. Add salmon, mayonnaise, lemon juice, and celery. Blend
well. With motor still running, add a heaping cupful of crushed
ice. Stir if necessary to get ice pulled down into blades. As soon
as ice is combined with salmon, pour into a 6-cup mold which has
been rinsed in cold water. Refrigerate until firm, about 20 minutes;
unmold and serve. Makes 4 luncheon servings.

PICKLED PEPPERY SALMON

> 8 ounces canned salmon
> 2 ounces chopped scallions
> ¼ teaspoon coarse black pepper
> 1 or 2 chili tepines
> Wine vinegar

Flake canned salmon in fairly large pieces. Sprinkle with chopped scallions and coarse black pepper and add 1 or 2 chili tepines (little dry, hot red peppers — the kind you find in mixed pickling spices); add wine vinegar almost to cover. Cover and refrigerate 24 hours or more. Makes 2 luncheon servings.

SCALLOPED FISH EN CASSEROLE

A hearty Sunday luncheon dish using leftovers from the extra-large fish you cooked on Saturday.

> ⅔ cup cooked enriched elbow macaroni
> 2 ounces cooked fish, diced
> 1 ounce sharp cheddar cheese
> ½ medium green pepper, minced, or ½ cup canned
>   mushrooms, drained
> ½ cup evaporated skimmed milk
> Salt and pepper
> Paprika

Combine all ingredients in small casserole, mix lightly, and bake at 350° F. for 35-45 minutes. Makes 1 luncheon serving.

BROILED SHAD ROE

> 1 tablespoon imitation (or diet) margarine, melted
> 1 teaspoon lemon juice
> ¼ teaspoon minced parsley
> 6 ounces canned shad roe

Combine margarine, lemon juice and parsley; set aside. Broil shad roe on both sides till brown, and top-dress it at the table with margarine-lemon sauce. Makes 1 dinner serving.

SOLE ON RICE

½ cup cooked enriched rice
2 tablespoons tomato juice
1 teaspoon minced parsley
Dash allspice and garlic salt
1 medium tomato, chopped
Salt and pepper
8 ounces fillet of sole (or flounder), cut into 3-inch squares
Dash paprika
1 teaspoon margarine

In flameproof oven-to-table casserole or small foil pan, combine rice, tomato juice, parsley, allspice and garlic salt. Cover with chopped tomato sprinkled with salt and pepper. Broil 3 inches from heat. Meanwhile arrange fillet of sole in separate broiling pan, sprinkle with paprika and broil alongside rice-tomato mixture, until fish flakes easily (thin fillets need not be turned). Transfer fillets to top of tomatoes, spread with margarine and heat for 1 minute under broiler. Makes 1 dinner serving.

VARIATION
Luncheon Risotto: Omit sole and margarine. Add 2 ounces canned clams, 1 ounce grated sharp hard cheese, and 2 tablespoons bottled clam juice to rice-tomato mixture. Bake at 350° until cheese melts. Nice baked in clam shells.

TUNA A LA KING
Our tuna recipes are for the canned fish, but if you ever get fresh tuna or bonita steaks, bake, broil or poach them following the general directions given earlier in this chapter. Use just as you would the canned fish.

¼ cup cooked or canned mushrooms
½ cup skim milk
Salt and pepper
Dash paprika
4 ounces canned tuna
1 slice toast

Drain mushrooms and place in blender. Add milk and seasonings and puree. Heat with tuna in saucepan. Pour over toast and serve for lunch. Makes 1 serving.

TUNA SANDWICH SPREADS AND DIPS

> 4 ounces canned, drained tuna
> 2 tablespoons evaporated skimmed milk
> Dash red hot sauce
> 1 teaspoon chopped chives
> 1 teaspoon parsley
> Salt and pepper
> Dash paprika
> Celery ribs, cut into sticks

Combine all ingredients except celery in blender; blend at high speed until well chopped. If necessary, move ingredients from sides to center of blender container with rubber spatula so they reach blades. Serve with celery sticks. Makes 1 luncheon serving.

VARIATIONS

1. Combine 4 ounces drained, canned tuna (or salmon); 1 teaspoon dehydrated onion flakes; 1 rib celery, finely diced; 1 teaspoon prepared mustard; 1 tablespoon mayonnaise. Mash well. Serve on 1 slice toast.

2. Combine 2 ounces drained tuna; 1 *almost*-hard-cooked egg, chopped; 1 teaspoon dehydrated onion flakes, reconstituted in 1 tablespoon water; 1 rib celery, finely diced. Mix well. Egg should be boiled 6 minutes (after water boils) so yolk is not quite firm; soft yolk adds needed moisture.

HAWAIIAN BEACHCOMBER'S SALAD

> 8 ounces canned tuna, drained and flaked
> ½ cup diced celery
> 2 tablespoons chopped gherkins
> 1 medium banana, sliced
> 2 small slices pineapple (canned in its own juice), diced, plus
>   2 tablespoons juice
> 2 tablespoons mayonnaise
> 1 teaspoon dry mustard
> 2 cups shredded lettuce

Combine all ingredients except lettuce, mix thoroughly, and divide evenly into 2 large shells or salad bowls holding shredded lettuce. Makes 2 luncheon servings; for dinner, increase tuna to 12 ounces.

SALAD NICOISE

A nice chef's salad originated by a Nice chef in that famous French resort.

> 6-8 cups salad greens (2 or more kinds — romaine, iceburg, Boston, bibb, etc.)
> 2 ribs celery (with leaves), diced
> 1 cut clove garlic
> 8 ounces canned drained tuna
> 4 hard-cooked eggs, quartered
> 2 cups cooked (pickled if possible) green beans
> 1 medium green pepper, cut in rings
> 1 medium red pepper, cut in strips
> ½ cup shredded roast pimentos
> 1 tablespoon chopped chives
> 4 medium (3-ounce) potatoes, boiled (optional)
> 1 recipe Parsley-Vinaigrette Sauce (p. 229—count 1 tablespoon oil per serving)

Wash lettuce and celery leaves, drain and dry quickly. Wrap in clean towel and refrigerate until ready to use. Rub 4 large salad bowls or deep plates with cut clove of garlic. Divide equally into the bowls: shredded lettuce, torn into bite-size pieces, celery, tuna, eggs, green beans, green and red peppers and pimentos, potatoes (if you are using them) and sprinkling of chives. (All of this may be done in advance and refrigerated.) Have everyone toss his own salad and dressing at the table. Makes 4 luncheon servings.

VARIATIONS

1. You can be as clever and creative as you like in omitting or adding ingredients to this classic French chef's salad. Four ounces hard-sliced cheese may replace eggs. Wedges of tomato and slices of cucumber, capers and parsley, four ounces sliced cooked artichoke hearts, or drained cooked shredded beets could be added too.

2. You may omit eggs and add 8 more ounces tuna, so salad qualifies as one of required fish meals.

3. If you omit the potato, you may add croutons made from 4 slices of toast. Toss them in at the very end so they don't become soggy.

TUNA WALDORF SALAD

> 1 tablespoon lemon juice
> 1 medium red apple, unpeeled and diced
> 4 ounces canned tuna, drained and flaked
> ½ medium dill pickle, chopped
> 1 tablespoon chopped pimento
> ¼ cup chopped raw Chinese cabbage, or ½ medium
>   cucumber, peeled and chopped
> Lettuce

Sprinkle lemon juice on apple to keep it from turning brown. Combine with remaining ingredients and chill. Serve on bed of lettuce. Makes 1 luncheon serving.

TUNA OR SALMON DEVILKIN

> ¼ cup skim milk
> 1 slice enriched white bread, made into crumbs
> 2 ounces cooked or canned tuna or salmon
> 1 hard-cooked egg, mashed
> Salt
> ¼ teaspoon prepared mustard
> ¼ teaspoon Worcestershire
> Dash red hot sauce
> Dash imitation butter flavoring

Combine milk, bread crumbs, fish and egg. Add salt, mustard, Worcestershire, red hot sauce, and butter flavoring. Turn into a small baking dish or large shell and bake at 450° F. for 15 minutes. Makes 1 luncheon serving.

STUFFED-WITH-TUNA MUSHROOMS

    1 cup large mushrooms
    2 envelopes instant chicken broth and seasoning mix
    1 cup water
    4 ounces canned tuna, drained
    ½ teaspoon lemon juice
    ¼ teaspoon dill
    1 teaspoon dehydrated onion flakes
    Salt and pepper

Remove stems from plump mushrooms, slice stems and combine with caps in saucepan. Add broth mix to water, bring to boil, cover and simmer for a few minutes. Drain; reserve liquid and serve separately as hot broth. Transfer whole mushroom caps to shallow baking dish, hollow side up. Combine tuna, sliced mushroom stems, lemon juice, seasonings and enough of the reserved broth to moisten the stuffing. Mix well and pile high in caps. Place in baking pan with ½ cup water and bake at 375° F. for 10 minutes. Makes 1 luncheon serving.

TUNA, TOMATO AND ZUCCHINI MOLD

    2 envelopes (2 tablespoons) unflavored gelatin
    ¼ cup water
    4 medium tomatoes, diced
    2 tablespoons dehydrated onion flakes
    ¼ clove garlic, minced
    2 tablespoons chopped parsley
    ¼ teaspoon dried leaf oregano
    2 teaspoons salt
    1 cup shredded, scrubbed raw zucchini
    8 ounces tuna, drained and flaked

In small saucepan sprinkle gelatin over water. Place saucepan over low heat and stir until gelatin is fully melted and tomatoes are soft, about 3 minutes. Remove from heat; add onion flakes, garlic, parsley, oregano and salt. Chill until mixture is thickened. Fold in raw zucchini and tuna. Turn into a quart-size mold. Chill 3-4 hours or until firm. Makes 4 servings; supplement as required.

TUNA PROVENCALE

Combine 1 serving Ratatouille (p. 270 — count 1½ cups cooked #3B vegetables) with 4 ounces flaked tuna and serve hot or cold. Tuna is great mixed with other vegetables too, for example, with 1 cup crisp-cooked and halved Chinese pea pods. Season with soy sauce. Makes 1 luncheon serving.

WHITING (OR COD) CREOLE

In New Orleans and elsewhere in the South, cooked grits are a traditional accompaniment for any fish served Creole style.

2 pounds whiting or cod fillets
½-1 cup water
Salt and pepper
3 cups cooked enriched hominy grits
1 recipe Creole Sauce (p. 217 — count ½ cup tomato juice
    and ¼ of your daily #3B vegetable allowance, per serving)

Arrange fillets in shallow baking pan. Add water. Sprinkle lightly with salt and pepper. Bake at 400° F. for 15 minutes, or until fish flakes easily with a fork. Remove fillets carefully to a platter. Serve alongside hominy grits, and top with Creole Sauce. Makes 4 servings.

MARINER'S VEGETABLE PLATTER

2 boned and skinned whitefish (or other steaks), 8 ounces each
2 medium (3-ounce) potatoes, cut into quarters
4 ounces carrots, cut into quarters
4 ounces peas
2 ribs celery, cut into matchstick pieces
Salt and pepper
1 cup cauliflower florets
1 teaspoon minced chives

Poach whitefish, cool and set aside on large serving platter. Meanwhile, bring 2 cups salted water to boil in saucepan, add potatoes, bring water to boil again; add carrots, peas and celery. Cook until vegetables are tender, but do not overcook them. Transfer drained vegetables (reserve liquid) to serving platter, surrounding fish, and keep warm. Sprinkle with salt and pepper. Add cauliflower to the liquid remaining in pan and cook until very soft (an exception to our "cook only until firm" statement), then puree in blender. Pour over fish and vegetables; sprinkle with chives and serve at once. Makes 2 dinner servings.

ONCE-A-WEEK ONLY

LONG ISLAND CLAM CHOWDER

    1 medium (3-ounce) potato, peeled and diced
    ½ cup clam juice
    ½ cup tomato juice
    ½ cup water
    ½ cup finely diced celery
    1 tablespoon dehydrated onion flakes
    ½ envelope instant chicken broth and seasoning mix
    ¼ teaspoon garlic powder
    ¼ teaspoon thyme
    ½ bay leaf
    Dash cayenne pepper
    6 ounces cooked, minced clams

Combine all ingredients except clams in saucepan and simmer until potato and celery are tender, about 15-20 minutes. Add clams and heat thoroughly. Makes 1 dinner serving.

CLAM-VEGETABLE CHOWDER

Follow recipe above, but add 1 ounce each of diced carrots, okra, Brussels sprouts and green peas; cook until potatoes and vegetables are tender. It's "legal" to mix-and-match our #4 vegetables, and reap the benefits of variety. Makes 1 dinner serving.

NOTE: It's easy to multiply these chowder recipes to make enough for the family (or the freezer). Be sure, however, to divide evenly as directed on p. 22.

CRAB DIABLO
Wow!

> 1 pound cooked crabmeat (or halibut, salmon, cod, etc.)
> 1 medium green pepper, finely diced
> 1 medium red pepper, finely diced
> 4 tablespoons mayonnaise
> ¼ cup skim milk
> 1 tablespoon lemon juice
> ½ teaspoon dry mustard
> 1 teaspoon Worcestershire
> 2 drops of red hot sauce
> Salt and white pepper
> 1 slice toast, made into crumbs
> Dash paprika

Flake and pick over crabmeat (best to do it with your fingers) to remove bones. Combine with mayonnaise, skim milk, lemon juice, Worcestershire, mustard, red hot sauce, salt and pepper. Mix thoroughly. Divide mixture equally into 8 individual ramekins or shells. Sprinkle with crumbs and paprika. Put shells on a baking sheet and bake at 375° F. until piping hot, about 25 minutes. Makes 4 luncheon servings; supplement as required.

LOBSTER TAILS WITH BUTTERY SAUCE

For Boiled Lobster Tails: In saucepan, bring salted water to boil; add lobster tails. Cook for 5 minutes if thawed, 7 minutes if frozen. Remove from water and drain quickly under cold water. Cut away underside membrane, and pull away from shell in one piece.

For Broiled Lobster Tails: Thaw tails at room temperature. Cut out underside membrane, and holding tail firmly, bend backward toward shell side. This cracks the shell and prevents curling. Broil 6 inches from heat, shell side up, in preheated broiler, 2-3 minutes. Turn tails shell side down, baste with chicken bouillon if desired, and broil 3-5 minutes on second side.

Serve your 6 ounces of boiled or broiled hot lobster tails with a pipkin or tiny sauceboat of our Buttery Sauce (p. 224 — count 2 tablespoons imitation, or diet, margarine and 1 fluid ounce skim milk).

LOBSTER BUTTERMILK LOAF (SALMON, TUNA, ETC.)

    1 envelope (1 tablespoon) unflavored gelatin
    1 cup chicken bouillon
    3 fluid ounces (6 tablespoons) buttermilk
    2 tablespoons lemon juice, or mild vinegar
    ½ teaspoon onion salt
    ⅛ teaspoon red hot sauce
    6 ounces cooked, diced lobster, or flaked, canned salmon,
        tuna, etc.
    ½ cup finely chopped celery
    Parsley sprigs

Sprinkle gelatin over bouillon in small saucepan. Place over low heat, stirring until gelatin is dissolved. Remove from heat, add buttermilk, lemon juice, salt and red hot sauce. Chill until mixture is slightly thickened. Fold in fish and celery. Rinse a quart mold in water. Pour in gelatin-fish mixture and chill 3-4 hours until firm. Unmold on chilled plate and garnish with parsley sprigs. Makes 1 serving.

OYSTERS VANDERBILT EN CASSEROLE

If Oysters Vanderbilt made for one sounds just a little selfish, you can easily double or quadruple this recipe.

    4 ounces canned oysters
    ½ cup Tomato Sauce (1 cup tomato juice reduced by half)
    Pinch basil or poultry seasoning
    1 tablespoon dehydrated onion flakes
    Dash garlic powder
    1 slice enriched white bread, made into crumbs

Spread oysters in small casserole, combine Tomato Sauce with basil or poultry seasoning, onion flakes and garlic powder. Spoon onto oysters. Top with bread crumbs. Bake at 375° F. until piping hot. Makes 1 luncheon serving.

SCALLOPS

You may serve the sweeter and costlier bay scallops or the larger sea variety with allowed margarine and a sprinkling of minced parsley.

To Broil Scallops: If scallops are very large, cut them into thick slices or quarters. Dip them in chicken bouillon before you broil to keep them moist, and don't overcook — they should be done on both sides in 3-5 minutes.

To Poach Scallops: Scallops are easily overcooked. Moist and delicious one minute, they become tough and rubbery the next. See How to Poach Fish, p. 96, allowing no more than 4-6 minutes total cooking time.

SCALLOPS IN SHELL

    6 ounces poached scallops, cut into pieces
    ¼ cup mushrooms, diced
    2 tablespoons (1 fluid ounce) evaporated skimmed milk
    ½ teaspoon chopped chives
    Few drops sherry extract
    Salt and pepper

Combine scallops, mushrooms, milk, chives, sherry extract, salt and pepper in large shell (or ramekin). Bake at 350° F. for 20 minutes. Makes 1 dinner serving.

SCALLOPS CON CAPPERI (SCALLOPS WITH CAPER SAUCE)

    1 pound scallops
    1 cup chicken bouillon
    Paprika
    2 teaspoons margarine
    1 teaspoon lemon juice or vinegar
    1 tablespoon minced capers

Roll scallops in chicken bouillon and sprinkle with paprika. Broil until scallops are no longer translucent halfway through their thickness, basting at least once with bouillon. Turn, baste again, and brown second side. Do not overcook — scallops will be done in 4-7 minutes, depending on their thickness. Combine margarine, lemon juice and capers; serve over scallops. Makes 2 dinner servings.

SHRIMP SAVVY

Cut down cooking odor by shelling shrimp before it is cooked. Shrimp may be cooked before or after they are shelled (your choice, since gourmets disagree about which method best preserves flavor).

Remember to allow 2 ounces for shell and 2 ounces for shrinkage in cooking, per serving, when you buy shrimp. Poach shrimp for 3-5 minutes, or until shrimp turns pink. For frozen shrimp, follow directions on package. After shrimp are cooked, they may be refrigerated for a day or so, if necessary, in a tightly covered container in cooking liquid to keep them juicy.

SERVING SUGGESTIONS

1. *Shrimp Creole:* 6 ounces cooked shrimp, ¼ recipe heated Creole Sauce (p. 217 – count ½ cup tomato juice and ¼ of daily #3B vegetable). Makes 1 dinner serving.

2. *Newburg Sauce* is a classic sauce for shrimp too. Use 8 ounces cooked shrimp to 1 recipe Newburg Sauce (p. 231 – count ½ cup #3B vegetable, ¼ cup tomato juice and ¼ cup evaporated skimmed milk per serving). Makes 2 luncheon servings.

SHRIMP BISQUE

    1 cup clam juice
    ½ cup cooked cauliflower
    ¼ cup tomato juice
    1 tablespoon dehydrated onion flakes
    ½ bay leaf
    1 teaspoon Worcestershire
    8 ounces cooked shrimp, chopped
    ¼ cup cooked mushrooms, drained and sliced
    Salt and pepper
    ¼ cup evaporated skimmed milk
    1 teaspoon chopped parsley

Place clam juice, cauliflower, tomato juice and onion flakes in blender. Blend until smooth. Pour into saucepan. Add bay leaf, Worcestershire, shrimp and mushrooms. Simmer for 10 minutes. Season with salt and pepper. Add milk; heat thoroughly, but do not boil. Sprinkle with parsley and serve. Makes 2 servings.

SHRIMP OREGANATA
Easily doubled or tripled to serve hungry hordes.

4 ounces cleaned, poached shrimp
½ slice dry bread, made into crumbs
2 teaspoons finely minced parsley
1½ teaspoons vegetable oil
½ small clove garlic, mashed
¼ teaspoon oregano
Salt and cayenné pepper (optional)
Lemon wedges for garnish

Arrange shrimp in an individual shallow flameproof casserole. Combine remaining ingredients (except lemon wedges) in a small bowl and mix well. Add a few drops water or clam juice to moisten, and pile some of mixture around and on each shrimp, covering them thoroughly. Broil at moderate heat just long enough to brown crumbs. Serve hot with lemon wedges. Makes 1 luncheon serving.

SHRIMP AND RICE JAMBALAYA

1 cup tomato juice
1 cup water
1 envelope instant chicken broth and seasoning mix
1 teaspoon dehydrated onion flakes
1 teaspoon Worcestershire
Salt and pepper
½ bay leaf
1½ pounds poached, cleaned shrimp
¼ cup evaporated skimmed milk
2 cups cooked enriched rice

In saucepan combine tomato juice, water, broth mix, onion flakes, Worcestershire, salt, pepper and bay leaf. Cook until liquid is reduced almost to half. Stir in shrimp and milk and simmer gently, just enough to heat through. Pour equally into 4 bowls, each containing ½ cup rice. Makes 4 dinner servings.

SEAFOOD FONDUE

A do-it-yourself party that relaxes hostess and guests too. Provide fondue forks or bamboo skewers for each diner. Pre-weigh portions for members of Weight Watchers. Serve in individual dishes, all ready for cooking.

CHOOSE TO FONDUE

For each serving, choose an 8-ounce assortment of uncooked seafood from the following list:

Fresh lobster tail meat, cut in bite-size chunks
Bay scallops, or sea scallops cut in half
Fresh shrimp, shelled and deveined
King crab legs, shelled and cut in bite-size pieces
Any firm-fleshed fish such as halibut or haddock, cut in 1-inch squares

IN THE FONDUE POT

1½ cups clam juice
1½ cups boiling water
2 envelopes instant chicken broth and seasoning mix

Bring to boil the clam juice, water and broth mix. When bubbly, reduce to simmer temperature and invite guests to spear raw fish tidbits on to their fondue forks, and dip in this bubbly brew until fish is done to their taste. From 3-5 minutes should be enough. Do not put the fondue fork in your mouth ... it can burn. Switch to another fork for ....

OPERATION DIP AND EAT

Each guest dips cooked fish into one or more sauces, which are served in clam shells or small bowls around his dinner plate. Suggested sauces for each serving:

1 recipe Teriyaki Sauce, p. 221
2 tablespoons Cocktail Sauce for Seafood (p. 216 — count 3 fluid ounces tomato juice)
2 tablespoons heated imitation (or diet) margarine, spiked with lemon juice

Fruit

In this chapter you will find such once-forbidden fruits as bananas and grapes, plus dozens of concoctions so delectable you will want to invent occasions to serve and show them off. Everyone's favorites are here: Banana-Cheese Betty, dreamy sherbets, Strawberry Jelly, mousses and parfaits so light they melt in your mouth, fruit beverages in great variety, and fruit salads for every season. Those of you with a sweet tooth can have dessert every day, without your figure ever letting on.

RULES FOR USING FRUIT

1. Amounts:

> WOMAN: 3 fruits a day
>
> MAN AND YOUTH: 5 fruits a day

2. One fruit must be taken at breakfast. Select 1 daily from List #1 and the others from List #1 or #2.

3. Use fresh or frozen (unsweetened) fruit unless otherwise specified; the only canned fruit permitted is sliced pineapple packed in its own juice. Two tablespoons pineapple juice must be consumed with the pineapple.

4. *List #1:* Choose 1 fruit from this list daily.

> Cantaloupe, ½ medium
> Fruit juice: orange, grapefruit or tangerine, ½ cup (4 fluid ounces)
> Grapefruit, ½ medium
> Honeydew or similar melon, 2-inch wedge
> Orange, 1 small
> Strawberries, 1 cup
> Tangelo, 1 small
> Tangerine, 1 medium
> Tomato juice, 1 cup (8 fluid ounces)

NOTE: If tomato juice is used in this way — it is in addition to your daily bonus of 12 ounces tomato juice.

5. *List* #2: Choose daily from this list, if desired.

> Apricots (12 per pound), 3
> Berries (blackberries, blueberries, loganberries or raspberries),
>   ½ cup
> Boysenberries, ⅔ cup
> Caimito, 1 medium (available in Puerto Rico)
> Crab apple, 2
> Cranberries, 1 cup
> Gineps, 2
> Guava, 1 medium (available in Puerto Rico)
> Jobo, 1 medium (available in Puerto Rico)
> Mandarin orange, 1 medium
> Mandarin orange sections, ½ cup
> Nectarine, 1 medium
> Paw Paw, ¼ medium
> Peach, 1 medium
> Pineapple (fresh), ¼ medium
> Pineapple (canned in its own juice), 2 small slices (or 1 large)
>   with 2 tablespoons of juice
> Plums (any type), 2 medium or 1 large
> Rhubarb, 2 cups raw or 1 cup cooked
> Sour sop, ⅓ cup
> Sweet sop (or sugar-apple), ½ cup
> Ugli fruit, 1 medium

You may choose from the following daily if desired:

> WOMAN: As 1 of your 3 fruits
> MAN: As 2 of your 5 fruits
> YOUTH: As 3 of your 5 fruits

Apple, 1 medium
Pear, 1 medium

Remember please that in all recipes serving more than one, foods must be evenly divided; follow directions on p. 22.

6. *List* #3: Once a week, if desired, you may substitute one of the following for one of your daily fruits. Do not choose the same fruit every week.

> WOMAN AND MAN: On the day you make this choice, do not include an apple or pear among your fruits
> YOUTH: On the day you make this choice, do not include more than 2 apples or 2 pears among your fruits.

Banana, 1 medium
Grapes (any type), 1 cup
Sapote (marmalade plum), ¼ cup diced
Sweet cherries, ½ cup pitted or ¾ cup unpitted

BAKED APPLES

> 4 medium baking apples (firm variety such as Rome Beauty, Northern Spy, Rhode Island Greening, Winesap, etc.)
> ¾ cup dietetic carbonated beverage (e.g. black cherry, raspberry, ginger ale, etc.)

Wash and core apples. To keep skins from bursting, pare them one-third of the way down or slit skins around apples about half way down. Arrange in baking dish, pour beverage over them and sprinkle with cinnamon. Bake uncovered at 400° F. 45 to 60 minutes or until tender. Makes 4 servings.

BAKED FRESH FRUIT
Baked fruits add variety to your meals. These go well with fish or meat.

> 12 apricots, 4 medium peaches, or 4 medium pears
> ½ cup boiling water
> ¼ cup brown sugar replacement
> 2 teaspoons lemon juice
> ¾ teaspoon cinnamon
> ¼ teaspoon each cloves, nutmeg and ginger

Halve fruit and remove pits or cores. Arrange, hollow side up, in shallow baking dish. Combine remaining ingredients and sprinkle over fruit. Bake uncovered at 400° F. about 20 minutes for apricots, 30 minutes for peaches, 45 minutes for pears, or until tender. Makes 4 servings.

BROILED FRESH FRUIT
Watch fruit carefully to avoid scorching.

> 4 medium apples, cored and sliced ¼ inch thick; or 4 medium green-tipped bananas, peeled and halved lengthwise; or 4 medium peaches, peeled, halved and pitted
> 1 tablespoon lemon juice
> ½ teaspoon flavor extract (coconut, walnut, etc.), optional

Brush both sides of fruit with lemon juice and arrange in foil-lined broiler pan. Broil until tender, turning once. Allow about 5 minutes for apples; 4-5 minutes for bananas; 10-12 minutes for peaches, or until tender. Sprinkle with flavor extract before serving, if desired. Makes 4 servings.

APPLE SQUARES

> 2 medium apples, cored, peeled and thinly sliced
> Artificial sweetener to equal 13 teaspoons sugar
> ½ teaspoon cinnamon
> 1 cup cream-flavored dietetic carbonated beverage
> 4 eggs, separated
> 1⅓ cups instant non-fat dry milk

Add apples, sweetener to equal 4 teaspoons of sugar and cinnamon to carbonated beverage; cook 5 minutes. Set aside. Beat egg whites until stiff; add dry milk and continue beating until well blended. Set aside. Add remaining sweetener to egg yolks and mix well. Fold yolk mixture into egg whites. Pour half of the egg mixture into a 9 x 9-inch baking pan, arrange apples on top, and pour remaining mixture over apples. Bake at 350° F. for 30 minutes or until lightly browned. Cool on rack. Makes 4 servings.

"JELLY" APPLES

Your overweight youngsters will want you to make plenty of these bright sticky treats for the Halloween party.

1 can (12 fluid ounces) black cherry-flavored dietetic
    carbonated beverage
1½ envelopes (4-5 teaspoons) unflavored gelatin
Few drops red food coloring
6 medium apples

Boil 1 cup beverage until bubbles are gone. Soften gelatin in remaining beverage, then stir into hot beverage. Add food coloring and stir well. Refrigerate till mixture is thickened. Put sticks into apples and dip into gelatin mixture. Place in freezer. Dip every 15 minutes and return to freezer. After 6 coats, transfer to shallow pan lined with wax paper. Chill leftover gelatin for dessert. Makes 6 servings.

REFRIGERATOR APPLE "BUTTER"

To spread on your slice of breakfast toast.

2 tart medium apples
2 cups water
Artificial sweetener to equal 6 teaspoons sugar
¼ teaspoon cinnamon
⅛ teaspoon allspice
⅛ teaspoon powdered cloves
1½ teaspoons unflavored gelatin
¼ cup water

Pare, core and quarter apples. Combine in blender with water, sweetener and spices. Blend till mixture is smooth. Cook over low heat till thickened, approximately 45 minutes. In blender container, sprinkle gelatin over ¼ cup water. Transfer boiling apple mixture to blender; puree. Store in refrigerator, evenly divided into 4 small jars. Makes 4 servings.

APRICOT BUTTERMILK MOLD
Also delicious made with 4 ripe medium nectarines or peaches to replace the apricots.

12 apricots (1 pound), pitted
½ cup boiling water
¼ cup cold tea (or water)
2 teaspoons unflavored gelatin
1 cup buttermilk
Artificial sweetener to equal ¼ cup sugar
½ teaspoon lemon extract
½ teaspoon vanilla extract

Cook apricots in boiling water in covered saucepan until tender (about 5 minutes). Drain, reserving cooking liquid. Pour tea into blender container, sprinkle gelatin over it, and add hot liquid left from cooking apricots. Run blender to dissolve gelatin. Add remaining ingredients including cooked apricots. Blend until fruit is pureed. Pour evenly into 4 small molds and chill until firm, about 3 hours. Unmold. Makes 4 servings.

BANANA-CHEESE BETTY
A dish for all seasons—but not for more than once a week.

1 envelope (1 tablespoon) unflavored gelatin
1 cup cream-flavored dietetic carbonated beverage
Artificial sweetener to equal 2 tablespoons sugar
1 teaspoon cinnamon
1 medium banana, peeled and sliced
½ teaspoon vanilla, or banana, extract
⅔ cup ricotta cheese
1 slice enriched white bread, made into crumbs

Sprinkle gelatin over beverage in small saucepan. Place over low heat and stir constantly until gelatin dissolves, about 1 minute. Refrigerate until mixture is thickened. Combine sweetener and cinnamon; sprinkle banana slices with half of cinnamon mixture. Stir vanilla or banana extract and remaining half of cinnamon mixture into ricotta cheese. In baking dish, make layers of banana slices, gelatin mixture, ricotta cheese, and bread crumbs. Repeat layers. Bake at 325° F. for 1 hour. Serve chilled. Makes 1 luncheon serving.

BAKED BANANA

1 underripe medium banana
Dash lemon juice
Artificial sweetener to equal 4 teaspoons sugar
Dash ginger or cinnamon (optional)

Bake banana in its skin at 375° F. about 25-30 minutes on a baking sheet or outdoor grill. Peel skin, sprinkle with lemon juice and sweetener; add a dash of ginger or cinnamon, if desired. Serve as a meat accompaniment. Makes 1 serving.

CHERRY COUPE

1 envelope (1 tablespoon) unflavored gelatin
1 can (12 fluid ounces) cherry-flavored dietetic carbonated
  beverage
Artificial sweetener to equal 2 teaspoons sugar
1 teaspoon cherry extract
2 cups sweet cherries, pitted
1 recipe Easy Whipped Topping (p. 199 — count ¼ cup skim
  milk per serving)

Sprinkle gelatin over ¼ cup cold beverage in small saucepan. Place over low heat, stirring constantly until gelatin dissolves, about 3 minutes. Stir in remaining beverage, sweetener and extract. Place ½ cup cherries in each of 4 stemmed glasses. Top with gelatin mixture. Chill until firm. Serve with fluffs of Whipped Topping divided equally. Makes 4 servings.

CRANBERRY, APPLE AND ORANGE RELISH

2 cups cranberries
1 small orange, unpeeled, sliced
1 medium apple, unpeeled and cored
Artificial sweetener to equal 1 cup sugar

Clean and pick over cranberries. Using meat grinder or blender, grind together cranberries and orange. Add sweetener. Mix well, let stand at least 2 hours and serve in a relish bowl. Makes 6 servings.

CRANBERRY SHERRY SHERBET

It's fun to have neighbors dropping in for a personal greeting during Christmas holidays—here's a festive treat to share with them.

4 cups raw cranberries
2¾ cups water
1 envelope (1 tablespoon) unflavored gelatin
Artificial sweetener to equal 1 cup sugar
¼ cup lemon juice
Pinch of salt
Sherry extract

Cook cranberries in 2½ cups water over low heat until they are very soft. Puree in blender with cooking liquid, or mash well. Soften gelatin in remaining water. Add to hot berries with sweetener, lemon juice and salt. Stir well to dissolve gelatin. Pour into freezer trays (without divider) and freeze until mushy, stirring occasionally, about one hour. Use at once or beat well with fork until mixture is smooth. Return to trays and freeze until consistency of ices (not solidly frozen). If necessary, let soften slightly in refrigerator for 20 minutes before serving. Spoon equally into 8 pretty stemmed dessert glasses, with a few drops sherry extract sprinkled over each. Makes 8 servings.

CRANBERRY JUICE THANKSGIVING COCKTAIL

4 cups raw cranberries
4 cups water
1 teaspoon cinnamon
2 small slices pineapple (canned in its own juice) plus 2
  tablespoons juice
½ cup orange juice
Artificial sweetener to equal 1 cup sugar
Cracked ice (optional)
Dietetic carbonated beverage, any flavor (optional)

Combine cranberries, water and cinnamon, and cook over low heat until berries are very soft, about 15 minutes. Puree pineapple and juice in blender, add berries with cooking liquid, orange juice and sweetener. Blend well. Serve in 8 glasses straight over cracked ice, or combine half and half with carbonated beverage of your choice. Makes 6 servings.

CRANBERRY GELEE

> 1 envelope (1 tablespoon) unflavored gelatin
> 1¼ cups water
> 2 cups raw cranberries
> Artificial sweetener to equal ½ cup sugar, or to taste

Soften gelatin in ¼ cup of the water. In saucepan, cook cranberries in remaining water until skins pop. Add gelatin and sweetener, stirring to dissolve gelatin. Pour into mold. Chill until set. Makes 4 servings.

CRANBERRY HORSERADISH RELISH
To serve with leftover turkey.

> 1 cup raw cranberries, chopped
> ⅓ cup grated horseradish
> Dash lemon extract
> Dash ginger

Combine and let stand 2 hours. Serve with cold meats or turkey. Makes 4 servings.

BROILED GRAPEFRUIT

Cut 1 medium grapefruit in half, and with a knife loosen pulp; remove seeds and tough center membrane. Sprinkle ¼ teaspoon rum flavor or strawberry extract and brown sugar replacement over each half. Broil for 10 minutes, or until fruit is hot and gold-flecked. Makes 2 servings.

SEACOAST GRAPEFRUIT SALAD

> ½ medium grapefruit
> 6 ounces cooked, flaked fish (salmon, halibut, etc.)
> 1 tablespoon chopped celery
> 1 tablespoon tomato juice
> 1 tablespoon dehydrated pepper flakes
> 1 teaspoon dehydrated onion flakes
> Lettuce

Carefully cut out grapefruit sections, and remove all white membrane from shell. Combine remaining ingredients; add to grapefruit sections. Line grapefruit shells with lettuce. Spoon grapefruit mixture back into shells. Makes 1 serving.

"PLANTER'S PUNCH"

½ cup unsweetened grapefruit juice
Artificial sweetener to equal 1 teaspoon sugar
Dash aromatic bitters
½ teaspoon rum extract
Few drops cherry extract
¾ cup crushed ice
Fresh mint

In tall glass, stir well grapefruit juice, sweetener, bitters, and rum and cherry extracts. Add crushed ice, serve with long straw and dangle sprig of fresh mint over sides of glass. Makes 1 serving.

MY MAI TAI

If you're serving Teriyaki beef or chicken, you'll want to make this Hawaiian specialty. For a touch of the luau, slice a stick from the center core of a quartered pineapple; save the remaining fresh fruit for dessert.

½ cup grapefruit juice
Artificial sweetener to equal 2 teaspoons sugar
½ teaspoon rum extract
⅛ teaspoon orange extract
Crushed ice
Sprig mint
Pineapple stick (see note above)

Combine grapefruit juice with sweetener and extracts. Pour into large (12-ounce or 15-ounce) old-fashioned glass mostly filled with crushed ice. Garnish with mint sprig and pineapple stick. Makes 1 serving.

GREEN GRAPE JELLY

To spoon over an omelet, to spread on toast, or to fill celery ribs. Be sure to use all of this at one time, as once-a-week fruit cannot be divided.

> 1 envelope (1 tablespoon) unflavored gelatin
> ½ cup lemon-lime flavored dietetic carbonated beverage
> 1 cup seedless grapes

Sprinkle gelatin over ¼ cup beverage and set aside to soften. Combine remaining ingredients in small saucepan, place over low heat and cook until grapes are tender and skins burst — about 10 minutes. Mash well to make a smooth spread. Stir in softened gelatin. Chill until jelled. Makes 1 serving.

VARIATION

Strawberry Jelly: Soften gelatin in ½ cup strawberry-flavored dietetic carbonated beverage in saucepan. Place over low heat, stirring to dissolve gelatin. Add 1 cup crushed strawberries and ¼ teaspoon strawberry extract. Chill until jelled. Makes 4 servings. Use other "legal" fruits to make homemade "jellies".

MANDARIN AND TANGERINE TREATS

Mandarin orange, including tangerines, are citrus fruits closely related to, but not of the same species as the real orange. Call them cousins, not sisters, and use the sectioned fruit interchangeably in any of our recipes.

1. Serve segments of 1 medium tangerine on a bed of mixed greens — iceberg lettuce, romaine and chicory. Sprinkle with cinnamon or coconut extract and garnish with shredded tangerine skin (outer part only, no white pulp). Makes 1 serving.

2. In small saucepan, heat ½ cup cooked bean sprouts or enriched rice in 2 tablespoons chicken bouillon. Remove from heat, add sections of 1 medium tangerine and sprinkle lightly with curry powder or cinnamon. Garnish with flower made by cutting tangerine skin into thin strips, then curling into rosette. Delicious with broiled chicken or fish. Makes 1 serving.

NECTARINE "DAIQUIRI"

1 ripe medium nectarine
¼ cup dietetic carbonated ginger ale
3 ice cubes, crushed
½ teaspoon rum extract
Dash lemon juice or lime juice

Combine ingredients in blender and blend until smooth. Serve in brandy snifter or glass, with straw. Makes 1 serving.

JELLED ORANGE CUP WITH CANDIED ORANGE PEEL

1 envelope (1 tablespoon) unflavored gelatin
2 cups orange-flavored dietetic carbonated beverage
2 small oranges, separated into segments (reserve peel)
Artificial sweetener to equal 4 teaspoons sugar

Sprinkle gelatin over 1½ cups beverage in small saucepan. Place over low heat, stirring constantly until gelatin dissolves. Remove from heat. Divide orange segments into 4 dessert glasses. Pour in gelatin mixture. Chill until firm. Meanwhile, make Candied Orange Peel: Remove membrane from reserved orange peel. Cut peel into matchstick pieces. Cover with water, bring to a boil and discard water. Repeat once or twice more to remove bitterness from peel. Pour remaining beverage into pan with the orange peel, and cook until peel is soft and beverage is absorbed. Cool. Sprinkle with sweetener and use as topping for Orange Cup. Makes 4 servings.

ORANGE FREEZEADE

1 small orange, peeled, seeded and quartered
⅓ cup instant non-fat dry milk
¼ teaspoon vanilla extract
Artificial sweetener to equal 6 teaspoons sugar
6-8 ice cubes

Combine all ingredients in a blender. Blend until smooth. Divide evenly into 2 chilled dessert glasses. Serve at once. Makes 2 servings.

VARIATIONS

Pineapple Freezeade: Use ¼ fresh medium pineapple cut in chunks, instead of orange. Or use 2 small slices pineapple (canned in its own juice) plus 2 tablespoons juice.

Four-Fruitade: Combine in blender the following: ½ cup (4 ounces) orange juice, 2 small slices pineapple (canned in its own juice) plus 2 tablespoons juice, 1 cup strawberries, and 1 medium peach. Blend. Add 4 ice cubes, one at a time, blending after each addition till frothy. Divide evenly into 4 glasses. Makes 4 servings.

BLENDER LETTUCE-ORANGEADE

Refreshing also with watercress. Omit lettuce and use up to ½ bunch cleaned watercress, stems removed.

> ½ cup orange juice
> Artificial sweetener to equal 2 teaspoons sugar
> 4 large fresh lettuce leaves, washed
> 2 sprigs fresh parsley
> Crushed ice

Combine all ingredients in blender. Blend until lettuce and ice are well mixed. Divide into 2 large glasses. Makes 2 servings.

PUERTO RICAN PUNCH

The "kick" in our drinks comes from the strong-flavored extracts, not from alcohol.

> ¼ cup orange juice
> Dash bitters
> 1 tablespoon lime or lemon juice
> ½ teaspoon rum extract
> Crushed ice

Combine ingredients and serve in an 8-ounce highball glass mostly filled with crushed ice. Makes 1 serving.

CARIBBEAN COCKTAIL

> ¾ cup boiling water
> 1 envelope instant chicken broth and seasoning mix
> ¾ cup tomato juice
> ½ cup orange juice

Combine water and broth mix. Add tomato and orange juices. Shake well. Serve on the rocks. Makes 1 serving.

MINTED PEACH AND CUCUMBER SALAD

1 medium peach
1 medium cucumber, scrubbed
½ cup buttermilk
2 teaspoons chopped, fresh mint leaves
Salt and pepper
Dash of dill and artificial sweetener

Slice the peaches into a small glass bowl. Cut cucumbers in half lengthwise, remove seeds and dice into bowl. Add remaining ingredients and mix thoroughly. Refrigerate till well chilled, about 1 hour. Delicious with roast leg of lamb. Makes 2 servings.

POACHED FRUIT (PEACHES, PEARS, ETC.)

1 cup water
1 thin slice lemon peel
3 or 4 whole cloves
½ teaspoon allspice
6 whole ripe medium peaches, blanched and peeled (see note)
¼ teaspoon strawberry extract

Combine water, lemon peel, cloves and allspice. Bring to boil. Add peaches. Simmer gently until peaches are tender but still firm. Cool in syrupy cooking liquid. Add extract. Serve well-chilled. You can cook fresh pears or apples in much the same way. Core and cut fruit in half before poaching. Makes 6 servings.

NOTE: To blanch ripe peaches, plunge into boiling water for one minute, then into cold. Skins can then be peeled off easily.

PEACH COBBLER

1 slice enriched white bread
1 medium peach, peeled and sliced
Dash cinnamon
1 cup skim milk
1 egg
Artificial sweetener to equal 8 teaspoons sugar
¼ teaspoon vanilla extract

Break bread into small pieces and arrange in a shallow baking dish (4-6 inches in diameter). Arrange peach slices over the bread and sprinkle with cinnamon. Pour milk into blender, add egg, sweetener, and vanilla. Blend at high speed about 30 seconds. Pour milk mixture over peaches and bread. Lift a few pieces of the bread up to make peaked crush. Bake at 325° F. about 30 minutes. Makes 1 luncheon serving.

PEAR AMANDINE MOUSSE (FROSTY DESSERT)

> ¼ cup cold water
> 1 envelope (1 tablespoon) unflavored gelatin
> ¼ cup boiling water
> 1 medium pear, cored and quartered
> ⅓ cup instant non-fat dry milk
> ½ teaspoon almond extract
> Artificial sweetener to equal 6 teaspoons sugar
> 6-8 ice cubes

With fast-setting recipes like this one, it's a good procedure to set out all the measured ingredients beforehand. Pour the ¼ cup cold water into blender and carefully sprinkle gelatin into it; let stand a few minutes for gelatin to soften. Pour in boiling water and turn on blender at low speed to dissolve gelatin. Add ¾ of the pear, non-fat dry milk, extract and sweetener. Blend until smooth. Add ice cubes, one at a time, blending after each addition. Pour mousse equally into 2 large dessert cups. Cut remaining ¼ of pear into finely diced pieces and use as garnish. Makes 2 servings.

VARIATION
Substitute 1 medium peach, 1 medium nectarine, 1 large plum, ½ cup pitted sweet cherries or 1 medium banana for pear. Omit almond extract and use brandy, orange, cherry, coconut or other flavor extract. Follow recipe.

A PRETTY PEAR
Pair fruit with cheddar cheese for a Sunday breakfast treat.

1 medium pear
Lemon juice
1 ounce grated sharp cheddar cheese
1 teaspoon margarine
2 cloves

Cut pear in half lengthwise. Remove core, using a sharp knife, then rub fruit with lemon juice to keep it from browning. Mash grated cheese with margarine. Stuff cheese mixture into pear cavities, heaping high in the middle. Stick a clove at the stem end of each pear half and chill for 30 minutes. Makes 1 serving.

BUTTERFLY PINEAPPLE SALAD
Surprise your guests with a picture salad. This one is a butterfly, and there's plenty of room for improvisation.

1 large slice pineapple (canned in its own juice) — see note
Lettuce leaves
½ medium green pepper
Long thin pimento strip
Capers
1 teaspoon mayonnaise

Cut pineapple slice in half and place on flat bed of lettuce leaves, curved sides facing each other for wings. Cut a long oval shape out of green pepper, reserving trimmings for garnish. Set pepper between pineapple halves to make a body. Use 2 long strips of pimento in a V-shape to make the feelers. Sprinkle a few capers and reserved chopped green pepper for wing spots. Add mayonnaise at the tail, and it's ready to serve. Makes 1 serving.

NOTE: You must consume 2 tablespoons juice from can.

PINEAPPLE FLUFF

1 ripe medium pineapple
1 envelope (1 tablespoon) unflavored gelatin
¼ cup cold water
¼ cup boiling water
1⅓ cups instant non-fat dry milk
2 teaspoons lemon juice
1 teaspoon vanilla extract
2 teaspoons coconut extract
½ cup ice water
Artificial sweetener to equal 8 teaspoons sugar
Few drops yellow food coloring

Peel and dice pineapple. Place in saucepan and cover with water. Cook until tender. Drain and chill pineapple. Sprinkle gelatin over ¼ cup cold water to soften; add boiling water and stir until gelatin is dissolved. Allow to cool. Meanwhile, combine remaining ingredients in a chilled bowl and beat until mixture begins to thicken. Pour in gelatin mixture and mix well. Place in freezer and freeze for 10 minutes. Remove from freezer and beat in pineapple with electric mixer. Pour evenly into dessert glasses and chill. Makes 4 servings.

PINEAPPLE-PEACH SHERBET

You can create dozens of different sherbets, as delicious as the classic ones but modified with your figure in mind. The basic ingredients are: fruit, blended to a pulp; liquid (could be water, fruit juice, skim milk, evaporated skimmed milk, buttermilk or even a dietetic carbonated beverage); artificial sweeteners and flavoring extracts, if desired.

1 medium peach, quartered
2 small slices pineapple (canned in its own juice) plus
    2 tablespoons juice
½ cup buttermilk
Artificial sweetener to equal ¼ cup sugar
1 teaspoon raspberry extract

Puree peach, pineapple, and pineapple juice in blender. Add remaining ingredients and blend again. Transfer to ice-cube tray (without dividers) and freeze fruit mixture about 30 minutes, or until the texture of water ices, not frozen into a block. Use immediately. Or beat and return to freezer. Refrigerate for 20-30 minutes before serving. If mixture freezes into a block, beat lightly. Serve in 2 stemmed wine glasses, to be licked from a spoon or sipped from a straw. Or serve in little lettuce leaf cups as a fruit course. Makes 2 servings.

VARIATION

A very small amount of gelatin is often added to a sherbet to keep its texture smooth. Soften ½ teaspoon gelatin in the 2 tablespoons of cold pineapple juice, add 2 tablespoons water and dissolve over low heat, stirring constantly. Then add to pureed fruit in blender, and follow recipe. Makes 2 servings.

PINEAPPLE-STRAWBERRY SOUR CREAM PARFAIT

Ribbons of strawberry red twirl around your glass in this festive parfait.

2 cups cottage cheese
2 small slices pineapple (canned in its own juice) plus 2 tablespoons juice
2 cups strawberries, hulled
½ teaspoon strawberry extract

Make Sour Cream by putting cottage cheese and pineapple into electric blender; blend at low speed until pineapple is crushed and cheese creamed. Refrigerate until chilled. Mash half the berries with the strawberry extract. Empty into bowl; slice remaining strawberries and add to bowl. To serve, layer even amounts of cheese mixture and strawberries in parfait (or highball) glasses. Makes 2 servings.

PICKLED PLUMS

1 cup water
½ cup cider vinegar
¾ cup brown sugar replacement
8 medium plums, pitted and halved
¼ teaspoon ground cloves
¼ teaspoon whole allspice
1 stick cinnamon
½ clove garlic

Bring the vinegar, water, cloves, allspice, cinnamon and garlic to boil in a saucepan. Add plums and cook for a few minutes or until tender. Transfer plums to jar or bowl, strain liquid over them and store in refrigerator. Makes 4 servings.

RASPBERRY ITALIAN ICES

One cup fresh or frozen unsweetened boysenberries, blackberries, blueberries, or loganberries may be substituted for the raspberries in the following recipe.

> 1 cup raspberries
> 1 cup water
> ½ teaspoon lemon juice
> Dash raspberry extract
> Artificial sweetener to equal 8 tablespoons sugar

Mix all ingredients thoroughly. Freeze till mushy, then serve at once or beat with electric or rotary beater till fluffy and freeze again. Serve firm but not solid. Makes 2 servings.

RHUBARB WHIP

Cook 2 cups fresh or frozen sliced rhubarb in ½ cup fruit-flavored dietetic carbonated beverage. Soften 1 envelope (1 tablespoon) unflavored gelatin in ¼ cup cold beverage. Let stand a few minutes, then stir into hot cooked rhubarb. Mix well. Whip with electric mixer until frothy if desired. Transfer to mold. Chill in refrigerator. Makes 1 serving.

FRESH STRAWBERRY-RHUBARB RING

> 4 cups sliced rhubarb (fresh or frozen)
> ¾ cup water
> Artificial sweetener to equal ½ cup sugar (or to taste)
> 2 envelopes (2 tablespoons) unflavored gelatin
> ½ cup orange juice
> 1 teaspoon lemon juice
> 1 cup fresh strawberries

Cook rhubarb in covered saucepan with ½ cup of the water; let simmer 5 minutes or until soft, stirring gently once or twice. Add sweetener. Soften gelatin in ¼ cup cold water; stir into hot rhubarb. Add orange and lemon juices. Pour into wet ring mold. Let cool; then refrigerate for several hours. Unmold; divide into quarters. Makes 4 servings.

SERVING SUGGESTIONS
This recipe may also be made in 4 individual ring molds. Unmold and fill center of each mold with 4 ounces cooked flaked fish and 1 tablespoon mayonnaise.

STRAWBERRY POPS

A "legal" summer treat for the kids (and good for them, too). And even you can have some, if you hurry before it's all gone.

¾ cup buttermilk
1 cup strawberries, cleaned and hulled
Artificial sweetener to equal 2 tablespoons sugar
1 teaspoon vanilla extract (optional)

Combine buttermilk and strawberries in blender until mixture is smooth. Add sweetener and vanilla; blend. Pour into 2 cleaned frozen juice cans. Place in freezer; insert popstick once it is partially frozen. Return to freezer and freeze until firm. Makes 2 servings.

FRUIT SAUCES YOU MAKE IN MINUTES

Since commercially packed fruit sauces are not "legal" isn't it nice to know you can make your own? The basic method is as follows: Add fruit (do not peel unless directed to do so) to boiling water (or dietetic carbonated beverage) in saucepan, cover, return to boiling, then let simmer until tender, stirring occasionally. Add sweetener and seasoning, if desired. Put cooked fruit and liquid into the blender and blend until smooth. Serve hot or cold, but be certain that you are meticulous in dividing sauce equally. Save small screw top jars for storing individual portions.

Fruit	Liquid	Artificial Sweetener Equalling	Cooking Time After Adding Fruit
Apples, 6 medium, cored and sliced	⅓ cup	¼ cup sugar	12-15 minutes
Apricots, 18 pitted (1½ lbs.)	½ cup	¾ cup	5 minutes
Sweet Cherries, 3 cups pitted	1 cup	½ cup	5 minutes
Cranberries, 6 cups	2 cups	1 cup or more	15 minutes
Peaches, 6 medium, pitted and sliced	¾ cup	¾ cup	7-8 minutes
Pears, 6 cored and sliced	⅔ cup	⅓ cup	10 minutes (20 minutes for hard varieties)
Pineapple, 1 medium peeled, cored and sliced	⅔ cup	½ cup	8-10 minutes
Plums, 12 medium	¾ cup	⅔ cup	5 minutes
Rhubarb, 6 cups sliced	¾ cup	1 cup	3-5 minutes

Optional seasonings, to be added during last few minutes of cooking if desired: a little ground cinnamon, nutmeg and cloves; a teaspoon of dehydrated orange or lemon peel; for a tart sauce, 2 teaspoons lemon juice or mild vinegar. Makes 6 servings.

CANNING FRUITS

Few of the commercially packed fruits in jars are "legal", but there's no reason why you can't preserve your own produce — and your figure too. Replace the canning syrup called for in your recipe with a solution made from water and granulated sugar replacements (the ones which are equal in volume to sugar, that is, 1 cup replacement equals 1 cup sugar). If you are new at preserving fruits, send for booklet "Home Canning of Fruits and Vegetables," U. S. Government Printing Office, Washington, D. C., 20¢.

To prevent discoloration of fruit, you may use ascorbic acid (its use for canning is permitted) following manufacturer's directions; or use a mixture of 3 tablespoons lemon juice to each quart of water.

> To replace light syrup, use 2 cups granulated artificial sugar replacement in 4 cups water (for apples, sweet apricots, berries, pears, plums).
>
> To replace medium syrup, use 3 cups granulated artificial sugar replacement in 4 cups water (for tart apples, apricots, cherries, grapes, peaches).
>
> To replace heavy syrup, use 4¾ cups granulated artificial sugar replacement in 4 cups water.

Combine artificial sugar replacement and water in saucepan. Stir to dissolve. Bring to boil before adding to fruit. You will need 1 to 1½ cups of this solution for each quart jar. Be certain to label jars with date and number of servings of fruit as permitted on Program.

FROSTED FRUIT PUREE WITH "RUM" SAUCE

> 1 cup strawberries, sliced
> 3 ripe apricots, pitted and diced
> 2 medium plums, pitted and diced
> 1 medium peach, pitted and diced
> Artificial sweetener to equal ½ cup sugar
> ¼ cup cherry-flavored dietetic carbonated beverage
> 1 teaspoon vanilla extract
> ½ teaspoon strawberry extract
> 1 cup skim milk
> 2 teaspoons rum extract
> ½ teaspoon almond extract
> ½ cup crushed ice

Combine fruits, half of sweetener, beverage, vanilla and strawberry extracts in blender, and puree. Pour ¼ of mixture into each of 4 dessert dishes. Chill in freezer for 40-50 minutes or until mixture is half frozen, thick but mushy. To make "Rum" Sauce, combine remaining ingredients in blender; blend until smooth. Serve at once evenly divided over each portion of fruit puree. Makes 4 servings.

UNUSUAL FRUIT SALADS

1. Puree in blender 1 cup ripe blackberries, blueberries, loganberries or raspberries with ¼ cup cherry-flavored dietetic carbonated beverage and ½ teaspoon lemon juice. Pour into refrigerator tray (remove divider) or bowl and freeze to consistency of ices. Serve over shredded lettuce in stemmed dessert glasses for instant enjoyment. Makes 2 servings.

2. For an unusual first course, slice a peeled, ripe medium banana over shredded lettuce on a chilled salad plate. Sprinkle lightly with lemon juice and cover with ¼ cup Cocktail Sauce for Seafood (p. 216 — count 6 fluid ounces tomato juice). Makes 1 serving.

3. In small saucepan, sprinkle 1 teaspoon unflavored gelatin over ¼ cup chicken bouillon, place over low heat and stir until gelatin dissolves. Add 1 medium unpeeled red apple, cored and cut into dice, and ½ medium dill pickle, chopped. Pour into small ring mold or coffee cup (rinse mold in cold water just before use). Chill. Unmold on watercress bed as dinner side dish. Makes 1 serving.

4. Just before use, rinse 1 cup ripe strawberries in strainer, drain and remove hulls. Put into serving bowl. Peel 1 small orange over the bowl (to catch juices), cutting away white membrane. Cut orange into sections. Dice meat from ½ medium cantaloupe and add to bowl with 1 ripe medium pear, diced. For a "juicier" salad, stir in ¼ cup (or more) of a cherry or berry-flavored dietetic carbonated beverage. Add ½ teaspoon cherry extract and ¼ teaspoon almond extract, and serve at once, garnished with mint sprigs. Makes 4 servings.

5. For that long night of TV watching, it's still a good idea to prepare a colorful munching bowl made up of any fruit or vegetables left from your daily allowances. Cut fruit into bite-size pieces, add raw any unused #3B vegetables (cauliflower or broccoli florets, spinach leaves from which tough stems have been removed, shredded cabbage, etc.). Include radish roses, celery sticks or flutes, sprigs of watercress, and fingers of pimento.

GINGER ALE MOLDED FRUIT SALAD

    1 envelope (1 tablespoon) unflavored gelatin
    1¾ cups dietetic carbonated ginger ale
    ½ cup diced celery
    ½ cup blueberries, blackberries, raspberries or loganberries
    1 small orange, cut into small pieces
    ½ medium grapefruit, cut into small pieces
    2 small slices pineapple (canned in its own juice) plus 2
       tablespoons juice
    Artificial sweetener to equal 2 tablespoons sugar
    1 tablespoon lemon juice
    Salt
    Dash ground ginger

Sprinkle gelatin over ½ cup cold ginger ale in saucepan. Place over low heat, stirring constantly until gelatin dissolves. Remove from heat, add remaining ingredients, mix well and pour into a 2-quart ring mold. Chill until firm. Unmold. Divide evenly. Makes 8 servings.

Liver

If you've only had broiled or baked liver for dinner, and patés at parties, we think you're in for a treat once you discover liver in all its versatile flavors and cooking styles. I've included enough recipes so you can go on for months without repeating one! Try marinating liver, or cooking it Portuguese style in a skillet. Or make a soufflé or a Hungarian dumpling. Flavor liver recipes with a ginger, curry or our Teriyaki Sauce. Invite liver to the party as a flavorful paté . . . or take it to the beach barbecue, kabob style. There's really no end to the interesting variety you can get from a few kinds of liver. Try them all — try all the recipes, too.

RULES FOR USING LIVER

1. Amounts (net cooked weight):

> WOMAN AND YOUTH: 4 ounces for lunch
> 6 ounces for dinner
> MAN: 4 ounces for lunch
> 8 ounces for dinner

2. Liver must be eaten at least once a week, either for lunch or dinner. It may be taken more often. If so, consider it as a Group C meat, which may be broiled, baked, roasted or panbroiled (without added fat). If liver amount is split, you may not count it as one of your required liver meals.

3. Liver from any meat or poultry that's allowed on Program may be used. This includes chicken and calf liver (the tenderest and most delicately flavored); lamb (not often available), steer and baby beef liver (usually tender and of good quality); and the more robust kinds of liver, which include mature beef, turkey, rabbit and venison livers. This last group of livers are frequently marinated for 30 minutes before they are cooked. Or they may be covered with boiling water, drained after a few minutes, dried and cooked as directed in the recipe.

152

HOW TO BUY LIVER

To allow for shrinkage in cooking, we recommend that you buy 2 extra ounces of liver per serving (i.e., 6 ounces raw for luncheon will produce 4 ounces net cooked weight). For general use, liver should be ordered cut into slices ⅓-inch thick, but this is a matter of preference.

HOW TO PREPARE LIVER

Store liver in the refrigerator, and use it as quickly as possible, preferably within 24 hours, as it is highly perishable. Just before cooking, wipe it clean with a damp cloth or paper towels. Remove membranes and veins. Cut into strips, if necessary, using a pair of scissors or a sharp knife. To make slicing easier, raw liver may be put into freezer for about 20 minutes until it is firm, then cut, or prepared as indicated in recipe.

HOW TO COOK LIVER

Panbroil sliced liver in a non-stick or heavy heated skillet, until done on both sides, but still pink inside, about 4-5 minutes in all. Diced vegetables such as green pepper, onion, celery, etc. may be added to the skillet once liver is browned, then simmered with a little boiling water till vegetables are tender. Season with salt and freshly ground pepper before serving.

Broil sliced liver quickly (1-2 minutes per side) using fairly high heat, about 3 inches from source of heat. Spread with a teaspoon of margarine, and sprinkle with lemon juice and minced watercress before serving.

Bake whole liver at 350° F. until it is tender, 40-50 minutes. Weigh portions, and serve still juicy. For a meal-in-one oven dish, surround liver with vegetables such as sliced onions, carrots, tomatoes, green pepper and even sliced potatoes; all in allowed amounts. Whole liver may also be cooked in a large covered skillet on top of range.

Boil liver by dropping strips or slices into boiling salted water. Cook briefly at fast simmer until just done; don't overcook it.

To marinate liver, cover with chicken bouillon or with dietetic ginger ale and let stand 30 minutes. Drain and cook as above.

CHICKEN LIVER PATE

> 8 ounces sliced onion
> 1 pound chicken livers, cut in half, or liver sliced ⅓-inch-
> thick
> 1 envelope instant chicken broth and seasoning mix
> Salt and pepper
> ¾ teaspoon poultry seasoning
> Lettuce leaf cups

Layer onions slices in a saucepan or non-stick skillet (with cover) and top with washed liver. Cover and steam until onions are soft and liver is done (but still slightly pink and moist inside), about 15-20 minutes. Sprinkle broth mix over onions. Let cool, then transfer liver, onions and liquid in pan to blender container, and puree (or put through fine blade of meat chopper). Stir in salt, pepper, and poultry seasoning. Chill and serve cold in lettuce leaf cups. Makes 2 dinner servings.

VARIATIONS

1. *Brandied Molded Chicken Liver Pâté.* Season pureed liver mixture above with ¾ teaspoon brandy extract. Sprinkle 1 tablespoon unflavored gelatin over 1½ cups chicken bouillon in small sauce pan; heat gently, stirring to dissolve gelatin.

Pour a thin film of gelatin into individual molds (ramekins, custard cups, even a plastic egg tray) and refrigerate until set. When gelatin is firm, divide liver evenly into mold, pushing it away from the sides. Pour more gelatin around the sides of the mold and refrigerate till completely set. Unmold on lettuce.

2. For baked pâté (dinner for 2) transfer pureed liver and onion mixture into 2 ramekins, or casseroles. Arrange slices from 1 truffle cut thin, on top. Set casseroles in a baking pan, add water to come halfway up the sides of the ramekins, and bake at 400° F. for 1½ hours. Cool in refrigerator. Spread 1 tablespoon vegetable oil on top

of each portion and serve with bowls of endive, lettuce, celery strips etc. Spread pâté on leaves. Each casserole makes 1 dinner serving.

3. Liver juices can come on strong but cook it in ginger ale to add just the right amount of sweetness. Add ½ cup dietetic carbonated ginger ale to skillet and cook until tender. Blend and season as above. Makes 2 servings.

4. Chopped liver can be used to stuff tomatoes instead of lettuce leaves. Wash and dry 2 firm medium tomatoes. Cut a thin slice from stem end and scoop out pulp, leaving a thick shell. Season inside with salt and pepper. Combine 6 ounces broiled, ground chicken (or other) livers with scooped-out tomato pulp, season with ½ teaspoon onion flakes and salt and pepper. Pack firmly into tomato shell. Then place stuffed tomatoes in a shallow saucepan containing 3 tablespoons water. Cover pan and cook at medium heat for 8-10 minutes. Don't let water evaporate completely; add a tablespoon or two as needed. Two stuffed tomatoes make 1 dinner serving.

FOIE DE VEAU VERONIQUE (CALF LIVER WITH GRAPES)
A ten-minute gourmet meal.

> 1 pound calf liver, sliced ⅓ inch thick
> Salt and freshly ground pepper
> 2 teaspoons lemon juice
> 1 cup seedless green grapes
> 2 teaspoons margarine
> 2 teaspoons minced parsley

Using a knife or kitchen scissors, cut liver into 1-inch strips. Season lightly with salt and freshly ground pepper. Cook quickly in non-stick skillet. As soon as strips are brown on all sides, divide equally into 2 serving plates; keep hot. Pour lemon juice and grapes into skillet, and mash a few of the grapes to release their juices. Heat quickly, remove from heat and divide evenly over liver strips. Stir 1 teaspoon margarine into each serving. Garnish with parsley. Makes 2 dinner servings.

LIVER AND VEGETABLES IN ONE POT

2 ounces peas
2 ounces onion, diced
½ cup eggplant, diced
½ cup mushrooms
½ cup zucchini or green beans
½ clove garlic, mashed
½ cup tomato juice
1 teaspoon salt
Dash cayenne pepper
½ pound liver, sliced ⅓-inch thick
⅔ cup cooked enriched elbow macaroni
1 tablespoon minced parsley

Combine all ingredients except liver, macaroni and parsley in saucepan, bring to boil, lower heat and simmer covered about 15 minutes. Cut liver into strips 1-inch wide, cover with boiling water, let stand 5 minutes, drain and dry. Add to saucepan and cook about 5 minutes, or until liver strips are done. Stir in macaroni and parsley just before serving. Reheat if necessary. Makes 1 dinner serving.

CALF LIVER WITH SCALLION SAUCE

1 pound calf liver, sliced ⅓-inch thick
4 tablespoons vinegar
3 tablespoons soy sauce
Artificial sweetener to equal 3 tablespoons sugar
1 envelope instant chicken broth and seasoning mix, or 1
    teaspoon poultry seasoning
Dash fennel seeds
4 ounces scallions, cut into pieces ¼-inch thick

Wash liver and wipe dry. Combine vinegar, soy sauce, sweetener, broth mix and fennel seeds. Spread about 2 tablespoons of the mixture on the liver slices and let stand. Combine remainder of the mixture with scallions, and reserve. Broil liver quickly on both sides and transfer to serving plates. Pour reserved scallion mixture evenly over each liver portion. Makes 2 dinner servings.

ISCAS (PORTUGUESE-STYLE LIVER AND POTATO DISH)

8 ounces beef liver, sliced ⅓-inch thick
¾ cup beef bouillon
2 tablespoons lemon juice, or wine vinegar
1 teaspoon dehydrated onion flakes
1 teaspoon salt
2 crushed peppercorns
1 clove crushed garlic
1 clove
½ bay leaf
1 medium (3-ounce) potato, peeled and halved

With scissors or knife, cut liver into strips 1-inch wide and put into a mixing bowl. Combine beef bouillon, lemon juice or vinegar, onion flakes, salt, peppercorns, garlic, clove and bay leaf and pour over liver. Let marinate for 30 minutes. Meanwhile, cook the potato in boiling salted water in a small saucepan. Drain and dry liver strips, reserving marinade. Cook liver in non-stick skillet for 2 minutes on each side. Transfer to earthenware serving dish. Drain cooked potato and cut into large dice. Add to liver. Pour reserved marinade into the skillet, reduce quickly over high heat for 2 minutes, then pour over liver and potatoes. Makes 1 dinner serving.

COUNTRY-STYLE SCALLOPED LIVER

6 ounces liver, sliced ⅓-inch thick
1 slice bread, made into soft crumbs
1 tablespoon dehydrated onion flakes
1 medium tomato, sliced
Salt and pepper

Broil liver, cut into ¼-inch strips and set aside. Sprinkle half the crumbs into a shallow individual casserole. Add a layer of liver, a sprinkle of onion flakes, a layer of tomatoes; season with salt and pepper. Add remaining liver and repeat layers, ending with bread crumbs. Bake at 350° F. for 40 minutes. Makes 1 luncheon serving.

SWEET AND SOUR LIVER

¼ fresh medium pineapple, cubed
½ medium green pepper, cut in lengthwise strips
1 tablespoon lemon juice or vinegar
1 tablespoon soy sauce
Artificial sweetener to equal 2 teaspoons sugar, or to taste
2 teaspoons minced chives or dehydrated onion flakes
1 clove garlic mashed
½ envelope instant beef broth and seasoning mix
1 slice fresh ginger root or dash ground ginger
Dash red hot sauce
6 ounces liver, sliced ⅓ inch thick and cut into strips

Combine all ingredients except liver in a saucepan. Simmer uncovered 10 minutes. Pour boiling water over liver, let stand 3 minutes, drain and dry. Add liver to saucepan and cook till liver is done. Makes 1 dinner serving.

LIVER PATTIES AND PINEAPPLE RINGS
Festive and colorful for a company lunch.

8 small slices pineapple (canned in its own juice) plus 8
  tablespoons juice
1½ pounds ground steer or chicken livers
2 slices bread, made into crumbs
¾ cup skim milk
¾ teaspoon salt
½ teaspoon thyme
2 cups cooked enriched rice
1 tablespoon minced parsley
Freshly ground pepper

Arrange pineapple slices on a non-stick baking sheet; reserve juice. Combine liver, crumbs, milk, salt and thyme; mix well. Shape into patties the size of the pineapple rings; top pineapple with patties. Bake at 400° F. until patties are brown on top; turn them gently with spatula and brown second side. (If you prefer, the patties and pineapple rings may be put under the broiler to brown; be sure to turn each patty to brown the second side). Meanwhile, heat reserved pineapple juice in saucepan, add rice and toss well to heat and separate the grains. Divide rice evenly into 4 luncheon plates and sprinkle with parsley. Serve liver and pineapple over rice. Pass pepper mill at the table. Makes 4 luncheon servings.

LIVERS TERIYAKI IN A FONDUE POT

To make eating liver more fun, serve it on a fondue fork! You'll need a fondue pot, skillet, or chafing dish—preferably electric. Set each portion of meat on a plate in front of each person with a fondue fork and dinner fork for each setting. (Fondue forks get too hot for eating purposes.) Sauces in individual bowls or fondue plates with separate compartments are essentials. The fondue pot should be set on a tray, within easy reach of all. There's a certain amount of splashing of hot liquid, so be careful. A simple salad, one of the #4 vegetables, and a fresh fruit for dessert will complete an unbeatably good meal. For each serving:

> 8 ounces chicken (or other) liver, cut into bite-size squares, ⅓-inch thick
> 1 recipe Teriyaki Sauce (p. 221)
> 3 cups beef bouillion
> 2 or more sauces
> 1 recipe Teriyaki Sauce (p. 221)
> ½ recipe Cauliflower White Sauce (p. 230 — count 1 cup #3B vegetable and ½ cup skim milk per serving)
> ½ recipe Pimento Dressing (p. 217)

Wipe liver clean with paper towel, and blanch by dropping into boiling water for 3 minutes. Cut into bite-size pieces, and transfer to bowl. Add Teriyaki Sauce and refrigerate at least 2 hours. At dinner time, pour bouillon into fondue pot and bring to boil. Keep just below boiling point throughout dinner. Drain and dry liver; set on plate. Each diner spears a liver square on his fondue fork, dunks it into hot liquid in the pot, and cooks it to his taste. He then transfers liver to dinner plate and, with dinner fork, dunks it into one of the sauces. This continues until all liver is cooked. Makes 1 dinner serving.

RISI E BISI CON FEGATINI

Prepare 1 recipe Risi e Bisi (p. 70). Just before serving, stir in 6 ounces broiled, diced chicken livers. Makes 1 dinner serving.

WESTERN LIVER SCRAMBLE

2 ounces cooked, diced liver
½ medium tomato, diced
½ medium green pepper, chopped
1 tablespoon tomato juice
¼ teaspoon dehydrated onion flakes
Salt and pepper
Dash cayenne pepper
1 egg, beaten

Combine tomato, green pepper, tomato juice, onion flakes, salt and pepper. Simmer in skillet until liquid is evaporated and pepper is soft. Add diced liver and stir in egg, scrambling to taste. Makes 1 luncheon serving.

MARINATED CHICKEN LIVERS AND BUTTER BEANS

8 ounces chicken livers
Boiling water
½ cup cooked butter beans or lima beans
1 serving Tomato French Dressing (p. 228 — count 1½ fluid ounces tomato juice and 1 tablespoon vegetable oil)
½ cup cooked fennel, or 2 ounces cooked sliced onions (optional)

Cut livers in half, cover with boiling water and bring water to boil again. Simmer until livers are just cooked, about 3 minutes after water boils. Drain, cool slightly and dice. Add cooked beans and fennel or onions, if desired; cover with Tomato French Dressing. Marinate in refrigerator for 30 minutes, or longer. Serve chilled. Makes 1 dinner serving.

LIVER SOUFFLE

4 ounces cooked liver, diced fine
½ cup skim milk
½ slice bread
2 eggs, separated
¼ teaspoon salt
2 cups tomato juice cooked down to half volume

Combine liver, milk and bread. Add slightly beaten egg yolks and salt. Mix well. Beat egg whites until stiff and fold into liver mixture. Divide equally and transfer to 2 small soufflé dishes. Bake at 400° F. until puffy and brown. Serve with Tomato Sauce. Makes 2 luncheon servings.

CHICKEN LIVER CHOP SUEY

½ pound chicken livers
½ cup celery, sliced in matchstick pieces
½ medium green pepper, sliced in matchstick pieces
4 ounces fresh peas
½ cup boiling water
1 envelope instant onion broth and seasoning mix
1 cup canned bean sprouts, rinsed and drained
1 teaspoon soy sauce
Salt and pepper
Chinese hot mustard (optional)

In non-stick skillet, panbroil chicken livers; dice, remove from skillet and set aside. To same skillet add celery, green pepper, peas, boiling water and onion broth mix. Cook, covered, until vegetables are soft. Stir in bean sprouts and liver; add soy sauce, salt and pepper. Serve hot with Chinese hot mustard, if desired (it's also called English mustard; make it by mixing dry mustard and a few drops of water to a paste). Makes 1 dinner serving.

LIVER AND APPLE SALAD

6 ounces cooked liver, diced
½ cup diced celery
½ cup cooked or canned bean sprouts, drained and rinsed
¼ medium green pepper, diced
1 medium apple, unpeeled, cored and diced
2 tablespoons diced pimento
1 envelope instant chicken broth and seasoning mix
1 tablespoon mayonnaise
1 teaspoon lemon juice

Mix all ingredients, except lettuce. Chill in bowl. Unmold on a bed of lettuce. Makes 1 dinner serving.

LIVER SAUCE NAPOLI

Serve over ⅔ cup cooked enriched spaghetti, or over 1 cup cooked bean sprouts or green beans. Broiled mushrooms or tomatoes are a nice accompaniment.

8 ounces liver
1½ cups tomato juice
2 teaspoons dehydrated onion flakes
1 teaspoon salt
⅛ teaspoon pepper
½ teaspoon oregano
Dash cayenne pepper

Cook liver in boiling water until just tender; drain and mash or chop fine. Meanwhile, cook tomato juice with remaining ingredients till reduced by half volume. Add chopped liver to tomato juice mixture, and let cook for 15 minutes longer. Makes 1 dinner serving.

HUNGARIAN LIVER DUMPLINGS IN SOUP

The liver should be cooked in a hot non-stick skillet or dropped into boiling water till done.

4 ounces cooked calf or chicken livers
2 slices enriched white bread, made into crumbs
⅓ cup instant non-fat dry milk
2 eggs
2 tablespoons fresh minced parsley
Salt and pepper
3 cups water
2 chicken bouillon cubes

Put liver through meat grinder, place in mixing bowl. Add bread crumbs, dry milk, eggs and parsley. Season with salt and pepper. Mix well. Combine water and bouillon cubes in saucepan, and bring to a slow boil. Divide liver mixture into 8 dumplings and drop four of them into bouillon. Cook for 5 minutes. Remove dumplings with a slotted spoon. Repeat with remaining dumplings. Place 4 dumplings in each of 2 soup bowls; pour bouillon into each bowl. Makes 2 luncheon servings.

BROILED LIVER AND WATERCRESS SANDWICH PLATTER

> 6 ounces liver, sliced ⅓ inch thick, or chicken livers, halved
> 1 tablespoon margarine
> 1½ teaspoons minced watercress leaves (no stems)
> 1 slice enriched white bread, toasted
> Watercress sprigs
> Pepper

Preheat broiler; set liver about 2 inches from heat and broil for about 3 minutes per side, turning once. Liver tastes best when it is served medium rare — with a hint of pink inside. Transfer to plate. Mash together the margarine and minced watercress and spread it over the broiled liver. Cut toast into diagonals and set on plate. Garnish with watercress sprigs. Use pepper mill at the table. Makes 1 serving.

LIVER AND KIDNEY KABOBS

This split-liver meal is not to count as your required liver meal.

> 1 medium green pepper, cut in chunks
> 4 ounces liver, cut in 2-inch squares
> 4 ounces kidney (calf or lamb), cut in pieces
> 6 cherry tomatoes

Parboil the green pepper. Alternate liver and kidney pieces between tomatoes and pepper chunks on skewers. Grill. Makes 1 dinner serving.

To Grill Kabobs: Just be sure that all the ingredients you pick can be grilled, barbecued or broiled in the same length of time. If not, some of the slower-cooking foods should be parboiled first. Allow about 5-9 minutes for most combinations, but watch them carefully.

LIVER AND CUCUMBER KABOBS

> 6 ounces chicken liver, halved
> 1 medium cucumber, sliced thick, or 4 ounces bamboo shoots, sliced

The larger half of the livers (there are always two uneven sections to chicken livers) can be cut again. Alternate liver and cucumbers on skewers and grill as above. Makes 1 luncheon serving.

Meats and Poultry

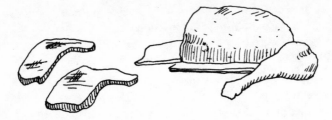

Come and get it — juicy summer barbecues and winter roasts that will warm your kitchen with their aroma. Poultry is here in all its glory too for gourmets and budget-stretchers alike. With our "legalized" international recipes and your slim new figure, you'll be an elegant hostess in more ways than one. But you'll have to restrain yourself — see rules which follow before feasting on our recipes.

GENERAL RULES FOR USING MEAT AND POULTRY

1. Amounts (net cooked weight):
   WOMAN, MAN AND YOUTH: 4 ounces for lunch
   WOMAN AND YOUTH: 6 ounces for dinner
   MAN: 8 ounces for dinner

For each serving, allow 2 ounces for shrinkage in cooking and 2 ounces for bone, in addition to cooked weight. Fresh and frozen meats are permitted.

2. Remove all visible fat before cooking.

3. Choose from items listed below, using the amounts allowed in the Menu Plan.

RULES FOR USING GROUP B MEATS
(See also General Rules for Using Meat and Poultry)

1. Select from this group three times a week, no more, no less, at either lunch or dinner.

2. Broil, bake or roast meats in this group: use a rack so all fat drips down. Do not boil, panbroil or fry. Frankfurters are excepted from this rule — they may be boiled if pierced first.

3. The following are classified as Group B Meats:

Beef
Caribou
Elk
Frankfurters
    (all-beef)

Gizzards
Kidney (beef)
Knockwurst
    (all-beef)

Lamb
Sweetbreads
    (beef)
Venison

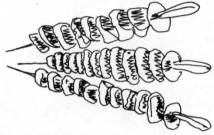

RULES FOR USING GROUP C MEATS
(See also General Rules for Using Meat and Poultry)

1. Choose as desired (but do not neglect your "must" meals).

2. You may broil, panbroil, bake, roast, steam or poach meats in this group (do not fry).

3. Poultry may be cooked with skin on, but remove the skin before you serve.

4. The following are Group C Meats:

Brains
Capon
Chicken
Cornish hen
Dove
Guinea hen
Heart
Kidney
    (calf, lamb)

Partridge
Peacock
Pheasant
Pigeon
Prairie chicken
Prairie hen
Quail
Rabbit

Sage grouse
Sage hen
Squab
Sweetbreads
    (calf, lamb)
Tripe
Turkey
Veal

GROUP B MEATS

HOW TO ROAST INEXPENSIVE CUTS OF BEEF

A great method to use for less costly roasts, but be sure they are choice quality, as graded by U. S. Department of Agriculture. They are tenderer if cooked to well-done state.

> Beef roast: rump, round, top sirloin, chuck, shoulder, etc.
> Marinade: a) 2 tablespoons soy sauce, 1 tablespoon Worcestershire, 1 cup boiling water and 1 envelope instant beef broth and seasoning mix; or b) Wine vinegar to half-cover roast

Remove visible fat from roast. Pour on one of the two marinades, and let stand at least 1 hour, turning meat often; the marinade acts as a meat tenderizer. Drain, reserving marinade. Insert meat thermometer in center of roast, and roast on rack set in roasting pan at 250° F., till done to taste. Baste every half hour with reserved marinade. Allow 45-60 minutes per pound for well-done meat (170° F. on meat thermometer).

HOW TO ROAST TENDER CUTS OF BEEF

Any of the bastes or marinades suggested under Inexpensive Cuts (preceding recipe) may be used. However, I prefer the natural flavor of unseasoned high-quality beef.

> Standing rib, filet mignon, shell strip, and sirloin steak

Remove all visible fat from beef roast, set on rack in preheated oven, insert thermometer in center of beef, and roast according to timetable below. When roast is done to your taste, remove from oven, let stand about 15 minutes, then slice, weigh and serve. Women and youth may have 6 ounces cooked meat at dinner; men, 8 ounces. Four ounces for everyone at lunch.

TIMING

The timetable below is for a roast at room temperature; allow more roasting time if roast is still frozen. Since there is considerable controversy about the benefits of high-temperature roasting (better flavor, say some) vs. moderate-temperature roasting (less shrinkage), I've given you a choice.

| 450° F. oven: | 10-12 minutes per pound for rare; 15-20 minutes per pound for medium; 25-30 minutes per pound for well done |
| 325° F. oven: | 18-20 minutes per pound for rare; 22-25 minutes per pound for medium; 28-35 minutes per pound for well done |

THERMOMETER READING

Rare: 140° F. Medium: 160° F. Well done: 170° F.

W TO BROIL STEAK

Tender steaks: filet mignon, porterhouse, T-bone, shell, sirloin, rib or spencer, club or minute

Less expensive steaks: Flank, skirt, Romanian tenderloin or chuck

Wine vinegar or lemon juice and sprinkling of herbs to taste or meat tenderizer (optional)

Remove all visible fat from steak. If using one of the less expensive cuts, marinate it for 1 hour in wine vinegar or lemon juice, with or without herbs (or sprinkle with meat tenderizer). Broil on rack set in broiling pan, lift out and serve. Weigh portions.

APPROXIMATE TIMING

Hamburgers and thin cuts of steak:
2-4 minutes per side for rare
5-6 minutes per side for medium
7-8 minutes per side for well done

1-inch-thick steaks:
4-6 minutes per side for rare
7-8 minutes per side for medium
10 or more minutes per side for well done

2-inch-thick steaks:
8-10 minutes per side for rare
10-15 minutes per side for medium
20 or more minutes per side for well done

BARBECUED SIRLOIN STEAK, PARTY STYLE

Thick steak grilled this way is juicy and quick — no burnt outsides and raw purple insides.

> 1 sirloin steak, 2 inches thick (5-6 pounds)
> 1 tablespoon Worcestershire
> 2 tablespoons soy sauce
> ½ envelope instant onion broth and seasoning mix

Remove all visible fat from steak. Combine Worcestershire sauce, soy sauce and onion broth mix. Spread mixture over both sides of steak. Let stand 2-3 hours (or overnight, if possible, so seasonings permeate beef). Drain steak and transfer to baking rack placed in a baking pan. Bake at 250° F. for 1 hour. When charcoal fire is hot, barbecue the steak about 4 inches from heat (or put under broiler), turning to brown both sides, about 10-15 minutes. Cut in diagonal slices and serve (weigh your portion). Makes 8-12 dinner servings.

SPEEDY STROGANOFF WITH NOODLES

> 8 ounces minute or cube steak, cut in strips
> 2 teaspoons dehydrated onion flakes
> ½ cup hot water
> ½ envelope instant chicken broth and seasoning mix
> ½ clove garlic, or ½ teaspoon garlic powder (optional)
> 2 tablespoons Catsup (p. 215 — count 3 fluid ounces tomato juice)
> ¾ teaspoons Worcestershire
> ½ cup canned sliced mushrooms, drained
> ¼ cup evaporated skimmed milk
> ½ cup cooked enriched noodles
> 1 teaspoon margarine

Broil beef strips on both sides. Transfer to saucepan with onion flakes, water, broth mix, and garlic. Cook 10 minutes. Stir in Catsup, Worcestershire and mushrooms; heat thoroughly. Stir in milk and heat gently. Serve over hot noodles, into which you've stirred margarine. Makes 1 dinner serving.

BARBECUED BEEF ON SKEWERS
Chicken may be done this way too.

½ cup vinegar
1 garlic clove, chopped
1 tablespoon chopped chili pepper
1 teaspoon powdered cumin
½ teaspoon salt
Black pepper
8 ounces steak, cut in cubes
1 medium green pepper, cut in wide strips
½ cup large whole mushrooms

Combine all ingredients except beef, green pepper and mushrooms to make marinade. Cut meat into bite-size pieces and marinate for 2 hours. Remove meat and place on skewer alternately with green pepper and mushrooms. Grill over charcoal until brown. Makes 1 dinner serving.

ROMANY BEEF GHIVETCH
(Baked Meat and Vegetable Casserole)

8 ounces boneless beefsteak
1 medium green pepper, seeded and sliced thin
2 ounces parsnip, sliced thin
1 rib celery, sliced thin
1 medium tomato, sliced
Salt and pepper
Dash allspice
1 cup boiling water
1 envelope instant onion broth and seasoning mix
½ cup cooked enriched rice

Cut the beef into ½-inch cubes and brown on rack under broiler, turning all sides. In small casserole, arrange layers of beef, green pepper, parsnip, celery and tomato slices. Sprinkle each layer with salt, pepper and allspice. Pour in boiling water and broth mix. Cover casserole and bake 1 hour at 350° F. Remove casserole, stir in rice and bake 15 minutes more. Makes 1 dinner serving.

CHINESE BEEF AND CABBAGE CASSEROLE

8 ounces boneless sirloin steak, ¼-inch thick, cut in strips
1 cup hot water
1 envelope instant beef broth and seasoning mix
1 cup celery, sliced thin
1 cup Chinese cabbage or broccoli
1 cup sliced mushrooms
1 small piece ginger, minced, or ¼ teaspoon powdered
Artificial sweetener to equal 1 teaspoon sugar
¼ cup soy sauce

Broil steak and set aside. In saucepan, bring water and broth mix to boil, add celery, cabbage, mushrooms, ginger and sweetener. Cook covered 15 minutes. Add broiled steak strips and soy sauce and heat quickly, but do not let meat boil. Makes 1 serving.

CARBONADO (BEEF STEW WITH FRUIT)

8 ounces diced or ground beef
1 medium (3-ounce) potato, peeled and diced
1 medium tomato
1 small chili pepper pod, or ¼ teaspoon chili powder
1 teaspoon dehydrated onion flakes
1 cup chicken bouillon
Salt and pepper
½ medium peach, cut in pieces
½ medium pear, cut in pieces

Make meat patties, brown under broiler, transfer to saucepan, crumble with fork, and add remaining ingredients except fruit. Stir. Simmer 25-30 minutes, or until potato is almost done. Add peach and pear; cook until fruit is soft. Discard whole chili pepper. Serve hot; makes 1 dinner serving.

VARIATION
Cranberry Stew: Omit peach and pear and add ½ cup cranberries with the potato; cook until potatoes and cranberries are soft.

ROAST BEEF SALAD

    6 ounces cooked roast beef, cut into slices ⅛-inch thick
    1 medium (3-ounce) potato, boiled and sliced
    1 gherkin, chopped
    2 ounces red onion, chopped, or 1 tablespoon chopped chives
    Salt and pepper
    Dash parsley
    1 tablespoon vegetable oil
    1 tablespoon wine vinegar
    Lettuce
    1 medium tomato, cut into wedges
    Watercress

Combine beef, potato, gherkin, onion (or chives), salt, pepper and parsley; stir in oil and vinegar. Chill for half an hour. Serve on bed of lettuce with tomato wedges and garnish of watercress. Makes 1 dinner serving.

HOW TO BROIL GROUND BEEF

In many of our recipes we call for cooked ground beef; here's how to broil it on a rack without losing it.

    6 or 8 ounces chopped lean beef
    Ice water

Shape beef into a hamburger patty, moistening it with ice water for extra juiciness. Broil 4 minutes on each side. Remove from broiler and crumble with a fork. Add to recipe as directed. Makes 1 luncheon or dinner serving.

NOTE: To store ground beef, keep loosely wrapped in refrigerator no more than 2 days; or store in freezer and use within 2-3 months.

CRUNCHY HAMBURGERS

1 pound ground chuck
2 cups bean sprouts, drained and rinsed
1 tablespoon Worcestershire, or soy sauce
1 teaspoon ground ginger
½ teaspoon salt
½ teaspoon garlic salt or powder
¼ teaspoon pepper

Combine all ingredients. Divide mixture into 4 equal portions; shape into patties. Broil on rack about 4 inches from source of heat for 8 minutes or until cooked throughout. Turn once. Makes 2 dinner servings.

MEATBALL RAGOUT

8 ounces chopped beef or veal
1 teaspoon dehydrated onion flakes
¼ teaspoon Italian seasoning spice
⅛ teaspoon garlic powder
½ cup cooked or canned mushrooms, stems and pieces
1 cup zucchini, sliced
1 medium green pepper, cut in strips
¼ cup celery, thinly sliced
1 cup tomato juice
1 envelope instant beef broth and seasoning mix, or 1 beef
    bouillon cube
1 tablespoon dehydrated onion flakes
¼ teaspoon thyme
¼ teaspoon garlic powder

Combine meat with onion flakes, Italian seasoning and garlic powder; shape into balls. Place on a rack and bake at 400° F. for approximately 10-15 minutes. Remove and set aside. Combine remaining ingredients in saucepan and simmer slowly. When mixture is reduced approximately one quarter in volume, add meatballs. Continue cooking until thick. Makes 1 dinner serving.

FAMILY FAVORITE MEAT LOAF
A festive meat loaf replete with shining glaze.

    1 pound ground beef
    1 cup evaporated skimmed milk
    2 tablespoons chopped parsley
    1 teaspoon lemon juice
    1 envelope instant onion broth and seasoning mix
    ¼ teaspoon dry mustard
    ⅛ teaspoon garlic powder
    ¼ cup Catsup (p. 215 — count 3 fluid ounces tomato juice
        per serving)
    1 teaspoon cherry extract

Combine all ingredients except catsup and cherry extract. Shape into a loaf and bake on rack in baking pan at 350° F. for 1½ hours. Combine catsup and extract to make glaze; blend well. Baste meatloaf with glaze several times during last 30 minutes of cooking time. Makes 2 dinner servings.

STUFFED PEPPERS (MEAL IN ONE POT)

    2 pounds ground beef or diced all-beef frankfurters
    Salt and pepper
    ½ cup tomato juice, cooked down to half volume
    4 medium green peppers (remove stems and seeds)
    4 cups shredded cabbage
    8 ounces leeks, sliced lengthwise
    8 ounces carrots; or half carrots, half peas

Shape ground beef into patties, and broil on rack until well done. Transfer meat to bowl, crumble with fork and season with salt and pepper. Moisten with thickened tomato juice, divide mixture and pack into peppers. Put cabbage into the bottom of a kettle. Add a layer of leeks and a layer of carrots. Place stuffed peppers on top and pour in enough boiling water to cover cabbage. Sprinkle lightly with salt, cover kettle tightly and simmer 45 minutes to 1 hour. Makes 4 dinner servings.

FRANKS AND BEANS

For a heartier flavor, you may substitute knockwurst for frankfurters in our recipes.

>8 ounces all-beef frankfurters
>¾ cup sauerkraut, drained
>2 tablespoons dehydrated onion flakes
>½ medium tomato, cubed
>1 teaspoon brown sugar replacement
>½ cup cooked lima beans
>Dash maple extract

Pierce frankfurters. Cook in boiling water for 10 minutes, drain, slice and place in flameproof serving dish. Add sauerkraut, onion flakes, tomato, brown sugar replacement, lima beans and maple extract. Heat until flavors mingle. Makes 1 dinner serving.

FAST AND FANCY FRANKFURTER STEW

Only all-beef frankfurters or knockwurst are approved. Frankfurters may be broiled, baked, roasted, or boiled (if pierced first).

>½ cup canned mushroom stems and pieces
>1 medium green pepper, cut into 1-inch strips
>1½ cups tomato juice
>1 tablespoon dehydrated onion flakes
>½ teaspoon Italian seasoning spice
>Salt and pepper
>Dash each garlic powder, celery salt, parsley flakes, and
>   thyme
>8 ounces all-beef frankfurters
>½ cup canned green beans, drained

Combine all ingredients except frankfurters and green beans. Simmer for 20 minutes. Cut frankfurters into 1-inch pieces and broil on a rack until golden brown. Add frankfurters and green beans to tomato juice mixture and simmer about 5 minutes. Makes 1 dinner serving.

HOT DOG-POTATO SALAD
Sweet and sour, German style.

16 ounces all-beef frankfurters
2 medium (3-ounce) potatoes, cooked and peeled
3 tablespoons dehydrated onion flakes, soaked in 2 tablespoons water
3 tablespoons wine vinegar
3 tablespoons water
2 teaspoons mustard
1 teaspoon celery seed
Artificial sweetener to equal 1 teaspoon sugar

Broil franks. Cool. Slice potatoes and hot dogs thin. Drain onion flakes. In large bowl, toss all ingredients until well mixed. Refrigerate for at least two hours for flavors to mingle. Serve hot, cold or at room temperature; divide evenly. Makes 2 dinner servings.

HOW TO PREPARE KIDNEYS

Beef Kidney (Group B)

Discard hard centers, tubes and fat. Soak kidneys in acidulated water (2 teaspoons lemon juice to a pint of water) for 1 hour. Drain, transfer to saucepan, cover with cold water and cook for 30 minutes, or until tender. Drain and pat dry. Cool and cook as desired. Cut into ⅓-inch slices, weigh. Broil alongside 1 medium tomato, cut in half and seasoned to taste, or stew gently in broiling water to cover for 1½ hours till tender. During the last half hour, for each serving, add 2 ounces sliced onion, 2 ounces carrots and ½ cup sliced mushrooms. Garnish with 2 teaspoons minced parsley and serve each portion with ½ cup hot enriched noodles.

Veal (Calf) and Lamb Kidney (Group C)

Remove hard centers and fat. Soak in acidulated water for 30 minutes. Drain and pat dry.

KIDNEYS DIABLO

    8 ounces cleaned veal or lamb kidneys, cut into ½-inch
       slices (see note)
    Salt and pepper
    Prepared mustard
    Dash cayenne pepper or few drops red hot sauce
    1 teaspoon vegetable oil

Sprinkle kidneys lightly with salt and pepper, and spread with mustard. Sprinkle with cayenne pepper or red hot sauce. Broil 3 inches from heat 7-9 minutes. Place in hot dinner plate, and drizzle oil on kidney. Makes 1 dinner serving.

NOTE: Six ounces cooked beef kidneys may be sliced and broiled following this recipe.

STEAK AND KIDNEY PIE
Pretty little meat pies, steaming-hot, will take all the winter frost out of you and the family.

    4 ounces broiled steak, cut into 1-inch cubes
    2 ounces broiled beef kidney, chopped
    ½ cup beef bouillon
    1 teaspoon dehydrated onion flakes
    1 medium (3-ounce) potato, boiled
    1 tablespoon skim milk
    Salt and pepper

Combine broiled steak and kidney with bouillon and onion flakes in individual casserole or soufflé dish. Mash potato, add milk, salt and pepper, and beat until light and fluffy. Spread mashed potato over meat mixture in casserole. Bake at 400° F. till potato topping is puffy and brown. Makes 1 dinner serving.

HOW TO ROAST A LEG OF LAMB
Lamb is a tender meat which roasts well (on the rotisserie too). Most of us overcook it, but in France it is served rare (pink inside, rather than all brown), and it's wonderfully juicy that way.

    1 teaspoon each coriander, cumin and turmeric
    Dash ground cloves
    Vinegar
    ½ leg of lamb

Combine coriander, cumin, turmeric and cloves with enough vine-gar to make a paste and spread on lamb. It may be left on several hours or overnight. Roast on rack at 325° F. (slow oven) for 25-35 minutes to the pound. If you use a meat thermometer, roast to medium rare (160°-165° F.). Weigh portion after carving; ½ leg will be enough for 5-6 servings.

VARIATIONS

1. Omit marinade above. Prepare the lamb roast by rubbing with cut garlic or lemon. Insert slivers of garlic and marjoram under the skin, using a pointed knife. Follow roasting directions above.

2. You'll certainly want to serve your lamb roast with one of our sweet and sour or minted sauces in the Sauces and Salad Dressings chapter.

LAMB BROCHETTES

> 2 pounds lean lamb
> 3 tablespoons soy sauce
> ½ teaspoon curry powder
> Dash artificial sweetener
> 8 small slices pineapple (canned in its own juice), each cut into 4 pieces, plus 8 tablespoons juice
> 1 cup fresh mushrooms (about 8)
> 8 ounces winter squash, cut in 1-inch slices
> 1 medium green pepper, cut into 8 squares
> 1 medium red pepper, cut into 8 squares
> 2 cups cooked enriched rice

Cut lamb in 1¼-inch cubes. Combine soy sauce, curry and sweet-ener. Pour over lamb, pineapple (reserve juice) and vegetables. Marinate 2 hours or more. Drain well, reserving marinade. Alter-nate lamb with vegetables on skewers and string a pineapple piece between each vegetable. Broil about 6 inches from heat source for 15 minutes, or until brown on all sides. Brush frequently with reserved marinade. Serve brochettes on bed of ½ cup rice sprin-kled with 2 tablespoons reserved pineapple juice. Makes 4 dinner servings.

MEDITERRANEAN LAMB CHOPS

> ½ cup lemon juice
> Dash each thyme, caraway seeds and minced parsley
> 4 lamb chops, 5 ounces each, with bone

Combine lemon juice, thyme, caraway seeds and minced parsley, and marinate lamb in this mixture for 1 hour. Drain. Broil on rack about 4 inches from heat source, turning once, about 8 minutes. Makes 2 dinner servings.

DOWN-HOME LAMB AND VEGETABLE STEW

In my autobiography, The Story of Weight Watchers, *I mentioned that "lamb stew night" at my mother's was always my favorite. So many members of Weight Watchers have asked me for a "legal" lamb stew that I've included this version, which has all the heartiness of mother's weekly melange. If only one could sprinkle it with that dash of nostalgia which is the best spice of all.*

> 1 pound stewing lamb (without bone or visible fat), cut in
> cubes
> 1 envelope instant onion broth and seasoning mix
> 2 ounces peas
> 2 ounces winter squash, turnips or okra, diced
> 1 cup boiling water
> 1 envelope instant onion broth and seasoning mix
> Salt and pepper
> 1 cup cooked lima (butter) beans, or 1⅓ cups cooked
> enriched macaroni
> Choice of seasonings: Herbs I like with lamb include parsley,
> basil, rosemary, thyme and curry

Broil lamb thoroughly on all sides on a rack. Meanwhile cook peas and winter squash in water with onion broth mix in covered saucepan for 10 minutes. Add salt, pepper and choice of seasonings. Transfer lamb to saucepan, cover and cook till very soft. Stir in lima beans (or macaroni) before serving and heat. If water evaporates during cooking, add more. Mix well, and divide evenly. Makes 2 dinner servings.

MOUSSAKA (GREEK-STYLE LAMB AND EGGPLANT)

2 cups eggplant, sliced ½-inch thick
Coarse salt
1 pound ground lamb
1 cup tomato juice, reduced by half
1 tablespoon dehydrated onion flakes
½ teaspoon grated lemon rind
1 clove garlic, crushed
½ teaspoon salt
¼ teaspoon pepper
Dash cinnamon
1 recipe Cauliflower White Sauce (p. 230 — count 1 cup
　#3B vegetable and ½ cup skim milk per serving)

Sprinkle eggplant with salt, and let stand about 30 minutes on a plate under a heavy weight. This will remove excess fluid. Meanwhile, brown lamb under broiler, lift out and combine with thickened tomato juice, onion flakes, lemon rind, garlic, salt, pepper and cinnamon; mix well. Wash, drain, and dry eggplant with paper toweling. Put eggplant slices over lamb mixture in shallow casserole. Spoon sauce on top. Bake covered at 375° F. for 30 minutes, or until top is brown. Makes 2 dinner servings.

LAMBURGERS

Start with an inexpensive cut of boned, sliced lamb (breast, shoulder, shanks) and remove all visible fat. Put through meat chopper. Season with onion salt, pepper, basil, marjoram or other herbs. Weigh. Moisten with cold water or club soda, shape into patties, and broil like hamburgers.

BROILED SWEETBREADS

2 pounds sweetbreads (calf or lamb)
1 quart water
1 tablespoon vinegar
1 teaspoon salt
½ envelope instant chicken broth and seasoning mix
½ cup hot water
2 tablespoons chopped parsley

Cover sweetbreads with water to which vinegar and salt have been added. Simmer 20 minutes; drain. Remove membranes, slice sweetbreads. Arrange on rack in broiler pan. Brush with bouillon (prepared by dissolving broth mix in water), and sprinkle with parsley. Broil about 4 inches from source of heat for 6 minutes or until sweetbreads are lightly browned, turning occasionally. Makes 4 dinner servings.

HOW TO STEAM CHICKEN

Have you ever steamed chicken? Put halved skinned chicken breasts in a colander set in a large kettle holding water *below* the level of the chicken. Cover kettle and let cook until chicken is soft. The tricky thing is to keep adding boiling water so the steam continues to rise, but never so much that the chicken touches water — it's the steam that does the cooking. Serve in any of the ways suggested for cooked chicken. Allow about 50% longer for steaming than for boiling. Chicken is done when it loses its pink shine. Remove skin and bone before serving. Check our chapter on Sauces for many delicious accompaniments.

Pressure-Cooked Chicken: Follow manufacturer's directions and use according to your Menu Plan. Be sure to remove skin.

HOW TO BAKE CHICKEN

Let chicken stand for 1 hour (or overnight) in refrigerator in one of the marinades suggested on p. 191. Chicken can be boned and skinned before or after it is baked. Drain chicken, saving marinade, and place on rack in pan. Bake at 350° F. (moderate oven) for 40-50 minutes, or until it is thoroughly cooked. Baste every 15 minutes with reserved marinade. To brown chicken, raise oven temperature to 400° F. for last 15 minutes. Chicken will be crisper if baked without a cover. However, if you like chicken that falls away from the bones, bake it in a shallow pan with a lid.

For an Italian accent, season the bird inside and out with salt and pepper and put 2 fresh sage leaves inside each cavity (substitute dried sage if you must, but it's not as good).

NOTE: Capon can be cooked by any method used in chicken recipes.

HOW TO ROTISSERIE CHICKEN

Yes, you may rotisserie chicken with the skin on (baste with bouillon), but remove skin before eating chicken. Orange Marinade (p. 191) makes a good baste. Allow 40-50 minutes. Try also skewering sage leaves with pieces of chicken or whole quail. Also delectable: wrapping chunks of chicken in fennel leaves before skewering on rotisserie spit.

SOUTHERN "FRIED" CHICKEN WITH DIXIE "GRAVY"
A familiar mid-Sunday meal done our way.

> 4 slices toast
> 1 teaspoon parsley
> ½ teaspoon poultry seasoning
> 4 skinned and boned chicken breasts (6 ounces each)
> 1 teaspoon salt
> ½ teaspoon pepper
> 1 cup skim milk
> ½ teaspoon imitation butter flavoring
> ½ cup water
> ½ envelope instant chicken broth and seasoning mix
> ½ teaspoon onion powder

Roll toast into crumbs with rolling pin or whiz in blender; mix in parsley and poultry seasoning. Sprinkle chicken with salt and pepper. Pour ½ cup of the skim milk into small bowl. Completely immerse each piece of chicken in milk; then roll in crumb mixture, making sure to use up all the milk and crumbs. Place chicken in non-stick baking pan. Bake at 375° F. (moderate oven) for 30 minutes. Lift out chicken. Meanwhile prepare our Dixie "Gravy" by combining remaining ½ cup milk with butter flavoring, water, broth mix and onion powder. Heat and serve with "fried" chicken. Makes 4 luncheon servings.

CREAMED CHICKEN IN PATTY SHELLS

Patty Shells

    1 egg white
    ⅛ teaspoon cream of tartar
    Pinch salt

Creamed Chicken Filling

    2 ounces cooked, boned and skinned chicken, diced
    ½ cup mushroom pieces
    2 tablespoons evaporated skimmed milk
    ¼ envelope instant chicken broth and seasoning mix
    1 egg yolk
    Strip of pimento

Line baking sheet with parchment paper, aluminum foil or brown paper. Combine ingredients for patty shells, and beat till egg white is stiff. Trace 3 circles about 2½ inches in diameter onto paper lining. Shape beaten egg white onto circles. With back of spoon, form a hollow in each one. Bake on lined sheet at 250° F. for 40 minutes, turn off heat and let stand in oven for 10 minutes. Remove patty shells from paper, using a spatula or pancake turner. To prepare filling, combine chicken, mushrooms, milk and bouillon in double boiler or in saucepan over very low direct heat. Stir in egg yolk and cook till thickened. Serve in patty shells with pimento strips for garnish. Makes 1 luncheon serving.

CHICKEN TETRAZZINI

    ⅔ cup cooked enriched spaghetti
    ½ cup cooked or canned mushrooms, sliced
    4 ounces peas
    6 ounces cooked, skinned and boned chicken, cut in pieces
    Salt and pepper
    Dash nutmeg (or thyme)
    ⅓ cup instant non-fat dry milk
    ½ cup water
    ½ envelope instant chicken broth and seasoning mix
    1 teaspoon dehydrated onion flakes
    Dash paprika

In small casserole, arrange layers of spaghetti, mushrooms (reserving a few slices), peas and chicken. Season with salt, pepper and nutmeg. Combine dry milk, water, broth mix and onion flakes; pour into casserole. Sprinkle top with paprika and reserved mushrooms. Bake at 350° F. until sauce is hot and bubbly, 20-30 minutes. Makes 1 dinner serving.

ARROZ CON POLLO

    1½ pounds cooked, skinned and boned chicken
    1½ cups water
    1 envelope instant chicken broth and seasoning mix
    3 medium tomatoes, diced
    1 green chili pepper, diced fine, or 1 shredded pimento
    2 tablespoons dehydrated onion flakes
    1 mashed clove garlic
    1 teaspoon salt
    ½ teaspoon chili powder
    ¼ teaspoon saffron
    2 cups cooked enriched rice

Dice chicken and set aside. Make a sauce by combining the next 9 ingredients. Cook rapidly for 15 minutes. Turn off heat, stir in rice and chicken, mix well and divide evenly. Serve hot. Makes 4 dinner servings.

VARIATION

Add 16 ounces cooked peas a few minutes before serving. Stir in ¼ teaspoon sherry extract, if desired.

JERUSALEM CHICKEN WITH OKRA

    1½ pounds steamed, boned and skinned chicken breasts
    4 ounces onion, sliced
    ½ clove garlic, crushed
    1 cup water
    1 envelope instant chicken broth and seasoning mix
    12 ounces okra, with ends trimmed off
    2 cups tomato juice
    Salt and pepper
    1 teaspoon cumin (optional)
    ½ teaspoon cinnamon

Cool steamed chicken and cut into dice. "Water fry" onions and garlic in saucepan containing 1 cup boiling water and broth mix. Cook at high heat until water evaporates and onions are golden. Add okra and pour in enough boiling water to half cover them. Cover pan and cook until okra is almost tender. Transfer chicken and cooked vegetables to casserole and cover with tomato juice. Sprinkle with seasonings. Cover and bake at 300° F. for 1½ hours. Makes 4 dinner servings.

CHICKEN CACCIATORI

    1 cup mushrooms, sliced
    1 tablespoon dehydrated onion flakes
    ½ cup water
    1 envelope instant chicken broth and seasoning mix
    4 cups tomato juice, reduced to half volume
    24 ounces cooked, skinned and boned chicken, cut up
    ½ teaspoon basil
    Dash each garlic power and oregano
    Salt and pepper
    2⅔ cups cooked enriched spaghetti

Cook mushrooms and onion flakes in water and broth mix in a small saucepan. When water boils away, let mushrooms brown lightly. Transfer to baking dish, add thickened tomato juice, chicken and seasonings, mix well, and bake at 375° F. for 30 minutes. Divide evenly in four dishes, each holding ⅔ cup spaghetti. Makes 4 dinner servings.

CHINESE CHICKEN SALAD

You could also serve this salad on a tomato rosette. Simply cut a tomato into 6 segments, but not all the way through. Open out like flower petals and flatten slightly.

    ½ cup cooked enriched noodles
    1 medium cucumber
    4 ounces shredded poached chicken
    ½ recipe Bean Sprouts Vinaigrette (p. 215 — count 1 cup
       bean sprouts)

Use a fine noodle for this recipe. Peel cucumber, cut in long strips and seed, then cut into shreds the same size as chicken. Toss all ingredients together. Makes 1 luncheon serving.

CHICKEN CHOW MEIN

2 cups celery, cut into matchstick pieces
2 tablespoons dehydrated onion flakes
2 cups boiling water
1 envelope instant chicken broth and seasoning mix
2 cups drained, rinsed bean sprouts
½ cup cooked or canned mushrooms
1-2 tablespoons soy sauce
6 ounces cooked, skinned and boned chicken, diced
½ cup Chinese "Fried" Noodles (p. 66)
1 teaspoon dry mustard, mixed to a paste with water

In shallow saucepan, "water-fry" celery and onion flakes in 1 cup of the water containing broth mix. When celery is soft and water evaporated, add bean sprouts, mushrooms, soy sauce and remaining boiling water. Heat gently, then turn off heat and add diced chicken. Mix thoroughly. Serve with "Fried" Noodles and English mustard (let paste stand 10 minutes). Makes 1 dinner serving.

TWO-MEAT BALLS

Everyone has a favorite recipe for meatballs, and here's mine. It's made from Group C meats, and can therefore be panbroiled.

½ pound raw, ground chicken or turkey breast
½ pound raw, ground veal
2 teaspoons dehydrated onion flakes, reconstituted in 1 tablespoon water
1½ teaspoons salt
¼ teaspoon pepper
½ teaspoon ground nutmeg, or a pinch of allspice (optional)
1½ cups boiling water
3 envelopes instant onion broth and seasoning mix

Combine all ingredients except water and broth mix; blend well. Add water, if necessary, to moisten mixture. With hands dipped in cold water, shape into small meatballs. Brown in non-stick pan on top of stove (or at 450° F. on a non-stick baking sheet) for about 15 minutes. Turn to brown all sides. Meanwhile prepare onion bouillon by combining water and onion broth mix; simmer 15 minutes. Lift meatballs from pan, transfer to onion bouillon and continue cooking for 1 hour. Can be served in a chafing dish for a party. Makes 2 dinner servings.

VARIATION

A tablespoon of our Chili Sauce (p. 216 — count 2 fluid ounces tomato juice) could replace water. Add a tablespoon of Chili Sauce to the onion bouillon too.

CHINESE CHICKEN WITH PINEAPPLE (Bo Lo Kai)

12 ounces cooked, skinned and boned chicken breasts
1 cup shredded Chinese cabbage
4 ounces bamboo shoots, sliced thin
½ cup celery
½ cup mushrooms
1½ cups water
2 envelopes instant chicken broth and seasoning mix
4 small slices pineapple (canned in its own juice), cut into chunks, plus 4 tablespoons juice
Artificial sweetener to equal 2 teaspoons sugar
1-2 tablespoons soy sauce
Dash pepper

Cut the chicken into thin diagonal strips and set aside. Cook cabbage, bamboo shoots, celery and mushrooms in ¾ cup water and 1 envelope broth mix. As soon as liquid boils out, add remaining water and broth mix, pineapple and pineapple juice, sweetener, soy sauce and pepper. Bring to boil, let liquid cook down about half and stir in chicken. Don't let the chicken strips boil — turn off heat; they'll warm in the sauce. Makes 2 dinner servings.

CHICKEN BUTTERMILK LOAF
A light and creamy luncheon dish for a hot summer day.

>1 envelope (1 tablespoon) unflavored gelatin
>1 cup cold chicken bouillon
>½ cup buttermilk
>2 teaspoons lemon juice
>½ teaspoon grated lemon rind
>½ teaspoon salt
>Dash red hot sauce
>8 ounces cooked, skinned and boned chicken, diced fine
>½ cup chopped celery
>1 tablespoon chopped parsley

In saucepan sprinkle gelatin over bouillon to soften. Place over low heat and stir until gelatin dissolves (about 3 minutes). Remove from heat; stir in buttermilk, lemon juice, lemon rind, salt and red hot sauce. Chill until mixture is consistency of unbeaten egg whites. Fold in chicken, celery and parsley. Turn into a 2½-cup mold or small loaf pan, which has been rinsed in cold water. Chill until firm. Unmold to serve. Makes 2 luncheon servings.

CHICKEN HASH

>12 ounces cooked, skinned, boned chicken, diced
>2 medium (3-ounce) potatoes, boiled and diced
>1 medium green pepper, chopped
>½ cup cooked, diced celery
>2 tablespoons diced pimento
>1 teaspoon dehydrated onion flakes
>1 cup chicken bouillon
>½ cup tomato juice, reduced by half
>2 medium tomatoes, sliced

Combine chicken, potatoes, pepper, celery and pimento in chopping bowl and chop fine. Divide into two oven-to-table dishes, add onion flakes, bouillon and tomato juice to each dish. Top with tomato slices and bake at 350° F. for 30 minutes. Makes 2 dinner servings.

POULE-AU-POT (CHICKEN-IN-THE-POT)

1 small roasting chicken
2 ribs celery, with leaves
2 quarts cold water
1 teaspoon salt
1 bouquet garni (3 sprigs parsley, 1 sprig dill, ½ bay leaf, tied in cheesecloth)
8 ounces carrots, finely diced
4 ounces parsnip, finely diced
4 ounces leek (white part), finely diced
2 envelopes instant chicken broth and seasoning mix
2 cups cooked enriched rice (optional)

Bake chicken on rack in roasting pan at 350° F. until just tender. Do not overdo. Remove skin and transfer chicken to a soup kettle with celery, cold water and salt. Bring to boil, and skim, if desired, to remove grayish scum that rises to top. Add diced carrots, parsnip, leek and broth mix to soup kettle. Bring to boil again, skimming as necessary. Cover kettle and simmer for 15 minutes, or until vegetables are tender. Serve soup separately; cut chicken into serving portions and serve with vegetables in bowls, each containing ½ cup rice, if desired. Makes 4 servings.

BROILED ROCK CORNISH HEN WITH "BRANDIED" CHERRY SAUCE

Rock Cornish hens should be completely defrosted before you use them. Thaw them overnight in your refrigerator, with the original wrappings on. If you're lucky enough to come by a pheasant, you can follow this same recipe.

1 Rock Cornish hen
2 tablespoons lemon juice
¾ cup chicken bouillon
Dash each of parsley, poultry seasoning and sage
1 cup sweet cherries, pitted
½ cup berry-flavored dietetic carbonated beverage
½ teaspoon brandy extract

Split thawed hen down the middle, brush with lemon juice and baste with chicken bouillon. Season to taste with parsley, poultry seasoning and sage. Broil, skin side down, on preheated broiler rack, turning to brown both sides. Allow 30-45 minutes in all. Remove skin, bone; weigh portions. Make "Brandied" Cherry Sauce: cover cherries with beverage and cook till cherries are soft. Stir in ½ teaspoon brandy extract. Spoon over Cornish hen, serve hot. Makes 2 dinner servings. Use leftover Cornish hen, if any, in one of our chicken salads or loafs.

HOW TO ROAST TURKEY

With so many markets offering turkey parts (including the delicious turkey breasts), you don't have to wait for a holiday to have it.

Roast the turkey uncovered in a slow oven (300° F.) until tender, allowing 25 minutes per pound for under 12 pounds; 20 minutes per pound for a larger turkey. Baste it every half hour or so with one of the recommended marinades (p. 191). Weigh boned and skinned portion before serving.

LEFTOVER TURKEY (OR CHICKEN)

1. It's one of the easiest foods to dress up. Try it diced with Daikon Sauce (p. 217).

2. Make an open-face turkey sandwich with Curried Mayonnaise (p. 226 — count 1 tablespoon mayonnaise and 1 tablespoon instant non-fat dry milk per serving).

3. Use for stuffed cabbage (p. 262) or grapevine leaves (p. 272).

4. Roast turkey can be sliced and weighed, then frozen in serving-size amounts. Defrost and use instead of chicken in any of the chicken recipes. For extended freezer storage, cover cooked turkey with stock made from boiling water and instant chicken broth and seasoning mix. Use the stock in the cooking, when turkey is de-frosted.

5. Make this salad for a perfect summer luncheon: Overlap thin slices of cooked turkey or chicken (4 ounces) with slices of ½ cantaloupe or 1 small orange, on a bed of lettuce. Serve with home-made potato salad (p. 64).

TURKEY AND CELERY MOLDED SALAD

1 envelope (1 tablespoon) unflavored gelatin
2 tablespoons cold water
1½ cups hot water
2 envelopes instant chicken broth and seasoning mix
4 ounces cooked diced turkey
½ cup celery, diced
2 hard-cooked eggs, chopped
½ medium dill pickle, chopped
2 tablespoons mayonnaise
1 tablespoon chopped pimento
2 teaspoons lemon juice
½ teaspoon poultry seasoning

Soften gelatin in cold water, then dissolve in hot water with chicken broth mix added. Set aside to cool and thicken slightly (to texture of thick egg whites). Combine remaining ingredients; blend well. Combine with gelatin and transfer to a wet mold. Chill in refrigerator until set. Unmold. Makes 2 luncheon servings.

TURKEY MEAT LOAF

16 ounces cooked turkey, ground
8 ounces cooked chopped veal
1 cup canned sliced mushrooms, drained
3 slices enriched white bread, made into crumbs
½ cup chicken bouillon
¼ cup Catsup (p. 215 — count ¾ cup tomato juice)
1 tablespoon dehydrated onion flakes
½ teaspoon sage
½ teaspoon salt
Salt and pepper

Combine all ingredients in mixing bowl; mix well. Shape into loaf in 4 x 9-inch pan and bake at 375° F. for one hour. Let stand about 15 minutes before slicing; divide equally. Makes 6 luncheon servings.

MARINADES FOR POULTRY

Orange Marinade

> 1 cup orange-flavored dietetic carbonated beverage,
>   or 1 cup water with ½ teaspoon orange extract
> 1-2 tablespoons soy sauce
> Dash ground ginger or poultry seasoning, or few drops brandy
>   extract

Tart Tomato Marinade

> 3 cups tomato juice, reduced by half
> ½ cup lemon-lime-flavored dietetic carbonated beverage
> ¼ cup brown sugar replacement
> ¼ teaspoon onion salt

Tangy Marinade

> ½ cup boiling water
> 2 chicken bouillon cubes
> 2 teaspoons Worcestershire
> 2 teaspoons curry powder
> 1 teaspoon salt
> 1 teaspoon oregano
> 1 mashed clove garlic
> 1 crushed bay leaf
> ½ teaspoon paprika
> ⅛ teaspoon "legal" red hot sauce

Tarragon Marinade

> ½ cup boiling water
> 1 envelope instant chicken broth and seasoning mix
> 2 tablespoons lemon juice
> 1 teaspoon salt
> ½ teaspoon pepper
> 2 teaspoons fresh chopped tarragon leaf
>   or ½ teaspoon dried tarragon

Combine ingredients for marinade and spread over chicken (or other poultry, turkey roasts, etc.), coating both sides. Let stand for 1 hour or overnight, then broil, bake or barbecue as desired. Or prepare marinade; spread on chicken while it is being cooked, basting every 15 minutes or so.

BRAINS A LA KING

1 pound brains
5 cups water
1 tablespoon vinegar
1 teaspoon salt
1 cup instant non-fat dry milk
1 envelope instant chicken broth and seasoning mix
½ cup finely chopped celery
½ cup fresh mushrooms
8 ounces cooked or canned peas

Simmer brains for 20 minutes in 1 quart water with vinegar and salt. Drain. Combine dry milk, broth mix and remaining water. Add celery and mushrooms; simmer for 6 minutes. Remove membranes and separate brains into small pieces. Add to milk-bouillon mixture. Stir in peas. Cook slowly for 5 minutes. Makes 2 dinner servings.

HEART CHOP SUEY

Veal, beef or lamb hearts are full of nutrients, and cooked and seasoned properly, they will be as tender and tasty as any meat dish.

1½ pound heart
Boiling water
2 whole cloves
1 clove garlic
¼ cup chopped celery
10 peppercorns
1 large bay leaf
¼ teaspoon thyme
2 tablespoons lemon juice
1 cup sliced fresh mushrooms
Salt and pepper

Wash the heart in plenty of water and remove any fat, veins and membranes. Cover with boiling water and add cloves, garlic, celery, peppercorns, bay leaf and thyme. Bring to boil and remove scum with a spoon. Cook for 3 hours or until meat is tender. Add lemon juice and mushrooms, and continue cooking another half hour. Drain. Season with salt and pepper. Makes 3 dinner servings.

ROAST VEAL
Tastes like roast pork!

½ cup soy sauce
Artificial sweetener to equal 1 tablespoon sugar
Salt and pepper
¼ teaspoon garlic powder
4-pound veal roast (or leg of veal)

Combine all ingredients except veal and pour over veal roast in baking pan. Marinate for at least 1 hour, turning frequently. Drain, reserving marinade. Bake veal at 350° F. for 2 hours or until done to taste; baste with reserved marinade. Weigh portions and serve; makes about 8 dinner servings.

BAKED VEAL AND VEGETABLE CASSEROLE

1½ pounds veal, sliced thin and cut in 2-inch squares
2 cups chicken bouillon
4 ounces yellow turnip, diced
4 ounces onion, diced
4 ounces carrot, diced
½ cup mushrooms
1 teaspoon minced parsley
1 clove garlic, mashed
Dash marjoram

In saucepan cover veal with bouillon and poach gently. Cook until veal shows no trace of pink. Drain, wipe dry and transfer to casserole. Add remaining ingredients, mix well, cover casserole and bake at 325° F. for 1 hour. Makes 3 dinner servings.

BROILED VEAL CHOPS

A good quick recipe popular with members of Weight Watchers calls for tenderloin or rib veal chops (10 ounces raw per serving) sprinkled with seasoned salt and broiled until brown on both sides. Sometime try a sauce made of finely cut parsley and dill mixed with lemon juice and spread over the broiled chop. Garlic and tomato, mushrooms, marjoram and rosemary go well with veal.

POTTED VEAL BALLS

1½ pounds ground veal
¼ cup club soda
¼ teaspoon garlic powder
¼ teaspoon oregano
Salt and pepper
4 cups shredded cabbage
1 medium green pepper, cut up
1½ cups tomato juice
1 teaspoon lemon juice
Artificial sweetener to equal 2 teaspoons sugar
1 clove garlic, mashed
¼ teaspoon basil

Combine ground veal with club soda, garlic powder, oregano, salt and pepper, and form into small balls. Cook veal balls on all sides in non-stick skillet. Remove and set aside. In a large pot, make a bed of shredded cabbage, top with green pepper, add tomato juice, lemon juice, artificial sweetener, garlic and basil. Put veal balls on top and bring to a boil. Lower heat to simmer for a little over an hour. Cook uncovered; the juice boils down to make a thicker sauce. Makes 3 dinner servings.

EGGPLANT AND VEAL ALLA MACCHERONI

2 cups peeled eggplant, sliced
Salt and pepper
6 ounces cooked, ground veal
1 cup beef bouillon
1 tablespoon dehydrated onion flakes
1 teaspoon Italian seasoning spice
⅔ cup cooked enriched macaroni shells

Season eggplant with salt and pepper. Brown under broiler, turning once. Transfer to individual casserole. Combine remaining ingredients in a small saucepan, and continue cooking until mixture thickens. Pour over eggplant in casserole. Bake at 350° F. for 15 minutes or until thoroughly heated. Serve over macaroni shells. Makes 1 dinner serving.

TACOS

Roast beef could be substituted for the browned veal.

    6 ounces raw ground veal
    1 teaspoon chili powder
    1 teaspoon dehydrated onion flakes
    ¼ teaspoon salt
    ¼ teaspoon onion powder
    ¼ teaspoon paprika
    Dash red hot sauce
    1 slice bread
    Toothpicks
    ½ cup shredded lettuce
    1 tablespoon Pimento Dressing (p. 217)

Brown veal in non-stick skillet. Add seasonings (next 6 ingredients) and cook 5 minutes. Lift veal out of skillet. Toast bread lightly. Spread meat mixture over one-half of the slice, fold and hold in place with toothpicks. Combine lettuce and 1 tablespoon Pimento Dressing and use to cover taco. Makes 1 luncheon serving.

VEAL BIRDS

Bake a fruit (pineapple slices?) along with the veal.

    8 ounces veal steak, cut thin as for scallopini
    ½ teaspoon poultry seasoning
    ½ cup cooked enriched rice
    2 teaspoons dehydrated onion flakes, reconstituted in
      2 tablespoons water
    1 medium green pepper, chopped
    1 medium tomato, chopped
    1 teaspoon parsley
    ¼ teaspoon oregano
    Dash garlic powder

In saucepan cover veal with water and poach gently until veal softens and loses its pink raw color. Drain, wash quickly and dry. Sprinkle poultry seasoning on rice, and add onion flakes. Spread rice mixture over the veal, roll up, and fasten with toothpicks or string. Transfer to small casserole or saucepan with remaining ingredients. Bake at 350° F. or cook over medium heat for 30 minutes. Makes 1 dinner serving.

Milk {Shakes, Creams, Toppings, Etc.}

Milkshakes? Bavarian creams? Ice creams? Sundaes? Even the names sound sinful on Weight Watchers Program — but of course we've taken out what's fattening and left lots of scintillating flavor. So if you've been unbearably tempted by soda-fountain treats, give in — but only to our very "legal" recipes.

RULES FOR USING MILK

1. Amounts:
    WOMAN AND MAN: 16 fluid ounces skim milk,
    or 12 fluid ounces buttermilk,
    or 8 fluid ounces evaporated skimmed milk
    YOUTH: 1 quart skim milk,
    or 24 fluid ounces buttermilk,
    or 16 fluid ounces evaporated skim milk

2. The skim milk we allow is the instant non-fat dry milk, re-constituted according to label directions; or skim milk labeled either "skimmed milk" or "modified" or "fortified skim milk" with no whole milk solids added. Do not use milk labeled "a skimmed milk product" or "99% fat free."

3. Your daily allowance of evaporated skimmed milk may be diluted with an equal amount of water to make a total of 16 ounces skim milk.

4. The buttermilk may be made from either whole or combination of skim and whole milk; Bulgarian buttermilk is not permitted.

5. You may use your milk at any time, at meal times, as snacks, at bedtime, in coffee or tea, or in our popular milk shakes and whipped toppings, but you must consume the amount allotted to you in your menu plan.

6. Mix-and-match your milk if you like. For example, a woman may use 1 cup (8 fluid ounces) skim milk and ½ cup (4 fluid ounces) evaporated skim milk to complete daily requirement.

7. Instant non-fat dry milk reconstitutes to the ratio of 1:3; therefore, if you stir 2 teaspoons dry milk into your coffee, you must count 6 teaspoons (1 fluid ounce) skim milk.

VANILLA ICE "CREAM"

¼ teaspoon gelatin
1 tablespoon cold water
½ cup evaporated skimmed milk
½ teaspoon vanilla extract
Artificial sweetener to equal 4 teaspoons sugar

Sprinkle gelatin over cold water in 1½-quart mixing bowl. Heat evaporated milk over very low heat or in the top part of a double boiler placed over hot water. When milk is hot but not boiling, add all of it, including thin skin which forms on top, to the mixing bowl. Stir well to dissolve gelatin, then chill thoroughly in freezer for a few minutes. Whip cold mixture with beater at medium speed until it stands in peaks but is not dry. Add vanilla and sweetener and beat just long enough to incorporate them. Put mixing bowl into freezer until mixture is almost frozen, 30-40 minutes. Divide into 4 equal portions and use at once. Or store frozen "cream" mixture, in 4 small bowls or in ice cube tray (without dividers), and use as desired. Let ice "cream" soften slightly in the refrigerator before serving. Makes 4 servings; count 1 ounce evaporated skimmed milk per serving.

VARIATION
Coffee Ice "Cream": Follow recipe for Vanilla Ice "Cream", but dissolve 1-1½ teaspoons instant coffee powder in evaporated skimmed milk in double boiler. Add dash of maple and black walnut extracts, if desired.

BLENDER QUICK CHOCOLATE ICE "CREAM"

For Chocolate "Eclairs" (yes!), use this as filling for 4 "pastry" cases (p. 27). For St. Patrick's Day "Eclairs" omit chocolate extract and brown food coloring; add ½ teaspoon peppermint extract, ¼ teaspoon almond extract, and green food coloring.

> ¼ cup chilled evaporated skimmed milk
> ⅓ cup instant non-fat dry milk
> Artificial sweetener to equal 6 teaspoons sugar
> 1 teaspoon chocolate extract
> Few drops black walnut or maple extract (optional)
> Brown food coloring (or red, green and yellow to make brown)
> 6-8 ice cubes

Combine milks, sweetener and extracts in blender; whip at low speed until smooth, carefully add food coloring to make chocolate brown. With blender on high speed, add ice cubes, one at a time, making certain each cube is incorporated in mixture before adding the next one. Transfer to freezing tray for ½ hour. Serve at once, or keep frozen and let soften 10 minutes before use. Makes 4 servings. Count 3 fluid ounces skim milk for each serving.

VARIATION

Lemon Ice "Cream": Follow recipe above but replace extracts with ¼ teaspoon lemon extract, 1 tablespoon lemon juice, a small piece of lemon rind; use yellow food coloring.

BEST WHIPPED TOPPING

Delicious and comparatively stable, so you can refrigerate it for an hour or more before use. If it fails, whip it again before serving.

> ¼ teaspoon unflavored gelatin
> 1 teaspoon cold water
> ½ cup evaporated skimmed milk
> ½ teaspoon vanilla extract
> Artificial sweetener to equal 4 teaspoons sugar

It's made almost exactly like our Vanilla Ice "Cream": Sprinkle gelatin over cold water in 1½-quart mixing bowl. Scald evaporated skimmed milk, add to mixing bowl and stir well to dissolve gelatin.

Chill in freezer for a few minutes. When mixture is very cold, add vanilla extract and sweetener, and whip with beater at medium speed until it stands in peaks. Divide into 4 portions. Refrigerate and use as desired. Makes 4 servings; count 1 ounce evaporated skimmed milk for each serving.

EASY WHIPPED TOPPING

This is made with non-fat dry milk and is not as stable as the Best Whipped Topping.

> ⅓ cup instant non-fat dry milk
> ⅓ cup ice water
> 2 teaspoons lemon juice
> Artificial sweetener to equal 4 tablespoons sugar
> ½ teaspoon nutmeg or flavor extract (vanilla, almond, black walnut, etc.)

Combine all ingredients in bowl and beat at high speed with electric mixer or by hand until mixture stands in peaks; it takes at least 10 minutes. Use immediately. Makes 4 servings; count ¼ cup skim milk per serving.

BAKED GRAPEFRUIT ALASKA

It's so rich you'll find it hard to believe we really allow it! Egg yolks and egg whites must be consumed at the same meal, so serve with Egg Foo Yung (p. 81) made with 2 egg yolks and 1 egg white.

> ½ medium grapefruit
> 1 egg white
> ⅛ teaspoon cream of tartar
> Salt
> Artificial sweetener to equal 2 teaspoons sugar (optional)
> 1 serving Vanilla Ice "Cream" (p. 197 — count 1 fluid ounce evaporated skimmed milk)

Preheat oven to 450° F. Cut the grapefruit segments away from the peel with a grapefruit knife and discard the tough membranes in the center. Be careful not to pierce the shell. Leave the segments and juice in the shell. Beat egg white, cream of tartar, salt and sweetener until whites are stiff (stand in peaks). Fill grapefruit shell with Vanilla Ice "Cream". Heap beaten egg white on the ice "cream" and set on foil tray or baking sheet. Bake on a high shelf in oven for about 5 minutes or until meringue is lightly brown and set. Makes 1 serving.

VARIATIONS

Baked Cantaloupe Alaska: Instead of grapefruit, use a ripe cantaloupe half, discard seeds, spoon in ice "cream," top with beaten egg white, then continue as for Grapefruit Alaska.

Baked Pineapple Alaska: Stack 2 small slices pineapple (canned in its own juice) in small baking dish; add ice "cream," sprinkle with 2 tablespoons pineapple juice, top with beaten egg white and bake as above.

PINEAPPLE BAVARIAN CREAM

Bavarian Cream: "a creamy dessert made with a flavored whipped gelatin mixture, into which a fluffy 'cream' topping is folded." By substituting two servings of fruit for the pineapple, and changing the flavors of the carbonated beverage (or even using water) you could make many different versions.

    1½ cups cream-flavored dietetic carbonated beverage
    1 envelope (1 tablespoon) unflavored gelatin
    4 small slices pineapple (canned in its own juice), diced,
        plus 4 tablespoons juice
    Salt
    Artificial sweetener to equal 4 teaspoons sugar
    1 recipe Best Whipped Topping (p. 198 — count 1 fluid ounce
        evaporated skimmed milk per serving)

Pour ¼ cup beverage into small saucepan. Sprinkle with gelatin and place over low heat; stir constantly until gelatin dissolves. Add diced pineapple, pineapple juice, remaining carbonated beverage, salt and sweetener. Mix well. Chill in refrigerator till thick and syrupy. Meanwhile prepare Best Whipped Topping. Fold gelatin mixture into topping and serve in dessert dishes. Makes 4 generous servings.

BLANC MANGE
Literally, "white food." It's an almond-flavored molded gelatin dessert.

> 1 envelope (1 tablespoon) unflavored gelatin
> 1 cup cold water
> 2 cups evaporated skimmed milk
> Artificial sweetener to equal 6 teaspoons sugar
> ½ teaspoon vanilla extract
> ¾ teaspoon almond extract
> ½ teaspoon cherry extract

Soften gelatin in 1 cup cold water. Scald (heat but do not boil) the milk. Add gelatin, stirring well until dissolved. Mix in extracts and sweetener. Refrigerate in crystal bowl until set. Makes 6 servings.

BOMBES
A bombe is a delectable concoction of sherbet (ices) and ice "cream", flavored to taste. Big festive metal bombe molds are available, but you can also make bombes in coffee cups, custard cups, etc.

> ½ recipe orange-flavor Milk Sherbet (p. 205 — count 1 fluid ounce evaporated skimmed milk per serving)
> ½ recipe Vanilla Ice "Cream" (p. 197 — count 1 fluid ounce evaporated skimmed milk per serving)

Line the sides and bottom of a small mold evenly with Orange Milk Sherbet, about ¼-1 inch thick. Set it in the freezer to harden. When the sherbet is hard, pack the center with Ice "'Cream". Cover mold with a sheet of wax paper or foil (or put the lid on it if it has one). Freeze up to 24 hours. To unmold bombe, dip it briefly into cool (never hot!) water. Loosen edges by running around, and invert on plate. Then set in freezer to harden, if necessary. Divide bombe into 2 portions. Makes 2 servings; count ¼ cup evaporated skimmed milk per serving.

SERVING SUGGESTIONS
Decorate unmolded bombe with mint leaves or other greens, or surround each serving with dice from ½ medium cantaloupe or ½ cup mandarin orange sections.

RASPBERRY CHIFFON

1½ cups raspberry-flavored dietetic carbonated beverage
1 envelope (1 tablespoon) unflavored gelatin
⅓ cup instant non-fat dry milk
Artificial sweetener to equal 1 tablespoon sugar

Freeze 1 cup of the beverage in ice cube tray with divider in place. Pour remaining carbonated beverage into small saucepan and sprinkle with gelatin. Place over low heat, stirring constantly until gelatin dissolves. Transfer to blender with dry milk and sweetener; blend well — and, with blender on, add frozen cubes of carbonated beverage, one or two at a time. Pour into dessert dishes and serve at once, or refrigerate. Makes 1 serving.

FRUIT SUNDAE (COUPE JACQUES)

A sundae with a French accent. It is similar to a parfait in that it combines ice cream or ices with fruit, sauce, or whipped cream, but it is usually served in a shallow dish.

1 recipe Vanilla Ice "Cream" (p. 197 — count 1 fluid ounce
    evaporated skimmed milk per serving)
½ cup blueberries
½ medium cantaloupe, diced
Artificial sweetener to equal 1 tablespoon sugar (optional)
¼ cup black cherry-flavored dietetic carbonated beverage

Prepare Ice "Cream" and put ¾ of recipe in freezer till firm but not hard. Refrigerate remaining ¼ of mixture to make Best Whipped Topping. Combine fruit, sprinkle with artificial sweetener, if desired. Boil carbonated beverage till it is reduced by half to make "syrup". Using 4 sundae cups or saucer-shaped stemmed champagne glasses, alternate layers of diced fruit with layers of Ice "Cream" and black cherry syrup; reserve a few pieces of fruit for garnish. Spoon on Whipped Topping (if Topping has collapsed, beat mixture once more); garnish with reserved fruit and serve. Use at once, or put in freezer 10 minutes or so, till ready to use. Makes 4 servings.

BANANA SPLIT WITH STRAWBERRY SAUCE

⅔ cup instant non-fat dry milk
¾ cup ice water
Artificial sweetener to equal ½ cup sugar (12 envelopes)
1 tablespoon vanilla extract
2 medium bananas
1 cup strawberries

Using a deep bowl, combine dry milk, ice water, artificial sweetener and vanilla extract. Beat at low speed of electric mixer for 1 minute, then beat at high speed until mixture is the consistency of thick cream, about 10 minutes in all. Chill in freezer for 3 hours or until mixture has the texture of ice cream.

Peel bananas and cut in half lengthwise or crosswise, depending on shape of dish. Put halves into 2 banana-split (or shallow dessert) dishes; top each dish with 1 small scoop of frozen milk mixture. Reserve about ¾-1 cup of the milk mixture and leave at room temperature to soften. Put dishes back in freezer to stay firm. Beat reserved milk mixture until it is the texture of whipped cream. Reserve 6 berries; gently mash remaining berries to release juice. Pour mashed strawberries and whipped milk mixture over banana split; garnish with 3 strawberries. Makes 2 servings. Count each serving as 1 cup milk, 1½ fruits.

FRUIT GLACE

½ cup blueberries, or 1 medium peach
Water
Dash lemon juice
1 serving Vanilla Ice "Cream" (p. 197 — count 1 fluid ounce evaporated skimmed milk)
Crushed ice

In covered saucepan cook fruit with a few tablespoons water and lemon juice till soft. Transfer fruit and cooking liquid to blender, and blend at medium speed. With a spoon, fold fruit puree into Ice "Cream" and pour over crushed ice in tall glass. Makes 1 serving.

CHOCOLATE MILK SHAKE

    1 cup skim milk
    1 teaspoon chocolate extract
    Few drops brown food coloring (optional)
    Artificial sweetener to equal 2 teaspoons sugar (or to taste)
    3 ice cubes

Put milk, extract, food coloring and artificial sweetener in blender and run for about 30 seconds or until mixture froths. With blender on, add ice cubes, one at a time. Serve frothy and cold in tall glasses. Makes 1 serving.

VARIATIONS

Double-Strength Milk Shake: Use ⅔ cup non-fat dry milk and 1 cup water to replace 1 cup skim milk. Omit food coloring. Continue as above. Flavor extracts may be varied to taste.

Mocha Milk Shake: Use ⅓ cup non-fat dry milk and 1 cup strong coffee to replace 1 cup skim milk. Continue as in basic recipe. You may add a light dusting of nutmeg and cinnamon, if desired, before serving.

Super Milk Shake: Use ⅓ cup non-fat dry milk and 1 cup dietetic carbonated beverage (any flavor). Extracts and sweetener may be omitted. Proceed as in basic recipe.

Fruit Shake: Add one of the following to basic recipe: 1 medium banana, or 1 cup strawberries, or ½ cup blueberries, 1 medium peach, or fruit of choice. Blend for 30 seconds as in basic recipe above. Omit chocolate extract and brown food coloring; add ½ teaspoon vanilla extract or other flavoring.

Orange Shake: Whiz in blender the following: 1 cup skim milk, ½ cup orange juice, 1 small orange (peeled and cut up), 2 tablespoons lemon juice, artificial sweetener to equal 2 teaspoons sugar, and 4 ice cubes. Makes 2 servings.

ICE "CREAM" SODA

    ¼ cup skim milk
    ¾ cup flavored dietetic carbonated beverage
    1 serving Vanilla Ice "Cream" (p. 197 — count 1 fluid ounce
       evaporated skimmed milk)

Use large old-fashioned ice-cream soda glass or highball glass. For each serving, combine milk and beverage, add Vanilla Ice "Cream." Remember the straws. Makes 1 serving.

APRICOT PARFAIT

Parfait means perfect and here's the perfect dessert, if served soft and creamy, not frozen into a block. Spoon these into tall highball glasses rather than the smaller parfaits so that you can get your whole serving of Best Whipped Topping or Ice "Cream".

> 12 apricots
> ¼ cup water or cream-flavored dietetic carbonated beverage
> Artificial sweetener to equal 1 teaspoon sugar (optional)
> 1 recipe Best Whipped Topping (p. 198 — count 1 fluid
>   ounce evaporated skimmed milk per serving)

Cook apricots in water sprinkled with artificial sweetener, if desired, till fruit is soft, but not overcooked. Spoon alternate layers of Best Whipped Topping and cooked apricots into each of 4 tall highball glasses. Transfer to freezer and chill for 15 minutes or use at once. Makes 4 servings.

VARIATION

Gelatin Parfaits: Prepare 3 different Dessert Gelatin Whips (p. 240), using varied colors and flavors of dietetic carbonated beverages (chocolate, orange and raspberry are a good combination). When gelatins are set, prepare 1 recipe Best Whipped Topping and divide to make 4 equal servings. Spoon layers of fluffy gelatin into 4 parfait glasses, alternating each one with a layer of Best Whipped Topping; end with Topping. (Refrigerate leftover gelatin for another treat.) Serve parfaits at once or refrigerate briefly before serving. Makes 4 parfaits; count 1 fluid ounce evaporated skimmed milk per serving.

MILK SHERBET

> ⅓ cup non-fat dry milk, or ½ cup evaporated skimmed milk
> 12 fluid ounces dietetic carbonated beverage (any flavor)

Combine dry milk and carbonated beverage in bowl. Mix thoroughly. Pour into ice cube tray (divider removed) and freeze to a mush, 40-60 minutes. Serve at once, or transfer to bowl and beat rapidly until smooth and creamy. Return to tray; freeze. Defrost in refrigerator 15-30 minutes before serving, so sherbet can be spooned out. Makes 4 servings.

PEACH MINT "CREAM"

    1 cup buttermilk
    2 medium peaches, pitted
    Artificial sweetener to equal 2 tablespoons sugar
    ¼ teaspoon mint extract
    Green food coloring (optional)

Whirl everything in blender. Freeze till mushy and reblend, then serve in 2 large dessert cups. Makes 2 servings.

CHOCOLATE "RUM" DESSERT WHIP

Our dessert whips contain skim milk whipped into a froth, gelatin, sweetener and flavor extract. You can vary your recipes as you wish, if you will just keep this basic formula in mind: 1 envelope (1 tablespoon) unflavored gelatin can stiffen or set 1 pint liquid.

    ¼ cup cold water
    1 envelope (1 tablespoon) unflavored gelatin
    ¼ cup boiling water
    1 cup skim milk
    Artificial sweetener to equal 6 teaspoons sugar
    1 teaspoon chocolate extract
    ¼ teaspoon rum extract
    Few drops brown food coloring
    4-6 ice cubes (for quick setting)

Sprinkle gelatin over cold water in small saucepan and place over low heat, stirring until gelatin dissolves. Transfer to blender with remaining ingredients, except ice cubes. With blender on, add cubes one at a time. Spoon into 4 dessert or custard cups and use at once. Makes 4 servings.

VARIATIONS

Mocha Whip: Dissolve gelatin as above. Transfer to blender with ⅓ cup instant non-fat dry milk, 1 teaspoon maple extract, ½ teaspoon instant coffee and ½ cup hot water (omit skim milk and extracts in basic recipe).

Creamy Vanilla Whip: Use ⅓ cup non-fat dry milk, ¾ cup cream-flavored dietetic carbonated beverage and ½ teaspoon vanilla extract (omit skim milk and extracts listed above).

FOAMY HOT SAUCE

> ½ cup cold skim milk
> 1 teaspoon unflavored gelatin
> Artificial sweetener to equal 2 teaspoons sugar
> ¼ teaspoon flavor extract (vanilla, rum, orange, etc.)

Pour milk into saucepan. Sprinkle with gelatin and let soften for several minutes. Beat with rotary beater over low heat several minutes, until sauce is hot and foamy. Stir in sweetener and extract. Serve over baked fruits, etc. The sauce can be kept in saucepan over low heat and whipped again just before serving. Makes 4 servings; count each serving as 1 fluid ounce of skim milk.

CHOCOLATE MINT (OR "BRANDY") MOUSSE

> ¼ cup cold water
> 1 envelope (1 tablespoon) unflavored gelatin
> ¼ cup boiling water
> ⅔ cup instant non-fat dry milk
> Artificial sweetener to equal 6 teaspoons sugar
> 1 teaspoon chocolate extract
> ½ teaspoon mint or brandy extract
> 1½ teaspoons brown food coloring
> 6-8 ice cubes

Put cold water in blender, add gelatin to soften. Add boiling water and blend a few seconds. Add dry milk, sweetener, extracts and coloring, and blend until smooth. Add ice cubes one at a time and blend after each addition. Pour into 4 dessert glasses. Serve at once or chill if desired. Makes 4 servings; count ½ cup skim milk per serving.

FRUITY ICE FROTH

1 cup hulled strawberries
1½ cups orange juice
1⅓ cups instant non-fat dry milk
¼ cup lemon juice

Combine strawberries and ½ cup of the orange juice in the blender. Whirl until smooth and set aside. Combine remaining orange juice and dry milk in a large bowl. Beat with an electric or rotary beater until fluffy, about 5 minutes. Add lemon juice gradually, beating mixture until it holds soft peaks. Fold in pureed strawberries. Pour into freezer container and freeze until firm. Remove from freezer, beat well, cover closely with foil, and return to freezer. Defrost for 15 minutes before serving in dessert bowls. Makes 8 servings; count ½ fruit and 4 fluid ounces skim milk per serving.

EGGLESS NOG

The rum, nutmeg and sweetened milk produce a nectar that recalls the holiday favorite.

⅓ cup water
⅓ cup instant non-fat dry milk
¼ teaspoon rum extract
¼ teaspoon vanilla extract
Dash nutmeg
4 ice cubes, crushed
Artificial sweetener to equal 2 teaspoons sugar

Place all ingredients in blender, and blend at low speed. Serve immediately. Makes 1 serving.

PEACH NECTAR

1 medium peach, diced
½ cup evaporated skimmed milk
2 tablespoons club soda

Mix ingredients in blender till everything is smooth; use immediately. Makes 1 serving.

BUTTERY MILK

1 cup lukewarm skim milk
1 tablespoon lemon juice
Dash of imitation butter flavoring
Salt

Combine ingredients; let stand 5 minutes, then beat with rotary beater. May be used in our recipes as substitute for commercial buttermilk, but count it as regular skim milk. Makes 1 cup.

TOMATO FRAPPE

1 cup buttermilk
3 cups tomato juice
1 teaspoon dehydrated onion flakes
¼ teaspoon celery salt
¼ teaspoon celery seed
Red hot sauce to taste
1 envelope instant chicken broth and seasoning mix, or 1
    chicken bouillon cube
Ice cubes
Lemon or lime wedges

Combine first 7 ingredients in blender. Blend until smooth. Serve very cold in chilled glasses over ice cubes. Garnish with lemon or lime wedges. Makes 4 servings, each containing ¼ cup buttermilk.

PINA COLADA

⅓ cup instant non-fat dry milk
½ cup water
Artificial sweetener to equal 2 teaspoons sugar
1 small slice pineapple (canned in its own juice) plus
    1 tablespoon juice
¼ teaspoon (or more) coconut extract
¼ teaspoon rum extract

Put ingredients in blender and mix for about 30 seconds. Serve over ice cubes. Makes 1 serving.

PURPLE COW

¾ cup buttermilk
½ cup blueberries
Artificial sweetener to equal 2 teaspoons sugar
1 teaspoon lemon extract
3 ice cubes

Place all ingredients, except ice cubes, in blender. Blend. Add ice cubes one at a time, blending well after each addition. Pour into dessert cup. Makes 1 serving.

VARIATION
Purple Cow Dessert Sauce: Prepare as above, omitting ice cubes. Pour over 1 serving Vanilla Ice "Cream" (p. 197). Count whole dessert as 1 fluid ounce evaporated skimmed milk and 6 fluid ounces buttermilk. Makes 1 serving.

TAHITIAN CREAM COOLER

1 cup evaporated skimmed milk
⅔ cup instant non-fat dry milk
Artificial sweetener to equal 10 teaspoons sugar
1½ teaspoons coconut extract
1½ teaspoons rum extract
8-9 ice cubes

Blend first 5 ingredients. Add ice cubes a few at a time until completely blended. Mixture should be smooth and creamy. Makes 4 servings; count 1 cup skim milk per serving.

PINK LADY

1 cup skim milk
½ teaspoon rum extract
Artificial sweetener to equal 2 tablespoons sugar
3 ice cubes
Drop red food coloring

Mix ingredients in blender. Serve in tall stemmed glass. Makes 1 serving.

CHOCOLATE "BRANDY" ALEXANDER
You'll have to cut out the alcohol till you've cut down to size. In the meantime, make it brandy extract.

> ½ cup evaporated skimmed milk
> 1 teaspoon chocolate extract
> ½ teaspoon vanilla extract
> ½ teaspoon brandy extract
> Artificial sweetener to equal 2 teaspoons sugar
> 3-4 ice cubes

Pour ingredients in blender, and blend, adding ice cubes one at a time. Serve frosty and frothy in highball glass or small brandy snifter. Makes 1 serving.

RUMOCHA TODDY
A dessert-and-drink combination, also great with anise extract.

> ¾ cup hot coffee
> Artificial sweetener to equal 2 teaspoons sugar (or to taste)
> ½ teaspoon rum extract
> 1 serving Best Whipped Topping (p. 198 — count 1 fluid ounce evaporated skimmed milk)
> Dash cinnamon

Place a spoon in an 8-ounce glass and add hot coffee sweetened to taste. Stir in rum extract, add Topping and a sprinkling of cinnamon. Makes 1 serving.

SPANISH CREAM
A molded dessert of gelatin, flavoring and beaten eggs, served cold.

> 1 envelope (1 tablespoon) unflavored gelatin
> 3 eggs, separated
> 2 cups skim milk (count ⅔ cup skim milk per serving), scalded
> ¼ cup cream-flavored dietetic carbonated beverage
> Dash salt

Sprinkle gelatin over carbonated beverage in top part of double boiler. Place over low heat, stirring constantly until gelatin dissolves, about 3 minutes. Set top over bottom part of double boiler holding water. Add hot milk, egg yolks, salt. Cook, stirring constantly until mixture thickens. Whip egg whites until stiff and fold into hot mixture (hot mixture cooks the whites). Turn into mold or 3 individual crystal dessert dishes. Chill until firm. Makes 3 luncheon servings; supplement as required.

COFFEE TOFFY

    1½ teaspoons instant coffee powder
    ⅔ cup instant non-fat dry milk
    Artificial sweetener to equal 1 tablespoon sugar
    ½ teaspoon vanilla extract
    3 tablespoons water

Combine coffee, dry milk and sweetener. Sprinkle extract and water over dry ingredients. Stir until mixture forms dry paste that just holds together. With wet hands, shape mixture into small balls about 1-inch in diameter. Chill in freezer for at least 40 minutes. Makes 8 balls; count ¼ cup skim milk per serving.

COCONUT MACAROON COOKIES

    1⅓ cups instant non-fat dry milk
    2 medium apples, peeled, cored and grated (about ¾ cup)
    6 tablespoons brown sugar replacement
    ½ teaspoon cinnamon
    ½ teaspoon coconut extract

Combine all ingredients in mixing bowl; mix thoroughly. Drop by teaspoonfuls onto non-stick cookie sheet. Bake at 350° F. (moderate oven) for 18 minutes. Store in a tightly covered container. Makes 4 servings (about 2 dozen cookies).

Sauces and Salad Dressings

Sauces and salad dressings, some with fats and others without, are combined in this chapter for easy reference. Hot or cold, sweet, sour (or both at once), thick or thin, in all colors (white, green, pink, brown), bland or nippy, bumpy or smooth — there's really something for everyone here.

Some of the ingredients are free or unlimited — but you will have to count milk, bread, cheese, and occasionally a vegetable or fruit which may be tucked into the recipes.

RULES FOR USING FATS

1. Fats in the amounts included in your Menu Plan must be taken daily (at mealtime only):

> 1 tablespoon (3 teaspoons) mayonnaise;
> *or* 1 tablespoon (3 teaspoons) vegetable oil;
> *or* oils such as corn, cottonseed, safflower, sesame seed, peanut and sunflower;
> *or* 1 tablespoon (3 teaspoons) liquid vegetable oil margarine;
> *or* 2 tablespoons (6 teaspoons) imitation (diet) margarine

2. Fats may be mixed-and-matched; e.g., you may have 1 teaspoon margarine and 2 teaspoons mayonnaise daily.

3. Any product labeled "mayonnaise" and any oil labeled "vegetable oil" may be used.

4. Two types of margarine may be used. Molded margarines in stick form or by the pound may be used only if the first word on the label ingredient list is "liquid" followed by the name(s) of the vegetable oil(s) used. The second type of margarine which may be used includes those labeled "imitation and/or diet" margarine. These are usually sold in containers.

5. Fat must always be spread with a spatula or knife (not brushed on) so that none will be lost.

HOW TO COOK WITH FATS

Broiling:
   a) After a food has been broiled, the fat may be spread over it, and the food returned to the broiler for *no longer than one minute*.
   b) A combination of ingredients mixed together and topped with fats and "legal" bread crumbs may be placed under the broiler *just long enough to melt fats*. This mixture must be in a container with sides so you'll get your full fat allowance.

Baking:
   a) Fats may be mixed with other ingredients and baked in an *individual* casserole.
   b) When it is desirable to make more than one serving, you may add fats only if they are thoroughly mixed with all the ingredients.

Range Top:
   a) You may not fry with fats at any time.
   b) Margarine may be heated in a small container (e.g., a custard or soufflé cup) over hot water and then used as a sauce.
   c) Individual servings of food may be prepared with the fats, provided that they are thoroughly mixed into the ingredients and cooked in a double boiler, rather than over direct heat.

VEGETABLE AND HERB-BASED SAUCES

ALL-PURPOSE TOMATO BARBECUE SAUCE

   1 can (46 fluid ounces) tomato juice
   3 tablespoons vinegar
   2 tablespoons dehydrated onion flakes
   2 tablespoons prepared mustard
   1 tablespoon lemon juice
   1 tablespoon Worcestershire
   ½ teaspoon garlic powder
   ½ teaspoon barbecue spice
   3 tablespoons brown sugar replacement

Combine all ingredients in a saucepan. Heat slowly until reduced to half its volume (it becomes quite thick). Sauce may be stored in refrigerator and used as a baste or marinade as desired on chicken, beef or fish. Makes 1½ pints. Count 1 tablespoon of sauce as 2 tablespoons (1 fluid ounce) tomato juice.

BEAN SPROUTS VINAIGRETTE

2 cups canned bean sprouts, drained and well-rinsed
1 cup water
½ cup white vinegar
Artificial sweetener to equal 3 tablespoons sugar
1 tablespoon minced chives
1 garlic clove, minced
½ teaspoon salt
Pepper

Combine all ingredients in bowl and let stand for several hours, up to 2 days. Drain before serving. Use as a sauce, vegetable or salad. Makes 4 servings.

CATSUP

1 large can (46 fluid ounces) tomato juice
2 cups sliced celery
1 teaspoon each allspice, mace and celery seed
8 cloves
8 peppercorns
1-inch stick cinnamon
¼ teaspoon dry mustard
1 clove garlic
1 bay leaf
½ cup cider vinegar
Dash cayenne pepper
Salt (optional)
Artificial sweetener to equal 2 tablespoons sugar, or to taste

Boil first nine ingredients in electric skillet or wide saucepan (its large surface permits quick evaporation) until reduced by half. Stir frequently to prevent scorching. If there is much spattering, set cover atilt on pan. Put sauce through strainer and press out juice from celery, then put sauce back in skillet. Add all the remaining ingredients, except sweetener. Bring to boil and cook 10 minutes longer at fast-simmer temperature (stir — don't let it scorch). Stir in sweetener. Store in refrigerator to use as needed (it will keep for weeks), or bring some to your friends in the Weight Watchers class. Makes scant 2 cups. Count each tablespoon as 1½ fluid ounces of tomato juice.

VARIATIONS

Chili Sauce: Add 1 teaspoon crushed red (chili) pepper to Catsup when it is cooked, and simmer an additional 20 minutes. Count each tablespoon as 2 fluid ounces of tomato juice.

Cocktail Sauce for Seafood: Combine ½ cup Catsup, 2 teaspoons prepared horseradish, 2 teaspoons lemon juice, salt and pepper, few drops red hot sauce and a dash of chili powder (optional). Stir well. Chill. Makes ½ cup. Count 1½ fluid ounces tomato juice per tablespoon.

TOMATO SAUCE
King of Italian sauces.

> 4 cups tomato juice
> Optional ingredients: 1 cup beef bouillon, ¾ teaspoon Italian seasoning spice, 1 tablespoon dehydrated onion flakes, ½ teaspoon celery seed, artificial sweetener and cinnamon to taste

Make this using just the tomato juice, or add your choice of optional ingredients. Cook uncovered in shallow saucepan until reduced to about half volume. Makes 2 cups (4 servings); count 1 cup tomato juice per serving.

VARIATIONS

1. *Tomato Paste:* Cook tomato juice until very thick; omit optional ingredients.

2. *Tomato Sauce With Tomato:* Combine 1 cup Tomato Sauce and 1 sliced fresh or canned tomato. Cook for 15 minutes.

CREOLE SAUCE

2 cups tomato juice
1 medium cucumber, peeled and finely diced
1 medium green pepper, finely diced
3 tablespoons minced parsley
2 tablespoons dehydrated onion flakes
1 cup celery, finely diced
1 garlic clove
1 cup water or clam juice
1 envelope instant chicken broth and seasoning mix
1 teaspoon salt
½ teaspoon pepper

Cook tomato juice in open pan till reduced by half. Add remaining ingredients, bring to boil, then let simmer for 20 minutes. The vegetables should be crisp-tender. Serve over fish. Makes 4 servings.

DAIKON SAUCE
To serve hot with broiled and steamed fish or chicken.

⅓ cup soy sauce
1 cup water or chicken bouillon
1 cup grated daikon (radish), or White Icicle radish
Artificial sweetener to equal 1 teaspoon sugar
Dash lemon juice (optional)

Combine soy sauce, liquid and daikon in saucepan and simmer for 15 minutes. Add sweetener. Makes about 1½ cups.

PIMENTO DRESSING

1 jar (7 ounces) roasted pimentos, drained
2 tablespoons vinegar
2 tablespoons prepared mustard
Artificial sweetener to equal 4 teaspoons sugar

Combine all ingredients in blender container, and blend until smooth. Store in refrigerator and use as desired. Makes about 1 cup; 2 servings.

MINT SAUCE
For roast lamb and cooked vegetables — even fruit segments.

⅓ cup wine vinegar (or part lemon juice)
¼ cup boiling water
1 cup fresh mint leaves, washed, drained and chopped fine
3 tablespoons brown sugar replacement

Heat vinegar and water; pour over mint leaves. Add brown sugar replacement and let stand several hours. Makes 2-4 servings.

RUSSIAN DRESSING (NO MAYONNAISE)

¾ cup tomato juice
½ cup buttermilk
1 teaspoon red wine vinegar
¼ teaspoon dry mustard
Dash dehydrated onion flakes
Artificial sweetener to taste
Salt
1 medium pickle, diced fine

Simmer tomato juice until reduced to half volume. In blender, combine all ingredients except dill pickle and blend well. Add diced dill pickle; blend. Nice over artichoke hearts. Makes 2 servings.

SOUBISE (ONION) SAUCE
Richer made with ¾ cup water and ¾ cup skim milk.

4 ounces sliced onions
1½ cups water
1 envelope instant chicken broth and seasoning mix
Salt

Cook sliced onions in saucepan with water and broth mix, until onions are soft and water cooks down to half. Puree in blender, or put through strainer; season with salt. Use with sweetbreads, fish, lamb, veal or hamburgers. Makes 4 servings. For each serving, count 1 ounce #4 vegetable.

POLYNESIAN FRUIT AND VEGETABLE VINAIGRETTE

Serve in sauce dishes to accompany broiled fish and meat, and anything made with curry. A treat over rinsed bean sprouts, tossed greens or shredded beets.

2 small slices pineapple (canned in its own juice), cut into
   8 pieces each, plus 2 tablespoons juice
½ medium cucumber, peeled and cut in ½-inch-thick slices
½ medium green pepper, cut in 1-inch squares
½ medium red pepper, cut in 1-inch squares
½ cup canned, drained button mushrooms
2 tablespoons water
2 tablespoons vinegar
1 teaspoon soy sauce
2 whole cloves
1 clove garlic
¼ teaspoon ground ginger
Artificial sweetener to equal 4 teaspoons sugar

Combine pineapple, cucumber, peppers and mushrooms in small jar or bowl. Heat remaining ingredients and pour over cut-up fruit and vegetables. Refrigerate overnight or several days, turning several times. Makes 4 servings; each serving counts as ¼ of your daily #3B vegetable requirement and ¼ fruit.

SPINACH-VEGETABLE SAUCE FOR PASTA

4 medium tomatoes, diced
½ cup frozen chopped spinach, defrosted and drained
½ cup canned mushrooms, minced
1 tablespoon dehydrated onion flakes
1 tablespoon minced parsley
1 tablespoon cider vinegar
1 clove garlic, crushed

Combine ingredients in a large pan and cook until thickened, about ½ hour. Serve over cooked enriched pasta. Makes 4 servings. Count 1¼ cups #3B vegetable per serving.

TANGY FRENCH DRESSING (FAT FREE)

This is a bonus, as it's made without oil, but you may wish to add your 1 tablespoon at serving time.

> 1 cup tomato juice
> 2 envelopes instant chicken broth and seasoning mix
> 4 tablespoons vinegar
> 1 teaspoon prepared mustard
> 1½ teaspoons Worcestershire
> 2 teaspoons dehydrated onion flakes
> Artificial sweetener to equal 1 teaspoon sugar
> Dash each garlic powder and cinnamon

Combine all ingredients in blender and blend well; or shake in jar. Makes 2 servings.

VARIATION

Tangy Roquefort Dressing: Follow recipe for Tangy French Dressing; stir in 2 ounces crumbled or mashed Roquefort cheese and mix well. Serve over salad greens. Makes 2 luncheon servings; supplement cheese as required.

TARRAGON VINEGAR

You can buy commercially prepared tarragon vinegar, or you can make it, with no fuss or bother.

> 4 tablespoons chopped fresh tarragon leaves, or 2 tablespoons dried tarragon
> 1 cup mild vinegar

Combine tarragon leaves and vinegar, and bring almost to boil. Let stand overnight, strain and store. Use in salad dressings to accompany a roast chicken dinner. Makes 1 cup.

VARIATION

Garlic Vinegar: Omit tarragon. To hot vinegar, add 3 cloves garlic, lightly pressed with fork to release flavor. Let stand overnight or longer. Remove garlic before serving.

TERIYAKI SAUCE
Use as marinade, basting sauce or dip for broiled or baked fish, chicken, beef, liver, kabobs or fondues. A dash of dry mustard or Worcestershire will make it spicier.

¼ cup soy sauce
Artificial sweetener to equal 6 teaspoons sugar
1 small slice fresh minced ginger root, or dash ground ginger
1 mashed clove garlic
1 teaspoon lemon juice

Combine ingredients. Makes 1 serving.

BREAD SAUCES

BASIC WHITE BREAD SAUCE
This gold-flecked sauce can be used in dozens of different ways — as a base for making other sauces, in stuffings, soufflés, soups and fish chowders.

1 slice enriched white bread
1 cup skim milk
¼ teaspoon imitation butter flavoring (optional)
Salt and white pepper

Put bread in blender to make crumbs. In saucepan, scald milk (heat without boiling until tiny bubbles form around the edge), add bread crumbs and butter flavoring if desired. Simmer for 5 minutes. Season lightly with salt and pepper. Makes 1 cup; 2 servings.

VARIATIONS

1. *Cheese Sauce:* To 1 recipe sauce in saucepan, add 2 ounces grated hard cheese (American, cheddar, etc.) and 1 teaspoon Worcestershire. Heat. Season with salt, pepper and paprika. Serve over cooked vegetables.

2. *Horseradish Sauce:* Prepare sauce as above. Add 2 tablespoons prepared white horseradish, 1 tablespoon white vinegar, artificial sweetener to equal 1 teaspoon sugar, 1 teaspoon dry mustard and dillweed to taste. Good on cold fish or meats.

3. *Mushroom Sauce:* Add ½ cup sliced cooked or canned mushrooms, 1 teaspoon dehydrated onion flakes, and a dash of lemon juice to basic recipe. Serve with fish, meat, poultry or vegetables.

4. *Paprika Sauce:* Prepare sauce as above. Add 1 teaspoon dehydrated onion flakes and 1 tablespoon mild paprika. Heat till onion flakes are soft. Serve over our Roast Beef (p. 166).

FLORENTINE SAUCE

> 1 cup Basic White Bread Sauce (p. 221 — count ½ slice
>   enriched white bread and ½ cup skim milk per serving)
> ½ cup cooked chopped spinach
> Grated nutmeg
> Dash Worcestershire or red hot sauce
> Dash lemon juice
> Dash parsley, chives or marjoram (optional)

Add spinach to basic sauce. Season with grated nutmeg, Worcestershire or red hot sauce and lemon juice; cook about 10 minutes. Parsley, chives or rosemary may be added as optional touches. Makes 2 servings.

BROWN SAUCE

> 1 slice 100% whole wheat toast
> 1 cup water
> 1 beef bouillon cube, or 1 envelope beef broth and seasoning
>   mix
> 2 tablespoons Catsup (p. 215 — count 1½ fluid ounces tomato
>   juice per serving)
> Dash of Worcestershire
> Few drops brown food coloring (optional)

Cut up toast and put into blender to make crumbs. Heat water and bouillon cube in saucepan, add bread crumbs and simmer for 15 minutes. Stir in Catsup and Worcestershire to taste; simmer another 15 minutes. Add a few drops brown food coloring, if desired. Makes 2 servings.

RAVIGOTE SAUCE
For poached chicken or fish.

>1 slice bread
>2 tablespoons dehydrated onion flakes
>½ cup water
>1 envelope instant chicken broth and seasoning mix
>1 cup skim milk
>1 teaspoon prepared mustard
>1 teaspoon chopped chives
>1 tablespoon chopped drained capers
>Dash tarragon

Put bread in blender to make crumbs. In saucepan cook onion flakes in water with broth mix. When onions are soft and water evaporated, add skim milk and bread crumbs. Cook until sauce is thick, then stir in remaining ingredients. If desired, you may puree the sauce in the blender or put through strainer. Makes 2 servings.

MARGARINE SPREADS AND SAUCES

HERB SPREAD

>2 tablespoons imitation (or diet) margarine
>1 tablespoon minced watercress or minced herbs (fresh
>   parsley alone, or combined with fresh or dried chives,
>   chervil, dill, marjoram, tarragon)
>Salt and freshly ground pepper

Combine ingredients; Mix well. Serve over fish or lima beans. Makes 1 serving.

VARIATIONS

1. *Lemon Caper Spread:* Add 1 tablespoon minced, drained capers to 2 tablespoons margarine. Add dash of fresh lemon juice or few drops lemon extract. Try this over cooked broccoli. Makes 2 servings.

2. *Maître d'Hôtel Spread:* Mash 2 tablespoons margarine with 1 tablespoon minced parsley, 1 teaspoon lemon juice, dash salt and

white pepper. Beat with a fork until quite fluffy. Add to broiled fish just before serving. Makes 2 servings.

3. *Onion Spread:* Add 2 teaspoons dehydrated onion flakes reconstituted in 2 tablespoons water, 1 teaspoon soy sauce and dash red hot sauce to 2 tablespoons margarine. Mix well. Perks up broiled hamburger, liver, or baked potato. Makes 2 servings.

CINNAMON-SPICE SPREAD
For French Toast or omelets, or to glaze baked and broiled fruit. Vary the extracts to taste.

>   1 tablespoon margarine
>   1 teaspoon cinnamon
>   Artificial sweetener to equal 4 teaspoons sugar
>   Dash each cloves, nutmeg and ginger

Combine ingredients. Makes 1 serving.

VARIATIONS
Maple "Butter" Spread: To 1 tablespoon melted margarine, add 1 teaspoon brown sugar replacement and a dash of maple extract. Mix well. Makes 1 serving.

BUTTERY SAUCE (DAILY DOUBLE)
S-t-r-e-t-c-h your daily fat allowance.

>   ¾ teaspoon unflavored gelatin
>   1 fluid ounce (2 tablespoons) skim milk
>   2 tablespoons imitation (or diet) margarine
>   ¼ teaspoon imitation butter flavoring
>   Salt

Sprinkle gelatin over milk in custard cup; let stand to soften gelatin. Add margarine, set in a warm water bath, and cook over low heat until margarine melts. Stir in butter flavoring and sprinkle lightly with salt. Delicious when used warm as a dip for boiled or broiled lobster. Makes 1 serving.

MOCK BEARNAISE SAUCE

2 tablespoons imitation (or diet) margarine
1 tablespoon mayonnaise
1 tablespoon tarragon vinegar
⅛ teaspoon parsley
¼ teaspoon dehydrated onion flakes, in ¾ teaspoon water
Few drops imitation butter flavoring

Heat margarine in custard cup set in a hot water bath; when it is melted, add mayonnaise, vinegar, parsley and onion flakes. Stir vigorously and serve at once. It is delicious over poached eggs, poached fish and broiled steak or hamburgers. Makes 2 servings.

MOCK HOLLANDAISE SAUCE

2 tablespoons imitation (or diet) margarine
1 tablespoon mayonnaise
1 tablespoon lemon juice
¼ teaspoon salt
¼ teaspoon paprika

Heat margarine in custard cup set in hot water bath. When melted, stir in mayonnaise, lemon juice, salt, and paprika. Stir vigorously and serve immediately. Divide evenly. Good over cooked cauliflower, asparagus, etc. Makes 2 servings.

MAYONNAISE DRESSINGS

FRUIT SALAD MAYONNAISE

You must serve this on 2 small slices pineapple (canned in its own juice) or on fruit salad which contains your canned pineapple.

1 tablespoon mayonnaise
2 tablespoons unsweetened pineapple juice from canned-in-its-own-juice pineapple
Dash artificial sweetener
¼ teaspoon dehydrated orange peel

Combine ingredients. Makes 1 serving.

VARIATIONS ON A MAYONNAISE THEME

1. *Creamy Mayonnaise for Pasta:* Combine 1 tablespoon mayonnaise, 3 tablespoons Buttery Milk (p. 209), 1 teaspoon dehydrated onion flakes, and a dash each of black pepper, oregano, basil and garlic powder. Makes 1 serving.

2. *Curried Mayonnaise:* Add 1 tablespoon instant non-fat dry milk, ½ teaspoon curry powder and a few drops lemon extract to 1 tablespoon mayonnaise. You'll love this on a turkey or chicken sandwich.

3. *Green Mayonnaise:* Simply add 2 teaspoons or more very finely minced herbs (parsley, watercress and chervil, if available) to your 1 tablespoon mayonnaise. A pretty and flavorful topping for individual molded salads.

4. *Spicy Mustard Mayonnaise:* Combine 1 tablespoon mayonnaise, 1 tablespoon prepared mustard, a dash poultry seasoning and a drop of red hot sauce. Stir into your favorite chicken or tuna salad.

MAYONNAISE SAUCE
A twofer.

> ¼ teaspoon unflavored gelatin
> 2 tablespoons (1 fluid ounce) evaporated skimmed milk
> 1 tablespoon mayonnaise

In small custard cup, sprinkle gelatin over evaporated skimmed milk, and let stand to soften. Immerse lower half of custard cup in hot water bath, and heat gently to dissolve gelatin, stirring well. Add mayonnaise and mix well. Serve immediately in custard cup. Makes 1 serving.

TARTAR SAUCE
Use over shredded greens, cabbage, sliced cucumber or — classically — over fish.

> 1 tablespoon mayonnaise
> ½ tablespoon minced gherkin
> ¼ medium dill pickle, minced
> ½ teaspoon drained, chopped capers
> ½ teaspoon prepared mustard

Combine ingredients. Refrigerate until ready to serve; use with fish. Makes 1 serving.

THOUSAND ISLAND DRESSING

    1 tablespoon mayonnaise
    1 tablespoon Chili Sauce (p. 216 — count 2 fluid ounces
        tomato juice), or 1 tablespoon diced pimento
    ½ teaspoon dehydrated onion flakes
    ¼ medium dill pickle, minced
    ¼ teaspoon minced parsley

Combine ingredients. Refrigerate for at least 15 minutes before serving, so flavors blend. Makes 1 serving.

SPRING SALAD RADISH DRESSING

    ½ cup radishes
    1 tablespoon mayonnaise
    ⅓ cup cottage cheese
    1 tablespoon skim milk
    Salt and freshly ground pepper

Clean the radishes, trim both ends, and chop very fine. Place in small bowl. Combine mayonnaise, cottage cheese, skim milk, salt and pepper and mix well. Pour over radishes and let stand for 30 minutes so flavors blend. Stir before serving over shredded lettuce, baked potatoes or sliced tomatoes. Makes 1 luncheon serving; supplement as required.

OIL-BASED DRESSINGS

BASIC FRENCH DRESSING

Our French Dressing is a little stingy with the oil, but it's a basic recipe which can be enlarged in many ways. Some of the classic additions are given in the variations which follow.

    1 teaspoon wine, tarragon or garlic vinegar
    Salt and freshly ground pepper
    Dash each of paprika and dry mustard
    Dash artificial sweetener (optional)
    1 tablespoon vegetable oil

Stir vinegar with seasonings and sweetener, if desired. Add oil and mix again. Makes 1 serving.

VARIATIONS

1. *Tomato-Onion French Dressing:* Prepare French Dressing as above. Add 1 tablespoon Catsup (p. 215 — count 1½ fluid ounces of tomato juice), ½ envelope instant onion broth and seasoning mix (or ½ teaspoon dehydrated onion flakes). Excellent as a marinade over cooked green vegetables.

2. *Quick Vegetable Sauce:* Prepare French Dressing as above. Soak 2 tablespoons each dehydrated pepper and onion flakes for 10 minutes. Drain and add flakes and 1 medium tomato, diced, to French Dressing. Sprinkle in a liberal amount of garlic powder. Nice over cooked, sliced zucchini or other vegetables.

CHIFFONADE LUNCHEON SALAD DRESSING

    2 tablespoons tomato juice
    1 tablespoon vegetable oil
    1 tablespoon vinegar
    1 ounce cooked shredded beets
    1 tablespoon minced parsley
    2 teaspoons dehydrated onion flakes
    1 hard-cooked egg, chopped or mashed

In screw top jar, combine tomato juice, oil, vinegar, beets, parsley and onion flakes. Let stand 30 minutes. Add egg and serve over salad greens. Makes 1 luncheon serving; supplement as required.

TOMATO FRENCH DRESSING

    1 teaspoon unflavored gelatin
    2 cups tomato juice
    4 tablespoons vegetable oil (see note)
    4 tablespoons wine vinegar
    2 teaspoons Worcestershire
    1 teaspoon dehydrated onion flakes
    ¾ teaspoon dry mustard
    ¾ teaspoon salt
    ¼ teaspoon garlic powder
    Artificial sweetener to equal 2 teaspoons sugar

Sprinkle gelatin over ½ cup cold tomato juice in blender container and let stand 3 minutes to soften. Heat remaining tomato juice to boiling point, pour into blender and run to dissolve gelatin. Add remaining ingredients and blend once again to homogenize mixture. Divide equally into 4 screw top containers. Chill in refrigerator. Shake or stir well before use. Makes 4 servings, ½ cup each.

NOTE: The vegetable oil may be omitted from blender and stirred into individual servings just before use; it may be omitted entirely or reduced in amount, according to your preferences, provided you do not exceed 1 tablespoon oil daily.

PARSLEY-VINAIGRETTE SAUCE

Use cold as a sauce over broiled or cooked fish or shellfish. Delicious too as a marinade over cooked vegetables, and can be lightly warmed to serve with boiled chicken.

> 4 tablespoons vegetable oil
> 3 tablespoons vinegar
> 2 teaspoons minced parsley sprigs (stems removed)
> ¼ teaspoon dry mustard
> 1 ice cube
> ½ envelope instant chicken broth and seasoning mix (optional)

Combine ingredients in blender, and blend for 20 seconds, or until thick. Makes 4 servings.

PESTO (BASIL) SAUCE

Stir into ⅔ cup cooked enriched macaroni or spaghetti, or ½ cup cooked enriched noodles. Splendid also on sliced tomatoes, or served over poached fish.

> ½ cup fresh basil leaves, finely chopped or pounded in mortar
> 1 tablespoon vegetable oil
> ½ clove garlic
> 1 ounce grated Pecorino or Parmesan cheese
> ½ teaspoon salt
> Freshly ground pepper
> 1 teaspoon minced parsley (optional)

Combine ingredients in a bowl and let stand 1 hour before using. You can also make this in a blender. Makes 1 serving; supplement cheese as required.

MILK DRESSINGS

BUTTERMILK DRESSING (THICK)
Use as salad dressing just as you would use mayonnaise for cole slaw, to bind chopped foods, etc.

> 2 teaspoons unflavored gelatin
> 2 tablespoons cold water
> 2 teaspoons dehydrated onion flakes
> ¼ cup cider vinegar
> 1 teaspoon salt
> 1 teaspoon dry mustard
> ⅛ teaspoon black pepper
> 1 cup buttermilk
> Artificial sweetener to equal 1 teaspoon sugar

Soften gelatin in cold water in small saucepan. Stir in onion flakes, vinegar, salt, mustard, pepper. Heat, stirring to dissolve gelatin. Add buttermilk and sweetener. Refrigerate until set. Whip in mixer or blender before serving. Makes 4 servings.

CAULIFLOWER WHITE SAUCE
Nourishing, easy to make, and delicious, this can be used in dozens of different ways...as a thickener in casseroles, for soufflés etc.

> 1 cup skim milk
> 2 cups cauliflower florets
> ½ teaspoon salt
> ½ teaspoon imitation butter flavoring

Heat milk to simmer. Add cauliflower and cook until it is very soft, then puree in blender. Add salt and butter flavoring. If it is too thick, heat a few tablespoons of water and stir into sauce. Makes 2 servings.

VARIATION
Boil ½ cup clam juice uncovered for 5 minutes, stir in Cauliflower White Sauce and ¼ teaspoon minced capers. Serve hot with boiled or poached fish.

CELERY SAUCE

2 cups celery, sliced
1 cup chicken bouillon
1 tablespoon dehydrated onion flakes
Salt and pepper
¼ cup evaporated skimmed milk

Place celery, bouillon, onion flakes, salt and pepper in blender container and blend until smooth. Transfer to saucepan and cook over medium heat for ½ hour. Add milk, heat thoroughly, *do not boil*. Makes 4 servings.

CUCUMBER SAUCE

3 tablespoons instant non-fat dry milk
1 medium cucumber, peeled, chopped fine and drained
2 tablespoons vinegar
¼ teaspoon salt
Pinch cayenne pepper

Combine. Let stand for ½ hour. Nice with salmon. Makes 2 servings.

NEWBURG SAUCE

1 cup chicken bouillon
½ cup cooked cauliflower
¼ cup tomato juice
¼ cup clam juice
¼ teaspoon sherry extract
¼ teaspoon brandy extract
Salt and pepper
¼ cup evaporated skimmed milk
1 teaspoon fresh chopped parsley

Place bouillon, cauliflower, tomato juice and clam juice in blender; blend until smooth. Pour into saucepan, and place over low heat. Add sherry and brandy extracts; simmer for 10 minutes. Season with salt and pepper. Add milk; reheat but do not boil. Sprinkle with parsley and serve. Makes 1 serving.

HOW TO PEP UP YOUR MEALS WITH SPICES AND HERBS

Allspice. Delicately fragrant West Indian spice, it tastes like a blend of nutmeg, cinnamon and cloves. Whole, it's a favorite seasoning for pot roast, pickles and boiled fish.

Anise. For lovers of licorice, delicious sprinkled on a slice of French toast or on Meringue Kisses (p. 89).

Basil. Basil means King and this royal sweet herb adds the crowning touch to all tomato dishes. Gives zest to eggs, fish, soups, salads, stews — to peas, squash and green beans, too. Sprinkle on lamb chops before broiling. You must use the fresh leaves in making Pesto, the famous Genoese sauce (p. 229).

Bay Leaves. (Laurel). Classic seasoning for stews, soups, meats, pickles, sauces and fish. The flavor is sharp and the fragrance pungent (always remove after cooking).

Bitters (Aromatic). This liquid blend of herbs and spices is the distinctive ingredient in many hard drinks. Add a few drops to tomato and clam juice for a pick-me-up. Super in stewed fruits.

Caraway. This aromatic seed adds piquancy to sauerkraut, cheese, toast. Yummy sprinkled on liver, kidneys before cooking.

Capers. Cut capers into your fish sauces and sprinkle them over salads too. They taste something like piquant gherkins. You may prefer them drained and rinsed if bought in brine.

Cardamom. Native to India, these tiny brown seeds have a natural affinity for coffee. In pods, they are used in pickles. Ground, it's a happy companion to iced melon and other fruits.

Cayenne Pepper. Go easy with this fiery spice — a touch is enough! Hottest of the red hot peppers. Used with restraint, it will perk up eggs, sauces, vegetables and fish.

Celery Seed. It has almost the same taste as the celery vegetable. Gives a tonic taste to sauces and salads, soups and vegetables.

Chervil. Delicate, looks and tastes like mild parsley with a hint of onion. Sweet and aromatic, it combines excellently with other herbs. Delicious, when fresh, in soups, salads, egg dishes, sauces for fish and chicken.

Chili Powder. The ancient Aztecs are credited for this racy blend of hot peppers (chili, cayenne, paprika, etc.) along with other ingredients like garlic. Use discreetly to give zip to cocktail sauces and eggs, stews and meat loaves.

Cinnamon. Cassia replaces its cousin, cinnamon, in this country. Ground, and mixed with artificial sweetener, it's a favorite on French toast and pancakes, puddings and stewed fruits too.

Cloves. Wars have been fought over this warm, rich spice. Once used only by the wealthy — today everyone can enjoy it. It's for pickling, and adding spice to vegetables.

Coriander. Use this pungent herb sparingly. Seeds are milder than the leaves. Their lemon-peel-with-sage flavor gives character to pickles and poultry stuffing; good in tossed green salads, too.

Cumin. Cumin seeds add a piquant tang to meat dishes, beans, and sauces. Use whole or ground in soups, cheese, and stuffed eggs.

Curry Powder. An exotic blend of many spices, the standby of Indian cookery. Picks up leftover meats, stews, rice and fish dishes. Try it in French dressing . . . also with rice, shrimp, chicken, eggs, and vegetables.

Dill Weed. An all-around herb, the tender fresh and dried leaves as well as the seeds have a crisp flavor that peps up eggs, cheese, meat, salads, potatoes, chicken soups, and all Scandinavian fish specialties.

Fennel. Somewhat like anise in flavor. Gives a special fillip to apples, boiled fish (a must in bouillabaisse) and pickles.

Garlic. The indispensable seasoning, it is available in powder form, as a garlic salt, and, for least concentrated flavor, as fresh cloves.

Ginger. Aromatic, pungent, and a universal favorite. Its root gives zest to Oriental dishes. Ground, it perks up pot roast, canned pineapple and salad dressing.

Italian Seasoning Spice. You can buy this blend of rosemary, oregano, marjoram, thyme and sage; or mix your own. Use over fish, meat, poultry, liver, vegetables, salads, enriched rice or pasta.

Mace. The outer covering of the nutmeg seed, this spice is something like nutmeg in flavor, but softer, more savory. Whole, it improves stewed cherries, fish sauces and pickles.

Marjoram. Interchangeable with its sister-seasoning oregano, but sweeter, more subtle. Does creative things for peas, string beans and limas . . . for stews, soups, frankfurter dishes and fish sauces. Add a sprinkle to lamb while roasting for a gourmet-flavor touch.

Mint. Strong and sweet, tangy yet cool — everyone knows this aromatic herb has an affinity for lamb! But it gives an exciting lift to lots of other dishes too. Try it for flavoring soups and stews. For brightening fish sauces and beverages.

Mustard. Whole, the mustard seed gives interest to pickles and beets. Ground, with a little water, it is the hot sauce of the Orient. Prepared, it tones up sauces, and marinades.

Nutmeg. Nutmeg livens sauces, puddings, custards — good in cauliflower and spinach too.

Oregano. This is the Spanish word for marjoram, which it closely resembles in taste — though the flavor is stronger and pleasantly bitter. Indispensable in most Mexican and Italian dishes. Gives a nice nip to eggs and vegetables.

Paprika. Cool, mild and slightly sweet, this member of the pepper family gives golden brownness to fish — sprinkle it on before you broil it. Its brilliant red is pleasing on any pale food.

Parsley. Why restrict this noble herb to a perpetual garnish? Fresh or dried, it adds color and a distinctively mild and subtle flavor to all manner of dishes. It enhances salads, sauces, soups, meats, fish, vegetables, stews and dressings.

Rosemary. "Rosemary is for remembrance" — and its fresh, sweet flavor will make any dish memorable. See how it brightens lamb dishes, soups and stews, boiled potatoes, turnips and cauliflower too.

Saffron. The world's most expensive spice — a little goes a long way! Steep a pinch in hot water; gives intriguing taste and rich golden color to rice. Saffron is a "must" in our Arroz con Pollo (p. 183).

Sage. Aromatic, warm and faintly bitter, sage comes from Yugoslavia where it grows wild. An ingredient in poultry seasoning spice blend, it has a natural affinity for fowl. Try it in baked fish.

Savory. Team up dried savory with other herbs to give sprightly flavor to meats, chicken, soups, salads and sauces. Takes scrambled eggs out of the humdrum too.

Tarragon. Add this anise-flavored herb to vinegar to make tarragon vinegar. Add a touch — not too much! — to sauces, salads, chicken, meat and eggs. Adds piquancy to tomato and chicken.

Thyme. This warm pungent herb turns up in chicken stuffings, stews and meat loaf . . . in clam chowder, croquettes or — delicious! — sprinkled on sliced tomatoes. It's a prime ingredient in the blend sold as Poultry Seasoning.

Use as Desired

This chapter is devoted to recipes for the bonus foods, to be used as desired. In it, I've tried to stir your imagination by suggesting many different ways to incorporate them in your daily cooking, but you've a freedom to improvise beyond the limits of our book. With the following list of "who's counting" ingredients at your elbow, we now invite you to dream up your own ways of using them:

1. DIETETIC PRODUCTS — Two are permitted, in reasonably unlimited amounts:

> *Dietetic carbonated beverages:* Any dietetic carbonated beverage is permitted on the Program in an amount equal to 15 calories per day. If a 12-ounce container of beverage has only 3 calories, you may consume 5 containers in one day. If a 16-ounce bottle contains 8½ calories, you may drink 28 ounces per day. Any dietetic beverage that contains 3 calories per fluid ounce must be limited to approximately 5 ounces.

> *Artificial sweeteners:* There's no limit on the amount allowed (until you reach the Leveling Plan). However, many of the revised formulas for sugar substitutes have changed in caloric content. Check labels: If the packet (equivalent to 2 teaspoons or more of sugar) lists up to 4 calories, consider it "legal."

2A. UNLIMITED — Use as desired the following:

Clam juice

Club soda

Coffee

Dehydrated vegetable flakes (as seasonings), e.g. celery, chives, onion, parsley, *not* dehydrated vegetable flakes containing carrots or potatoes

Herbs, spices and other seasonings (e.g. shake-on type) for flavor. Shake-on seasonings in which either sugar or starch is listed as first ingredient are not permitted.

Horseradish (red or white)
Lemon and lime juice, fresh or reconstituted (for flavoring only)
Mustard, prepared or dry
Pepper sauce
Postum (limited to 2 cups daily)
Red hot sauce
Salt, pepper
Soy Sauce
Tea (mint, Gossip, rose hip, sassafras, unsweetened instant teas, and usual tea leaves)
Vinegar (all vinegars are "legal": Cider vinegar, made from apples, wine vinegar from grapes, malt vinegar from grain, etc.)
Water
Worcestershire

2B. LIMITED ITEMS

Bouillon cubes, instant broth and seasoning mixes: Not more than 3 per day.

Extracts and flavors (natural or with added imitation flavor): Use 2 teaspoons per day. Please note that we use the term "flavor extract" throughout the book to signify products labeled either "flavor" or "extract."

Unflavored gelatin: Up to 3 envelopes (3 tablespoons) per day. Kosher unflavored gelatin is permitted.

Tomato Juice: You may use up to 1½ cups (12 fluid ounces) daily, if desired.

COPING WITH THE COCKTAIL HOUR
You get your kicks by looking in the mirror after you've stayed away from the stronger beverages.

1. *Cherry-O:* Make ice cubes from 1 cup cherry-flavored dietetic carbonated beverage and 1 cup dietetic ginger ale. Crush cubes (can be done in blender) and serve in champagne glasses with a short straw for sipping. Makes 2 servings.

2. *Horse's Neck Highball:* Pour 1 cup club soda (or dietetic quinine water), dash aromatic bitters, and a dash lemon juice over ice cubes in an old-fashioned glass; garnish with twist of lemon or lime peel. Makes 1 serving.

3. *Skinny Devil:* It's made with 1 cup tomato juice, ½ cup clam juice, and a dash red hot sauce or cayenne pepper. Serve over ice cubes in an old-fashioned glass. Makes 1 serving.

4. *Banana "Daiquiri":* In individual ice cube molds make ice cubes from ¾ cup cream-flavored dietetic carbonated beverage (or double recipe to serve 2 if you're using a standard ice cube tray with dividers). When frozen, crush ice cubes and add ½ teaspoon banana extract, ½ teaspoon rum extract, and artificial sweetener to equal 1 teaspoon sugar. Serve in champagne glass with short straws. Makes 1 serving.

5. *"Champagne" Fizz:* Make ice cubes from 1 cup ginger ale to which you have added ¼ teaspoon each vanilla and sherry extracts. Crush cubes and serve in 2 champagne glasses with short straws. Makes 2 servings.

6. *Wassail Bowl:* Heat 1 quart root-beer-flavored dietetic carbonated beverage, add 1 teaspoon cinnamon, ½ teaspoon each ginger and nutmeg, and 6 teaspoons brown sugar replacement. Serve from punch bowl.

7. *"Margarita" in a Frosted Glass:* Prepare two frosted highball glasses: dip rim of each glass in lime or lemon juice, then into salt. Put in freezer until "frost" sets; then refrigerate till needed. Make ice cubes from 1 cup citrus-flavored dietetic carbonated beverage. When frozen, place cubes in blender with juice of one lime and artificial sweetener to equal 2 teaspoons sugar; blend well. Serve beverage over crushed ice in frosted glasses. Makes 2 servings.

8. *"Rum" and Cola:* Combine ¾ cup cola-flavored dietetic carbonated beverage and ¾ teaspoon rum extract. Pour over 3 ice cubes in a highball glass. Makes 1 serving.

9. *"Sangria":* Combine 1 cup grape-flavored dietetic carbonated beverage, ½ teaspoon burgundy or other wine-flavored extract, and ¼ teaspoon orange extract. Pour over ice cubes in tall glass; garnish with cinnamon stick. Makes 1 serving.

10. *Tommy Collins:* Combine ¼ cup dietetic quinine water, 1 teaspoon rum extract, artificial sweetener to equal 1 teaspoon sugar, and 1 teaspoon lemon juice. Serve over ice cubes in a tall glass with long straw.

11. *Creme de Menthe Frappé:* Mix artificial sweetener to equal 4 teaspoons sugar with 1 cup cold water, ¼ teaspoon peppermint extract and few drops green food coloring. Add crushed ice and stir. Serve in frosted cocktail glass with short straw. Makes 1 serving.

COFFEE AND TEA BREAKS

1. *Coffee "Brandy":* Combine ½ cup boiling water, 1 teaspoon instant coffee powder, artificial sweetener to equal 2 teaspoons sugar, ½ teaspoon brandy (or anise) extract and a twist of lemon peel. Serve in demitasse cup. Makes 1 serving.

2. *Iced Coffee:* Make ice cubes of regular coffee. Serve regular strength coffee over coffee ice cubes in tall glass. For a *Coffee Granita,* put everything into blender and whip to a froth.

3. *Chocolate "Rum" Sherbet:* Combine ¼ cup chocolate-flavored dietetic carbonated beverage and ¼ cup regular-strength coffee in ice cube tray; freeze till mushy. Serve in sherbet glass topped with ½ teaspoon rum extract. Sip from straw. Makes 1 serving.

4. *Hot Mint Tea:* Steep 1 teaspoon dried mint leaves (or 1 tablespoon crushed fresh mint leaves) in 1 cup boiling water for 15 minutes (for full flavor extraction). Sweeten to taste. Pleasant seasonings to be steeped with mint leaves: rose hips, sassafras leaves, whole cloves, aniseed, allspice, lemon peel, cinnamon stick, cardamom seeds; tea bag of usual tea leaves may be steeped along with the mint leaves, but for only 5 minutes.

5. *Mint Sherbet:* Freeze sweetened spiced mint tea in ice cube tray till mushy (if frozen solid, crush cubes before serving). Serve with straw in dessert glasses.

HOT AND COLD SOUPS

1. *Chicken Soup (or Bouillon):* Make it from ¾ cup boiling water, 1 envelope instant chicken broth and seasoning mix or 1 chicken bouillon cube, and ½ teaspoon dehydrated onion flakes (op-

tional). Heat in saucepan. For *Beef Bouillon,* use 1 envelope instant beef broth and seasoning mix or 1 beef bouillon cube, dash Worcestershire and ¾ cup water. Minced parsley, dill, chives or pimento; garlic powder, celery seed or a piece of bay leaf are optional seasonings.

2. *"Old-Fashioned" Vegetable Soup:* For a just-made taste, prepare a mixture of ¼ cup fresh minced herbs, lettuce or celery leaves. Add to ¾ cup liquid left from cooking your vegetables (or liquid from canned vegetables) with 1 bouillon cube.

3. *Mock Wonton Soup:* Toss ¼ cup raw shredded spinach leaves into Chicken Soup or "Old-Fashioned" Soup above and let wilt slightly. Serve at once.

4. *Bouillon Spritzer:* Combine ¾ cup boiling water and 1 envelope instant beef broth and seasoning mix; cool and make into ice cubes. Crush when frozen and transfer to highball glass; cover with 1 cup club soda. Hang a lemon wedge on the side of the glass for garnish. Makes 1 serving.

5. *Tomato Soup:* In saucepan combine 2 cups tomato juice; 1 rib celery, diced; 1 tablespoon dehydrated onion flakes; 1 teaspoon lemon juice; artificial sweetener to equal 1 teaspoon sugar; 1 beef bouillon cube; ½ teaspoon salt; and dash cayenne pepper or red hot sauce. Simmer 10-12 minutes, or until celery is tender. Transfer to blender and puree. Serve very hot, or refrigerate and serve in frosted glasses (wet rims of glasses, dip in salt and set in freezer until "frost" is set). Makes 2 servings.

6. *Madrilene (Jellied Tomato Soup):* Sprinkle 1 tablespoon gelatin over ¼ cup cold water or tomato juice. Place over low heat in small saucepan, stirring to dissolve gelatin. Add dissolved gelatin to 1¾ cups tomato soup (above), mix well, transfer to mold, and refrigerate until set. Spoon into individual bowls, cutting up gelatin to make sparkling cubes. Garnish with minced chives or parsley.

7. *Spiked Clam Juice on the Rocks:* Salt is generally unnecessary with clam juice, but add other seasonings to taste. Try half clam and half tomato juice. Or combine ¾ cup clam juice and dash each lemon juice, celery seed, cayenne pepper, red hot sauce or aromatic bitters with ice cubes in tall old-fashioned glass. Use a long stick of celery as a swizzle. Makes 1 serving.

GELATIN DELIGHTS

1. *Dessert Gelatin Whips:* Sprinkle 1 envelope (1 tablespoon) unflavored gelatin over ½ cup dietetic carbonated beverage (any flavor) in small saucepan. Place over low heat, stirring constantly until dissolved. Remove from heat and add 1½ cups of same flavor beverage. For a fluffy mold, whip to a froth in blender before molding. Or pour directly into moistened mold, and refrigerate until firm. Unmold onto serving plate. Diced fresh fruit or berries may be added if desired (in "legal" amounts, of course).

2. *Mint Jelly:* You'll need 1 envelope (1 tablespoon) unflavored gelatin, 2 cups club soda or lemon-lime-flavored dietetic carbonated beverage, artificial sweetener to equal 2 teaspoons sugar, 1 teaspoon mint extract and few drops green food coloring. Sprinkle gelatin over ½ cup beverage in small saucepan. Place over low heat, stirring constantly until gelatin dissolves, about 3 minutes. Remove from heat. Add remaining ingredients. Transfer to loaf pan or other mold which has been rinsed first in water. Refrigerate until firm. Serve in squares with roast lamb. Makes 4 servings.

3. *Gelatin Pick-Me-Up:* Combine 1 envelope (1 tablespoon) unflavored gelatin, ¾ cup tomato juice (hot) and dash aromatic bitters in blender; run blender for 30 seconds. Serve at once. Makes 1 serving.

TOMATO ASPIC

    1 envelope (1 tablespoon) unflavored gelatin
    2 cups tomato juice
    ½ teaspoon lemon juice
    Artificial sweetener to equal 1 teaspoon sugar
    Dash cayenne pepper, red hot sauce, or any desired #2A item
    ½-1 cup #3A vegetable, evenly diced or shredded (optional)

Soften gelatin over ¼ cup cold tomato juice in small saucepan. Place over low heat, stirring constantly to dissolve gelatin. Remove from heat. Add remaining tomato juice, lemon juice, sweetener and desired seasonings. Chill until slightly thickened. Fold in any desired #3A vegetable, pour into individual molds (coffee cups, for example) rinsed in cold water to make unmolding easier, and chill until firm. Makes 4 servings.

FLUFFY CHOCOLATE "PIE"
Grand illusions.

1 envelope (1 tablespoon) unflavored gelatin
1½ cups chocolate-flavored dietetic carbonated beverage
Artificial sweetener to equal 4 tablespoons sugar
½ teaspoon chocolate extract
¼ teaspoon imitation butter flavoring
Dash salt
Few drops brown food coloring

Sprinkle gelatin over beverage in saucepan and place over low heat, stirring to dissolve gelatin. Remove from heat; add remaining ingredients and mix well. Chill until slightly set. Whip again with rotary beater until thick. Transfer to a deep 9-inch pie plate. Chill until firm. Makes 2 servings.

VARIATIONS
1. *Fluffy Lemon "Pie"*: Follow recipe above, but substitute 1½ cups lemon-flavored dietetic carbonated beverage, ½ teaspoon lemon extract, 1 teaspoon grated lemon rind, and few drops yellow food coloring.
2. *Fluffy Strawberry "Pie"*: Use 1½ cups berry-flavored dietetic carbonated beverage and ½ teaspoon strawberry extract. One cup sliced strawberries may be arranged in pie plate before gelatin is poured in.

TIPS ON GELATIN

1. One tablespoon of gelatin will mold 2 cups of liquids and solids combined.
2. Always rinse mold quickly in cold water just before adding gelatin for easier unmolding.
3. If gelatin should become too stiff to permit folding in solid ingredients like fruit, place mold containing the mixture into a bath of hot water almost to the rim. Then fold mixture into softened gelatin and chill again.
4. Allow 2-3 hours for chilling in refrigerator (less if gelatin is all liquid, more if it contains solids).

Unmolding

1. Run a knife gently along the inside edge of the mold. Turn serving plate upside-down over the mold, and invert both mold and plate. Place a warm, wet towel around the mold; lift off mold.
2. Or dip mold almost to its rim into very warm water. Then quickly invert onto serving plate.

TEEN TREATS

1. *Lemonade:* Combine 1 cup water, 2 tablespoons lemon juice and artificial sweetener to equal 4 teaspoons sugar. Serve over ice cubes in large glass. Mint leaves may be floated on top. Makes 1 serving.

2. *Fruit-Flavored Snowballs:* Boil down 1 cup fruit-flavored dietetic carbonated beverage to half volume. Meanwhile, combine 4 cups cracked ice and 2 cups cold water in blender container. (To crack ice, wrap cubes in a towel and pound with rolling pin or hammer, or crush them in blender). Run blender till ice looks like snow crystals, then let drain quickly, and pile ice into 4 paper cups.

Drizzle 2 tablespoons of the thickened fruit-flavored beverage (you may stir in an appropriate flavor extract to taste) over each cone and serve promptly. Makes 4 snowballs.

Vegetables--Unlimited and Moderate Amounts

Vegetables play a big part in our program, and we want you to learn how to buy, prepare and cook them properly. You'll find valuable tips throughout this chapter, so please read our notes and recipes carefully.

You can learn to eat many a vegetable you aren't too fond of by toning down the flavor, mixing it with a vegetable you enjoy. Or you can use your boiled or baked potato (be sure you omit a slice of bread), mashing it with turnips, cauliflower, squash, etc. You can create new flavors too by baking your cooked vegetables with added seasonings, to make delicious puddings.

For greater variety, try cooking some vegetables you usually eat raw (celery, tomato, cucumber, etc.). In reverse, try raw those vegetables you usually cook. Have you ever tried raw cauliflower, broccoli or spinach tucked into a salad along with the lettuce? Or pickled? Or chopped and made into a luscious gelatin mold?

RULES FOR USING #3 VEGETABLES

1. Use vegetables raw or cooked; fresh, frozen (without sauce), or canned, either at meals or between meals (but *always* have at least one #3 vegetable at lunch).

2. You may eat all you want from Group A. Eat up to 4 cups raw or 2 cups cooked from Group B. Note that cucumbers, peppers, pickles and tomatoes are counted rather than measured. The number listed (e.g. 2 medium cucumbers) counts as the total daily requirement of #3B vegetables. However, you may mix and match; for example, on the day you use 1 medium tomato, you may also have up to 1 cup cooked or 2 cups raw #3B vegetables.

*3. Please note asterisks designating dark green, deep yellow and red vegetables. You must select from these marked vegetables at least 2-3 times weekly. Vary your selection from day to day.

3A. UNLIMITED

Celery
Chicory
Chilies (Peppers)
Chives
Escarole
Gherkins

Lettuce
Nasturtium
 leaves
Parsley
*Pimentos

Radishes
 (Daikon)
Truffles
Watercress
(Peppergrass)

3B. MODERATE AMOUNTS

Anise
Asparagus
*Bean sprouts
*Beans, green
Beans, wax
*Beet greens
*Broccoli
Cabbage (also
 Swamp
 Cabbage)
Cauliflower
Chard (Swiss)
Chinese cabbage
 (Bok Choy)
Chinese pea pods
 (Snow Peas or
 Chinese peas)
Chinese winter
 melon
 (Tonqua)
Collard Greens
Comfrey leaves
Cucumbers,
 2 medium

*Dandelion greens
Eggplant
Endive
 (including
 Belgian)
Fennel
Fiddlefern
 (Fiddlehead
 greens)
Finocchio
Grape leaves
*Kale
Kohlrabi
Mushrooms
*Mustard greens
*Peppers (green
 and red),
 2 medium
Pickles (dill,
 sour),
 2 medium
Poke salad greens
Sauerkraut
Sour grass

*Spinach
Squash (summer)
 Casserta
 Chayote
 Cocozelle
 Cymling
 Pattypan
 Scalloped
 Spaghetti
 Straight or
  Crookneck
 Vegetable
  Marrow
 Zucchini
Tomatoes, cherry
 (1-1½″ in
 diameter),
 approximately
 10-12
*Tomatoes (green
 or ripe),
 2 medium
Turnip greens

A. UNLIMITED

RAW CELERY FOR GARNISH AND SALAD

Preparing celery: Separate each rib from stalk (bunch) and trim away the base. (Cut off the green leaves and use them in salads, soups made from bouillon cubes and envelopes of broth mix, and as garnishes. They have a fresh, perky flavor.) Season with salt, pepper and anise and use them to stave off hunger pangs through the day.

Scrub the outer tough ribs with a vegetable brush and remove any strings. Wash quickly under running water, dry and cut into desired sizes.

Cutting celery: The fastest way to dice celery is to cut ribs into thin strips lengthwise (1/16 to 3/8-inch thick). Cut strips crosswise into fine dice. For julienne or matchstick pieces, cut strips ⅛ inch thick and 2 to 3 inches long. Celery may also be cut into horizontal or diagonal slices.

Fluting celery: Cut raw washed celery in half lengthwise, then into 4-inch lengths. Make parallel cuts, 1-inch deep and 1/16-inch apart, on one side of the celery. Repeat on the other side. Refrigerate covered with water until ready to use as salad trim, fish garnish, etc. The fluted ends will open to create a bow-tie shape.

TANGY CELERY LUNCHEON SALAD

> 1 stalk (bunch) celery
> 1 cup boiling water
> 1 envelope instant chicken broth and seasoning mix
> Shredded lettuce
> Chopped parsley
> Freshly ground black pepper
> 1 roasted pimento
> 1 teaspoon capers
> ⅔ cup cottage cheese, or 4 ounces drained tuna
> 6 cherry tomatoes, halved
> ½ recipe Tangy French Dressing (p. 220 — count ½ cup tomato juice)
> 1 tablespoon vegetable oil

Leave stalk whole, but wash gently and scrape strings from outside ribs. Trim away root end and slice across top, removing most of the outer leaves. Cut stalk lengthwise into 4 pieces. Cook covered in shallow saucepan with water and broth mix. When celery is tender (do not overcook), carefully transfer to large serving dish covered with a bed of shredded lettuce. Arrange celery radiating out from center (like spokes of a wheel). Sprinkle with chopped parsley and freshly ground pepper. Make several crosses of pimento strips along each length of celery, and dot with capers. Add a ball of cheese or fish, and make a border of cherry tomatoes. Combine Tangy French Dressing and oil. Mix well. Pour over salad and refrigerate to chill. Makes 1 serving.

BRAISED CELERY

A marvelous vegetable, totally neglected in this country (but not in France).

> 1 stalk (bunch) celery
> ¾ cup boiling water
> 1 envelope instant chicken broth and seasoning mix
> 1 tablespoon vegetable oil (optional)
> Garlic powder or well-mashed clove garlic

Cut thick celery pieces lengthwise into quarters, cut the inner pieces lengthwise into halves, then cut all into 3-inch lengths. Arrange in shallow casserole, cover with boiling water, sprinkle with broth mix, cover and simmer until celery is tender. Divide celery into 2 salad plates. Reduce liquid left in pan to half. Combine with oil and garlic, and divide over celery. Makes 2 servings.

CELERY BISQUE

> 1 cup celery, cut into pieces 3 inches long by ¼ inch wide
> ½ cup skim milk (or water)
> 1 envelope instant chicken broth and seasoning mix
> Dash rosemary
> Minced chives and young celery leaves for garnish

Combine celery and milk in enamel saucepan, and simmer gently until celery is done — still somewhat crisp, not limp and exhausted.

Allow about 12 minutes. Add broth mix and rosemary. Serve immediately, or transfer all or part of the mixture to blender and chop, not too fine. Serve hot in soup bowl with a sprinkling of minced chives and celery leaves. Makes 1 serving.

VARIATION

Celery and Potato Chowder: Cook 1 medium (3-ounce) potato, diced, in ¼ cup boiling salted water for 10 minutes. Add celery and milk and continue as above. A delicious chowder. Makes 1 serving.

CELERY PARMIGIANA

3 cups celery, cut into pieces 3 inches long by ¼ inch wide
¾ cup chicken bouillon
1 cup tomato juice, reduced by half
Onion salt
3 ounces mozzarella cheese, sliced thin
1 ounce Parmesan cheese, grated

Cook celery in chicken bouillon in covered saucepan until just tender, 12-15 minutes. Transfer half of celery to shallow casserole. Cover with ⅓ of thickened tomato juice and half of mozzarella cheese; sprinkle with onion salt. Repeat layers, ending with tomato juice and Parmesan cheese. Bake at 400° F. for 10-15 minutes, or until hot and bubby. Makes 2 luncheon servings.

CHILI PEPPERS (ALSO CHILE AND CHILLI)

The slender hot chili pepper, well-known in Mexico, is unlimited on Program, except, of course, for the restrictions their hot pungent flavor will impose on your palate. They are available fresh, dried whole, powdered or canned. The fresh pods, when used whole in soups, vegetable stews, etc., add a pleasant tang—it's the seeds that are so very hot—but discard the whole pods before serving. The dried whole chili peppers may be reconstituted in water to cover, then added to sauces and other foods as desired. Canned chilis are widely available. Chili powder is a blend of hot peppers, of which the main ingredient is the chili pepper.

Pimento is also unlimited — this is a mild, sweet, thick pepper sold in cans or jars.

NOTE: The other green or red peppers — large, sweet and broad — are #3B vegetables.

HOME-STYLE PICKLED GHERKINS
This small cucumber is not widely available, but it's easy to grow (vines are said to produce an "astonishingly large crop"), and easy to pickle.

> 1 pound fresh gherkins
> 1 cup cider vinegar
> ¾ cup water
> Artificial sweetener to equal ½ cup sugar
> 1 teaspoon pickling spices
> 1 teaspoon dehydrated onion flakes (optional)
> ½ clove garlic
> Turmeric

Cut washed pickles into ½-inch slices and pack in two sterilized pint jars or one quart jar. Bring vinegar, water and sweetener to boil; add to jar with remaining ingredients, filling to within an inch of the top. Cover and seal. Let stand in refrigerator 24 hours or longer before use. Store in refrigerator.

TOSSED SALADS

The following salad greens are unlimited: Bibb, Boston, celery leaves, curly-leaf chicory (not the blanched white kind known as Belgian or French endive or witloof), escarole, iceberg, and romaine. Do include at least two different kinds in your salad bowl.

Buy fresh green heads. Discard any tough, discolored outer leaves, but don't otherwise waste the nutrient-rich dark green outer leaves. Prepare and store your #3A vegetables as soon as you get them home from the market, and they'll be there when needed for runaway appetites.

Preparing and storing greens

Cut off the core and wash lettuce briefly in a colander under cold running water. (Leaves of solid iceberg lettuce will separate easily under the force of the water if you turn the lettuce core-side up). You may have to wash very sandy leaves of chicory or escarole one by one, to remove all hidden soil. When leaves are washed, invert them in colander to drain in sink, turning several times to release water trapped in leaves. Wrap the fairly dry leaves in cloth towels and refrigerate. Greens will keep crisp 2-3 days.

Tear leaves an hour or so before use, if you wish, and put into salad bowl, lightly covered with paper toweling. Leaves that are sliced or shredded (rather than torn) release juices, so these procedures are best done just before use.

For party preparation or carrying salad greens away from home (lunch or picnics), store the dry greens in a plastic bag. Just before serving, pour dressing into plastic bag, hold top tightly closed and shake well. Unless otherwise directed, salad dressings should be added to any salad at the last minute, just before use. Salad dressings with oil are for limited use, but we have moderately unlimited dressings here in abundance (see chapter on Sauces, Salad Dressings, pp. 213-234). For garlic flavor, add mashed clove of garlic to your salad dressing and let stand overnight. Or rub salad bowl with cut clove of garlic before use. For a stronger garlic accent, mash garlic clove(s) to a paste with salt, and mix into the greens or the dressing. Garlic powder or garlic salt (which might, however, produce too much saltiness for the amount of garlic you'd like) may be sprinkled over the greens. Sprinkle herbs of your choice, fresh or dried, over the greens before you serve them.

BRAISED LETTUCE

1 head Boston or romaine lettuce
½ cup boiling water
1 envelope instant chicken broth and seasoning mix
1 teaspoon minced parsley

Carefully wash lettuce. Discard any wilted outer leaves. Cover with boiling water and let stand 2 minutes. (Or steam it.) Drain, dry with towel, and let cool. Cut lettuce in half through the stem, then cut again into a total of 6 sections. Line a shallow pan with lettuce sections, press them down slightly. Sprinkle with broth mix, add ½ cup boiling water, cover pan with lid or aluminum foil, and cook 8-10 minutes. Sprinkle with parsley. Serves 6, but as lettuce is unlimited, you may have 2 or 3 (or more!) helpings yourself — as much as you can eat.

LETTUCE COUPE

>1 head lettuce
>2 cups tomato juice, buttermilk, or combination
>Onion or celery salt

Pour 1 cup liquid into blender with half of the lettuce leaves. Liquefy at low speed. Refill blender with remaining lettuce and liquid and blend once more. Serve immediately in juice glasses or chill. A dash of salt and a sprinkling of fresh minced herbs are last-minute additions. Makes 4 servings.

MOLDED LETTUCE

>1 head iceberg or other crisp lettuce
>½ medium green pepper, diced fine
>½ medium red pepper, diced fine
>2 teaspoons dehydrated onion flakes, reconstituted in
> 2 tablespoons water
>1 garlic clove, mashed well, or garlic powder
>2 recipes Mayonnaise Sauce (p. 226 — count 1 tablespoon
>mayonnaise and 1 fluid ounce evaporated skimmed milk
> per serving)
>Watercress or parsley sprigs
>Salt and freshly ground pepper
>Pimento strips

Shred lettuce fine to make 3-4 cups, tightly packed. Add green and red peppers, onion flakes, garlic and freshly made Mayonnaise Sauce. Mix well. Pack mixture into mold and refrigerate. Serve on platter with border of watercress or parsley sprigs. Garnish top of mold with strips of pimento. Pass salt and pepper mill at the table. Makes 4 servings.

STUFFED LETTUCE LEAVES

Follow directions for Stuffed Cabbage Leaves (p. 262), but cook lettuce leaves briefly (or steam them) no more than a few minutes, as they are not strong enough for prolonged cooking.

PARSLEY

Parsley is nature's taste complement for pungent onion and garlic, and a garnish we use freely. American markets usually carry two varieties: the curly American kind, and the Italian parsley, whose flat, jagged leaves resemble celery tops. To store parsley, break off the bottom part of stems, remove string which ties leaves into a bunch, and give them a quick bath in cold water. Drain leaves, dry in paper or cloth towels to keep parsley dry (excess moisture causes parsley to spoil).

BROILED FRESH PIMENTOS

Blister 2 pimentos (see p. 275). Peel off skin, discard seeds, and cut them in strips. For each serving, rub a bowl with garlic. Add peppers, 1 tablespoon vegetable oil, 1 tablespoon vinegar, and salt and pepper to taste. Let stand 2 hours.

Storing Pimentos: Pimentos (packed in vinegar, and roasted) also come in cans or jars; they spoil quickly once opened. Here's how to store them: drain off liquid in which they were packed, replace with fresh water and, optional, add ½ teaspoon vinegar and ⅛ teaspoon oregano or tarragon. Cover tightly and refrigerate. They will last for a week or more . . . if you don't put them on everything!

RADISHES UNLIMITED

The common red and white radish, the black radish, and daikon, the large Japanese radish, are unlimited on our program. They may be used interchangeably, unless otherwise specified. See also Daikon Sauce (p. 217).

1. *Cooked:* Peel and slice radishes, cover with boiling water and cook until tender, 8-15 minutes. Marinate in Tangy French Dressing (p. 220).

2. *Red Radish Roses:* Can be made a few days ahead. Use large round cleaned radishes. Slice off top ends. Make 5 cuts about ¼-inch deep all around the radish at the top end, make a second layer of cuts (petals) in an alternate row at the lower end of the radish. Put in water-filled container and refrigerate. Petals will open in half an hour.

3. *Red Radish Accordions:* Trim both ends of radish. Make parallel slashes all along the side of the radish about 1/16-inch or 1/8-inch apart not quite through to the opposite side. Refrigerate in water so cuts will open.
4. *Radish Puff:* Trim away radish top and slice it lengthwise almost through to the stem. Then slice it crosswise almost to stem. Refrigerate in water until it pops open — about ½ hour.

HORSERADISH SHERBET

1 recipe Best Whipped Topping (p. 198 — count 1 fluid ounce evaporated skimmed milk per serving)
3 tablespoons fresh, grated horseradish, or daikon
Artificial sweetener to equal 1 teaspoon sugar
½ teaspoon salt
¼ teaspoon orange extract

Make Best Whipped Topping. When stiff, fold in remaining ingredients and freeze in bowl. Defrost in refrigerator for a few minutes, then stir lightly with fork and serve, still icy, as a pungent dressing for boiled fish or beef. Makes 4 servings.

HORSERADISH RELISH

Horseradish roots
½ cup white vinegar
¼ teaspoon salt

Remove brown outer skin of horseradish roots. Cut up and put into blender, or grate enough roots to make 1 cup. Combine with white vinegar and salt. Pack into clean jar, cover and store in refrigerator.

TRUFFLES

Truffles are the trifles of the rich. Prized for their delicacy, these underground fungi bring to the table a scent of the wild where they are harvested by trained dogs and pigs. Truffles cannot be cultivated, and they don't even grow wild in the United States and England.

You can see why my local gourmet shop keeps them locked up in the safe. They are listed on our program as unlimited — so add them sliced to scrambled eggs, cooked chicken livers, or cooked enriched rice — if you can bear to eat anything that costs over a hundred dollars a pound.

WATERCRESS SOUP

> ½ cup watercress
> ½ cup water
> 1 envelope instant chicken broth and seasoning mix
> 1 teaspoon dehydrated onion flakes
> ½ teaspoon salt
> ½ cup skim milk

Wash the watercress and dry it well. Chop fine, both leaves and stems. In small saucepan, combine water, chicken broth mix, onion flakes and salt. Cook, stirring constantly to dissolve the mix; add skim milk and bring to boiling point. Stir in chopped watercress, turn off heat immediately, and serve in soup bowl with a sprig of watercress floating on top. Makes 1 serving.

CRUDITES

For party-goers or party-givers who want taste without waist, these raw crisp vegetables, called crudités in France, could be a favorite hors d'oeuvre. Prepare them an hour or more before use and refrigerate until party time. Provide individual platters for all with #3B and #4 vegetables measured or weighed in advance. These make great TV snacks too for late-show nibblers. Just before serving, pour 1 tablespoon oil on each platter.

Beans, Green or Wax (#3B): Use young and whole; or parboil and cut on diagonal.

Bean Sprouts (#3B): Prepare as vinaigrette, p. 215.

Broccoli (#3B): Bathe tiny raw florets in ice water containing 1 teaspoon lemon juice or vinegar. Drain and dry in towel.

Carrots (#4): Cut off slivers or strips using a paring knife. To make curls, roll up strips, secure with toothpick and put in ice water to set the curl.

Cauliflower (#3B): Dip tiny raw florets in ice water containing 1 teaspoon lemon juice or vinegar. Drain and dry.

Celery (#3A): Cut tender ribs into long slim fingers. Use raw or poach lightly in chicken bouillon. Or make into curls, just as you do carrots. Celery sticks look pretty served with the green leaves left on.

Celeriac — celery root (#4): Peel and cut in long strips, wash in water containing lemon juice, drain and dry. Can be made into curls or poached too, just as you do celery.

Chinese Cabbage (#3B): Use halved stalks or rolled-up leaf sections.

Chinese snow peas (#3B): Serve them whole and crisp.

Cucumbers (#3B): Use peeled or, if young, scrub and use unpeeled. With tines of a fork, make parallel gashes from top to bottom around the whole cucumber, then slice in rounds. Or cut long, thin strips. Soak slices or strips in salted ice water for ½ hour, then drain and dry. Sprinkle with chopped fresh dill or chives, if desired.

Fennel (#3B): Cut into slices and serve raw.

Kale (#3B): Serve this curly-leaved member of the cabbage family raw, individual leaves well washed and dried.

Kohlrabi (#3B): Peel it just as you would turnip, then serve in thin slices.

Lettuce (#3A): Use crisp firm leaves of chicory and an assortment of other available greens, well washed and dried.

Mushrooms (#3B): Pickled mushrooms (bought vinegar-packed in jars), drained. Or dip raw mushroom caps in lemon juice. Or cut through cap and stem in pretty slices, dip in lemon juice or vinegar bath and serve raw.

Parsley (#3A): Use large crisp sprigs, washed and dried.

Peppers (#3B): Use both red and green for color contrast. Seed and cut into lengthwise strips or rings.

Pimentos (#3A): Use for bright red color; nice shredded and used as light stuffing in celery ribs.

Spinach (#3B): Buy loose, with full dark color, wash carefully, dry well and serve raw. Cut out tough ribs with scissors, if necessary.

Radishes (#3A): Prepare radish roses, accordions or puffs, p. 251.

Scallions (#4): Trim off root end, but leave plenty of green leaf. Cut the thick ones in half, lengthwise. Leaf ends can be gashed to make scallion brushes.

Squash — Summer (#3B): Use young thin-skinned zucchini, lightly scrubbed but not peeled. Cut into fingers or slices, cover with boiling water and let stand for 2-3 minutes to soften. Drain and dry.

Tomatoes (#3B): Use whole cherry tomatoes, washed and dried. Or serve medium tomatoes, cut in quarters and sprinkled with basil, dill or (if you dare at a party) with garlic.

Watercress (#3A): Use large fresh sprigs, washed and dried, for their deliciously peppery taste.

Suggested platter of crudités for 1 serving:

> ½ cup raw broccoli florets
> ½ cup raw cauliflower florets
> ½ cup barely cooked crisp green beans
> 3 cherry tomatoes
> ¼ medium red pepper, cut into strips
> 1 ounce carrot curls
> 1 ounce scallions, or 1 ounce cooked artichoke hearts
> Celery ribs
> Endive fingers
> Radish roses
> Sprigs of watercress and parsley

Suggested dips for individual servings

> 1 serving Pimento Dressing (p. 217)
> 1 serving Tangy French Dressing (p. 220 — count ½ cup tomato juice)
> 1 serving Mock Hollandaise Sauce (p. 225 — count 1 tablespoon fat)

B. MODERATE AMOUNTS

ANISE

It's an annual herb with a licorice-like taste, and it's available from October to March. Look for a pearly-white, fresh-looking bulb with bright green, featherlike leaves. Store it in a refrigerator crisper; it will keep fresh for several days. The green leaves are delicious in salads or chopped and mixed with cottage cheese. If you can't find fresh anise, you might like the anise extract (but don't count it as a vegetable). Anise and fennel are very similar, but no need for you garden-growers to be confused; anise belongs to the Pimpinella family of herbs, and fennel is part of genus Foeniculum.

MOCK SPLIT PEA SOUP
Or, if you prefer — it's not "mock anything" — it's real asparagus and green bean soup.

>   1½ cups canned asparagus (reserve liquid)
>   1½ cups canned green beans (reserve liquid)
>   1 cup diced celery (with leaves)
>   4 sprigs parsley
>   2 cups chicken bouillon, or 2 cups water and 3 envelopes instant chicken broth and seasoning mix
>   ½ bay leaf
>   Dash Worcestershire or nutmeg
>   Salt and pepper
>   Few drops green food coloring (optional)

Combine asparagus, green beans (with 1 cup combined liquids), celery and parsley in blender and purée. Transfer to soup kettle with remaining ingredients. Bring to quick boil, then simmer for about 30 minutes. Serve hot in soup mugs. Makes 4 servings; count ¾ cup cooked #3B vegetables per serving.

ASPARAGUS VINAIGRETTE

½ cup tarragon vinegar
1 teaspoon minced parsley
1 teaspoon minced capers
Few drops lemon juice
1 cup cooked, drained asparagus

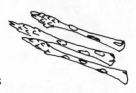

Bring vinegar to boil in saucepan; add minced parsley, capers and lemon juice. Pour over asparagus; marinate an hour or more. Delicious as a separate course, or with Fettucini Alfredo (p. 68). Makes 1 serving.

SPROUT YOUR OWN BEAN SPROUTS?

Why not? There's special equipment for this, but you don't really need it. Buy mung beans for sprouting. Use a porcelain or glass or other non-porous container, such as a wide-mouth jar. First, soak beans for several hours or overnight in water to cover. Pour off water and put just enough beans in one jar to make one layer deep. To keep beans moist, cover the mouth of the jar with a few layers of cheesecloth held tight with a rubber band. From this point on, keep the beans moist, but do not immerse in water. Any excess can be poured off right through the cheesecloth. Cover the jar with paper towels to keep light out and hasten the sprouting. Beans will sprout in six to eight days.

To harvest, just lift out the sprouts, rinse off the green pods, and drain. Store in a loosely covered container or even a colander so that air can circulate around them. They are as perishable as any green vegetable. For longer storage, plunge them in boiling water for 5 minutes, then in cold water. To keep, store fresh (or canned) bean sprouts in refrigerator container, cover with water and change the water daily. Or store in freezer in plastic containers. One pound of mung beans produces 6-8 pounds of sprouts; one-half pound of freshly sprouted beans cooked in boiling salted water for 10-15 minutes replace one-pound canned sprouts. But remember, this is a #3B moderate-amount vegetable, so measure it before use.

You can also find fresh bean sprouts in Chinese markets, or buy this invaluable food in cans. Use bean sprouts in fruit and vegetable salads, soups, stews, and casseroles and scrambled with eggs.

BEAN SPROUT SALAD

> 1 cup cooked or canned bean sprouts, freshened (see above)
> ½ cup shredded raw cabbage or cooked green beans; or
>   4 ounces canned bamboo shoots, sliced
> Shredded lettuce
> ½ recipe Sour Cream (p. 49 — count ⅓ cup cottage cheese)

Combine vegetables and greens. Serve with Sour Cream. Makes 1 serving; supplement as required.

To Freshen and Store Canned Bean Sprouts: Transfer canned sprouts to strainer, rinse several times under running water, and soak in a bath of ice water, using plenty of ice cubes, for about an hour. At that time, they should be crisp enough for use in salad. There's always the problem of what to do with leftover canned bean sprouts: Drain off liquid, rinse, cover with fresh water, and refrigerate in covered jar for up to one week; change water daily.

COOKED GREEN BEANS
We called these string beans when I was a girl, but they've bred the strings out of them. I hope you can find them at a nearby farm stand, at the peak of their delicate flavor. If so, prepare them as follows:

Trim off the ends, and cut into 2-inch pieces. Measure. Rinse quickly and put into skillet (in a shallow pan, you need no more than ½ cup boiling salted water). Bring to boil, cover pan and let simmer until they are done, but still green and crisp (10 to 12 minutes). For flavor, you could cook the beans with a sprig or two of fresh savory, basil, or marjoram (or 1 teaspoon dried herbs). Serve beans as a separate course in individual bowls, with allowed margarine, if you wish, and finely chopped parsley or basil for garnish. If young and fresh, green beans are first-rate without added seasoning. (To cook frozen green beans, follow directions on the package, measure, don't overcook.)

THREE-BEAN SALAD WITH OIL DRESSING
It sounds so fattening but it's "legal". One-half cup bean sprouts could replace lima beans.

>1 tablespoon vegetable oil
>1 tablespoon lemon juice
>1 tablespoon tomato juice
>1 tablespoon minced parsley
>1 tablespoon minced chives
>1 tablespoon marjoram
>½ cup cooked lima beans
>½ cup cooked wax beans
>½ cup cooked whole green beans

In bowl combine oil, lemon juice, tomato juice, parsley, chives and marjoram. Mix thoroughly and add beans. Toss lightly; chill. Makes 1 serving.

CHOPPED GREEN BEAN "LIVER"
A liverless paté.

>2 ounces sliced onions
>1 rib celery, diced
>2 cups fresh green beans, cut in 1-inch pieces
>1 cup water
>1 envelope instant chicken broth and seasoning mix
>2 hard-cooked eggs
>Lettuce
>2 tablespoons mayonnaise, or vegetable oil
>Salt and pepper

"Water-fry" onions, celery and green beans in uncovered saucepan with water and broth mix until vegetables are soft and liquid evaporated. Let cool. Chop vegetables and eggs together, or puree in blender. Serve on bed of lettuce on 2 individual plates, each topped with allowed mayonnaise or oil. Season with salt and pepper to taste. Makes 2 luncheon servings; supplement as required.

BEET GREENS

A green vegetable (some say even better than spinach) that you cook like spinach. Beets are available year round, with a peak in June and July. Look for fresh, green and tender leaves with a minimum of yellowing. Cut from root (#4 vegetable) and remove large tough stems and any damaged leaves. Wash thoroughly. You may use the most tender leaves for salads. Keeps for 2-3 days in the refrigerator.

COOKED BROCCOLI

Select broccoli that has a rich green color, a tight flower bud and a heavy head. Cut off the toughest part of the stem and any tough green leaves. Scrub or peel the stalk almost to the florets and cut deep gashes through the stalks to speed cooking. Separate large sections into uniform pieces. Cook by either one of the following methods:

1. Slice the tough stalks from the florets in 1-inch pieces and put in the bottom of the saucepan. Arrange florets on top. Pour in ½ cup boiling water for each 2 cups of broccoli (stalks and florets). Salt lightly. Cover pan and cook until stalks are tender when tested with fork, about 10 minutes. Florets should remain crisp and green.

2. *French Style:* Do not separate the stalks from the florets. Boil 3 quarts water in a large kettle containing 1 tablespoon salt. When water boils, put broccoli into a wire basket, dip basket into the water and bring to boil again. Lower heat and continue to boil gently for 5 minutes or until stalks are tender but broccoli still retains its firm texture and bright color.

If broccoli will not be served at once, cool it rapidly on a shallow plate in refrigerator (otherwise it loses its bright color). Or plunge basket quickly into a basin of ice-cold water. Cold, cooked broccoli is delicious with any of the Mayonnaise Sauces (p. 226), or Mock Hollandaise Sauce (p. 225). Or dress each serving with a great combination: 1 tablespoon melted margarine, 2 teaspoons lemon juice, and a few diced capers.

QUICK-COOKED CABBAGE

There was a time when everyone cooked cabbage until it turned an unappetizing brown in the pan. Below is a better way.

Select firm green heads; the greener the leaves, the more food value and flavor. Shred the cabbage just before use, wash quickly and put in pan with boiling salted water to cover. Bring to boil again, lower heat and cook uncovered until cabbage is just done, about 7 minutes if young, 12 minutes if mature. Salt, caraway seeds and marjoram are all good seasonings. Serve with Horseradish Sherbet (p. 252), if desired.

For a colorful cabbage plate, cook wedges of red cabbage in acidulated boiling salted water to cover. After 10 minutes, add wedges of green cabbage and continue cooking covered for about 10 minutes more, or until both cabbages are tender.

SWEDISH COLESLAW

6 cups (1 head) cabbage, finely shredded
1 tablespoon salt
4 celery ribs, diced
1 medium green pepper, diced
1 medium red pepper, diced
½ cup water
1 cup tarragon vinegar
Artificial sweetener to equal 3 tablespoons sugar
1 teaspoon celery seed
1 teaspoon prepared mustard

Layer cabbage in bowl, sprinkling each layer with salt and a bit of water. Set aside for 2 hours, then pick it up by the handful and squeeze out the liquid. Place the cabbage in another bowl; add celery and peppers. Toss. Meanwhile prepare dressing by combining water, vinegar, sweetener, celery seed and mustard; mix thoroughly, and pour over cabbage mixture. It will remain fresh for a few days in a covered plastic container. Garnish with tomato wedges, cucumber slices, pepper strips, etc. — counted, of course. Makes 6 servings.

STUFFED CABBAGE LEAVES

> 2 cups raw cabbage leaves
> Water

Filling

> 6 ounces cooked ground beef
> ½ cup cooked green beans, finely chopped
> 1 teaspoon dehydrated onion flakes
> 2 tablespoons beef bouillon
> Salt and pepper

Cooking Liquid

> 1½ cups tomato juice, reduced by half
> ½ cup water
> 1 teaspoon dehydrated onion flakes
> ½ teaspoon caraway seed
> 1 envelope instant chicken broth and seasoning mix
> Salt and pepper
> Artificial sweetener to equal 2 teaspoons sugar
> 1 cup shredded cabbage (optional)

Prepare leaves as follows: with the point of a paring knife, cut out the core of a young, green-leaved cabbage. Boil a kettle-full of water. Using large strainer or basket, immerse cabbage in boiling water to loosen outer leaves. Remove cabbage from water, plunge loosened leaves into cold water and dry on paper towels. Continue until necessary leaves are loosened. (Reserve remainder of cabbage for other use.) With scissors, cut away any tough ribs. Set leaves aside. Combine ingredients for filling; mix well. Place a heaping tablespoon on each cabbage leaf. Fold in the right and left sections, then roll up. Set aside, seam-side down. Boil ingredients for cooking liquid in shallow pot or electric skillet (if you have one). Transfer filled leaves to pot, seam-side down, and cook for 30 minutes. Serve with pot liquid. Makes 1 dinner serving.

Reminder: all mixtures serving more than one person must be divided evenly; follow the directions on p. 22.

SWEET-SOUR RED CABBAGE WITH APPLE

Red cabbage is slower-cooking than the green. Always add vinegar or lemon juice to water in which it is boiled; otherwise, it loses its bright color.

> 6 cups red cabbage
> 1½ cups boiling water
> 1 teaspoon lemon juice
> 1 teaspoon caraway seed
> 3 medium apples, peeled, cored and sliced
> ⅓ cup cider vinegar
> Artificial sweetener to equal 8 teaspoons sugar
> Dash cayenne

Shred cabbage and cook 10 minutes in boiling water containing lemon juice and caraway seeds. Add apples and cook 10 minutes longer. Drain off most of liquid. Add remaining ingredients. Serve hot. Makes 6 servings.

HOW TO COOK CAULIFLOWER

Buy a white head with tight compact buds. Granular or spreading florets are a sign of age. Cut off tough end. Break the cauliflower into quarters (leave the young green leaves), and wash through colander. Transfer to saucepan, stalk down, florets up. Pour in enough water to come about halfway up the stalk, cover, bring to boil, and simmer until stalk is tender (when tested with a fork) but still white, 12-15 minutes. Don't overcook; it will turn gray and mushy if you do. Measure. For seasoning, add rosemary, salt and pepper.

VEGETABLES AU GRATIN

> ½ tablespoon margarine
> ½ slice bread, made into crumbs
> 1 cup cooked vegetable (cauliflower florets, broccoli, green beans, etc.)

Melt margarine in top of small double boiler. Add crumbs; mix well. Stir in vegetable and shake pan (cover with plate) to distribute crumbs and fat evenly. Makes 1 serving.

SWISS CHARD

This is one of those neglected vegetables that we recommend enthusiastically because it is a good source of food value. Simply cut away the coarse end of the central rib and cook the leaves just as you would spinach. Don't overdo the cooking—leaves might get bitter. Add a little fresh garlic before serving. Swiss chard can be used in place of Chinese cabbage or spinach. Its flavor is more delicate, more subtle, than that of spinach, and you just might like it better. Measure it before you serve.

CHINESE CABBAGE

Chinese cabbage, also called Bok Choy, is another staple of Oriental diet that is allowed on our program. With green-yellow leaves and wide center ribs, it looks like celery or endive rather than cabbage. Its flavor is less pungent and peppery than ordinary cabbage.

In the Orient, the green parts of the leaf are usually used in salads or as a soup garnish (like spinach). The center mid-rib sections are often braised or steamed. They are quickly cooked (in 4-5 minutes), if shredded or cut as you do the common cabbage. You'll enjoy this delightful green if you can find it in your produce market; it's not always available. However, you can grow Chinese cabbage in your American garden. A garden catalog says you sow the seeds about 3 months before the first expected frost.

CHINESE CABBAGE SOUP

4 cups Chinese cabbage
4 cups boiling water
4 envelopes instant chicken or beef broth and seasoning mix
2 teaspoons soy sauce
2 thin slices ginger root
¼ teaspoon pepper
Dash artificial sweetener

Slice cabbage coarse, and combine with other ingredients in saucepan. Cover pot and simmer only until cabbage is done (Chinese soups are famous because most of them are cooked so quickly that the vegetables remain fresh and tasty). Serve hot. Makes 4 servings.

CHINESE PEA PODS

Also known as edible-pod peas or snow peas, they are as tender and sweet as young green beans. Both pod and peas are eaten, but the pods may be sliced before cooking. You can buy them frozen or, if you are an enthusiastic gourmet gardener, grow your own crop. Dwarf Gray Sugar, and Mammoth Melting Sugar are two varieties listed in seed catalogs; most authorities recommend the latter. I am told that you plant them early in the spring, as soon as the ground can be worked, and you must provide a 5-foot high trellis or chicken wire fence for them to climb on. The snow peas should be eaten when the seed just begins to show in the pod. They get tough and flavorless if pods are too large.

When cooking Chinese pea pods, stir vegetables gently as they cook, moving pea pods at bottom of pan to the sides and top where they will get less heat. Move uncooked vegetables to bottom for greater heat. Thus all are done simultaneously. The Chinese cook all their vegetables this way. That's why they never destroy the vegetable's green color, crunchiness and freshness.

Frozen pea pods are cooked within 2 minutes; don't overdo. Measure before you serve.

CHINESE WINTER MELON

Is it a melon? A squash? It's a tonqua (tonca, tonka), a refreshing vegetable sold whole or in a wedge. You can peel off the rind, discard the yellow seeds and cut the pulp into large dice. Cook it in a little water, or steam it, just as you do other tender produce. Season with salt and pepper and perhaps a touch of soy sauce, or sweeten artificially to taste.

CHINESE TONQUA SOUP

    1½ cups water
    2 envelopes instant chicken broth and seasoning mix
    1 cup diced tonqua (scoop out inside)
    Sliced ginger root, 1-inch piece, ½-inch thick (see note)

Bring water to boil, add broth mix, tonqua and ginger; simmer till tonqua is soft. Makes 2 servings.

NOTE: Fresh ginger has a deliciously spicy taste which the ground ginger only faintly resembles. The ginger root can be refrigerated for weeks, or frozen for months. Peel it before you cut it. If you can't find it at specialty food stores, use ground ginger.

SERVING SUGGESTIONS
Party-givers: This recipe can easily be multiplied. The tonqua shell makes a novel soup tureen. First cut a round or oval "lid" and save it to cover your tonqua bowl. Then scoop out and discard yellow seeds, leaving shell intact. Remove meat, dice it and cook as directed above. When soup is done, serve it hot in the tonqua shell.

COLLARD GREENS

These juicy blue-green leaves are grown primarily in the South. The flavor is somewhat like cabbage, and the cooking methods are similar. Follow package directions if you use frozen collards. Measure!

COMFREY LEAVES

Garden enthusiasts often grow this plant. Cook the leaves in soup; or dry them and use them as a tea, steeped as you would ordinary tea leaves. You've got to measure them, to include their total in your daily allowance.

CUCUMBER IN DILL SAUCE

Coarse (kosher) salt
1 medium cucumber, unpeeled and sliced thin
1 teaspoon dehydrated onion flakes, reconstituted in
    2 teaspoons lemon juice
1 recipe Mayonnaise Sauce (p. 226 – count 1 fluid ounce
    evaporated skimmed milk and 1 tablespoon mayonnaise), or
    ¼ cup buttermilk and 1 tablespoon mayonnaise (see note)
¼ teaspoon salt
⅛ teaspoon dry mustard
Freshly ground pepper
Dash artificial sweetener
Minced dill (fresh or dry) to taste

Sprinkle coarse salt over cucumber slices and let stand 30 minutes. Wash under cold water and dry lightly between paper towels. Combine in bowl with remaining ingredients and serve at once. Makes 1 serving.

NOTE: This dish may be prepared several hours ahead and served cold. If so, use buttermilk and mayonnaise; the Mayonnaise Sauce will jell if refrigerated.

SCALLOPED CUCUMBER

1 medium cucumber, peeled
1 medium green pepper, chopped
1 teaspoon parsley
Salt
1 slice 100% whole wheat bread, made into crumbs
½ cup skim milk, or chicken bouillon
1½ teaspoons margarine

Cut cucumber into thin slices. In a small casserole, arrange in layers with green pepper, parsley, salt and crumbs. Repeat layers. Pour in skim milk (it should come almost to top). End with a layer of crumbs. Bake at 375° F. till cucumber is soft, about 40 minutes. Dot with margarine and run under broiler for 1 minute. Makes 1 serving.

CUCUMBER "JELLY" CUBES

4 medium cucumbers
2 tablespoons vinegar
Salt and white pepper
1 envelope (1 tablespoon) unflavored gelatin
1 cup hot chicken bouillon
Few drops green food coloring (optional)
4 tablespoons mayonnaise
Pimento strips for garnish

Peel cucumbers, remove seeds and grate. Add vinegar and sprinkle with salt and white pepper. Let stand for 20 minutes. Drain off liquid, reserving 3 tablespoons. Soften gelatin in reserved liquid, then dissolve in hot chicken bouillon. Combine with grated cucumber, and add green food coloring to make a pale green. Pour into a sectioned ice cube tray, chill in refrigerator and, when firm, remove divider. Serve in separate plates over lettuce leaves; dot with allowed mayonnaise (one tablespoon per serving). Add a rolled strip of pimento for color, if desired. Makes 4 servings.

DANDELION GREENS

Everyone with a lawn knows it as a weed, but this tenacious lawn-spoiler is, nutritionally, a dandy, full of food value even when cooked. Gather leaves when you see them in spring from lawn or at your grocer's. Wash well, discard tough ends (some people cut them away from the roots with kitchen shears), and cook in boiling salted water. Or steam in a colander above (but not touching) water, until leaves are tender. Measure. It has a deliciously bitter taste, and you can give it soul by tossing it with a tablespoon of your allowed oil and a sprinkling of fresh garlic.

Raw dandelion greens, well washed and thoroughly dried, may be covered with a vinaigrette dressing and allowed to stand for about an hour, to wilt and soften before they are served. Dandelion leaves may also be steeped in water for 3-5 minutes; then strain and use as a tea, artificially sweetened.

EGGPLANT CAVIAR
Choose firm eggplant with dark, rich purple color and bright green cap. Wrinkled or flabby eggplant will be bitter. Cook with skin on, or peel just before use.

1 small eggplant
½ teaspoon salt
¼ teaspoon pepper
¾ teaspoon lemon juice
Dash red hot sauce or powdered ginger (optional)

Wash eggplant, discard green end, and bake whole on a shallow pan at 400° F., until it is soft to the touch at its broadest end, about 30 minutes. Cool cooked eggplant, then cut in half length-wise and scoop flesh from shell. Discard skin and excess seeds. Measure pulp and beat it to a puree, using a beater or blender, or chop finely by hand. Stir in seasonings, continuing to beat into a creamy mixture. Store in refrigerator until ready to use.

VARIATION

Just before use, stir in 2 ounces very finely chopped or pureed onion or ¼ cup finely minced celery. Add 1 tablespoon mayonnaise or vegetable oil.

SERVING SUGGESTIONS

Patlijan Salata (Turkish Chef's Salad): Heap 1 cup crisp shredded lettuce into a bowl and add ½ medium tomato, diced; ½ medium cucumber, diced; ½ medium green pepper, diced; 2 sliced hard-cooked eggs and ½ tablespoon diced capers. Make a salad dressing by combining ½ cup Eggplant Caviar (above), 1 tablespoon mayonnaise or vegetable oil and 1 tablespoon lemon juice. Mix well. Serve over salad. Makes 1 luncheon serving.

CAPONATA A LA SICILIANO (EGGPLANT)

> 1 large eggplant
> ¾ cup diced celery
> 1 large roasted pimento, chopped
> 3 tablespoons chopped parsley
> 2 tablespoons capers, drained and rinsed
> 1 clove garlic, mashed well
> ½ teaspoon oregano
> ⅛ teaspoon dill
> Salt and freshly ground pepper
> 4 tablespoons lemon juice or vinegar
> 4 tablespoons vegetable oil

In kettle, half-cover eggplant with boiling salted water and cook until it is tender, turning once. Let cool, peel off skin and cut into slices ¼-inch thick. Remove excess seeds. Cut each slice into strips about 1½ x ½-inch. Measure and store in small jars in 1-cup or ½-cup servings. Combine remaining ingredients, except oil, and mix well. Divide over eggplant. Add 1 tablespoon oil to each serving, screw top on jar and turn upside down or stir well to combine ingredients. May be used as antipasto in a bed of lettuce; as a side dish with meat or poultry; or as a spread over celery. Keeps for days in refrigerator. Makes 4 servings.

RATATOUILLE (MEDITERRANEAN VEGETABLE STEW)

Ratatouille can be folded into omelets, or topped with Swiss cheese and baked until cheese bubbles and melts, or served with a mound of cottage cheese or scrambled eggs for lunch. Delicious too with raw vegetables.

> 2 medium green peppers, cut in ½-inch squares
> 2 cups (1 small) eggplant, sliced, salted, drained, rinsed and cut in ½-inch cubes (see Note)
> 1½ cups water
> 2 cloves garlic, minced
> 2 tablespoons dehydrated onion flakes
> 2 envelopes instant chicken broth and seasoning mix
> 2 cups zucchini, cut in ½-inch slices
> 2 medium tomatoes, quartered
> Dash basil
> Salt and freshly ground pepper
> 2 ribs celery (remove strings and slice very thin)

In large shallow pan, arrange peppers and eggplant in groups, add water, garlic, onion flakes and broth mix and cook until vegetables are soft. Add zucchini and tomatoes. Sprinkle with basil, salt and freshly ground pepper. Cook until zucchini is done. Turn off heat and add very thin slices of raw celery. Cover pan. (Celery makes this a crunchy dish.) Delicious hot or cold. Makes 4 servings.

NOTE: This is standard procedure to remove excess moisture and bitterness from eggplant. Salt unpeeled slices; let stand at least 30 minutes, wash salt off under cold water, and press dry between paper towels.

EGGPLANT PARMIGIANA

> 2 cups eggplant slices (¾-inch thick), salted, drained and rinsed
> ½ recipe Tomato Sauce (p. 216 — count 1 cup tomato juice per serving)
> ½ ounce (1 tablespoon) Parmesan cheese, grated
> 1½ ounces sliced mozzarella cheese
> Salt and pepper

Cover eggplant with boiling water and cook 15 minutes. Drain. In small casserole, make layers of eggplant, Tomato Sauce, and mozzarella slices. Sprinkle each layer with salt and pepper. Top with Parmesan cheese. Bake at 350° F. for about 15 minutes or until eggplant is tender and cheese is bubbly. Makes 2 luncheon servings.

VARIATION

Eggplant Rollatine, Sicilian-Style: You may cut the mozzarella (or use cheddar) into "fingers" and roll the eggplant slices around them. Top with Tomato Sauce and Parmesan cheese and bake as above. Or use ⅔ cup cottage cheese to fill eggplant rolls, omitting mozzarella and Parmesan.

FENNEL

Fennel (finocchio) with its enlarged leaf base and anise-like flavor is excellent served raw in salads, or boiled like celery, which it resembles in appearance and use. Try it braised with Parmesan cheese. You can make it into soup too. To do this, give it long slow cooking till it practically dissolves. Then measure, liquefy in blender, combine with skim milk and serve cold. Try diced raw fennel as a filling for rolled fish fillets or red snapper. Fennel leaves added to Tomato Sauce make it something special to serve with spaghetti, mackerel, salmon too.

FIDDLEFERNS

In New England markets in spring, you might find Bracken fiddle-head ferns, sometimes called croziers because the young stalks come up curled like a bishops staff. Osmunda and the Ostrich Ferns also provide edible new stalks. Tie them in bundles of 6-8 fronds, measure, and steam them upright just like asparagus. They can be prepared in a colander, then set in a kettle (with lid) which holds boiling water. The water should not reach the greens, which are best cooked by steam only. Allow about 10 minutes. Measure before serving.

DOLMADES (STUFFED GRAPE LEAVES—GREEK STYLE)

If you use the commercial pack, separate leaves carefully and rinse in cold water to remove brine. Dry and measure 1 cupful. To use fresh grape leaves, pick tender, unblemished leaves, wash well and cover with boiling water. Let stand till wilted. Remove from hot water and cool leaves under cold water. Cut away tough stems, if any. Drain and dry with paper towels. Measure.

> 6 ounces cooked ground chicken
> ½ cup firm-cooked enriched rice
> 2 teaspoons minced parsley
> 1 teaspoon chopped fresh mint leaves, or ¼ teaspoon dried
> ¾ teaspoon onion salt
> ¼ teaspoon pepper
> 1 cup wilted or cooked grape leaves
> 1½ cups boiling water
> 2 envelopes instant chicken broth and seasoning mix
> 1 teaspoon lemon juice
> Dash each turmeric and cloves (optional)

Prepare filling: In bowl, combine chicken, rice, parsley, mint, onion salt and pepper. Mix well. Spread a heaping teaspoonful in the center of each leaf. Fold in sides, then roll up. Put any leftover filling or leftover leaves in a saucepan. Add stuffed leaves, seam side down, in layers, closely packed. Pour in boiling water, broth mix, lemon juice, turmeric and cloves. Place a heavy plate on top of rolls to hold them in place. Cover pan and let simmer for 1 to 1½ hours. Let cool in pan and serve rolled leaves with any liquid left in pan. Makes 1 dinner serving.

KALE

This nutritious leafy green fall vegetable, a member of the cabbage family, can be boiled; cook greens (the younger the better) for 12-20 minutes or until tender. Some people use the raw leaves chopped in salads. Measure before use. Store washed fresh greens in refrigerator crisper and use within 2-3 days.

KOHLRABI

The part you eat is the large bulb which grows above ground. It tastes rather like a mild, sweet turnip. Cut off all leaves and remove the root. Pare it and then slice it to serve raw in salad. Or cube and cook like turnip. Because of its bland flavor, it goes well with a White Sauce (p. 221 — count 1 slice bread and 1 cup skim milk) or with 2 ounces Parmesan or cheddar cheese sprinkled on top. Young kohlrabi is best; old plants tend to become woody. Buy 2 or more large kohlrabi for each serving . . . measure before use.

MUSHROOM-TOMATO SOUFFLE

Any cooked vegetable can be pureed or chopped fine and made into a soufflé as below.

> 1 cup mushrooms
> 1 medium tomato, sliced
> ½ cup skim milk
> ½ slice bread, made into crumbs
> Salt and pepper
> Dash nutmeg and cayenne pepper
> 1 egg, separated
> 1 tablespoon water

Wipe mushrooms clean with paper towel (or scrub lightly with brush and wipe dry with paper towel). Dice fine. Add to saucepan with tomato and milk and cook at low heat for 10 minutes. Stir in bread crumbs. Season with salt, pepper, a little nutmeg and cayenne pepper. Beat egg yolk with water and add to mushrooms; heat gently, then remove from heat. Beat egg white till stiff (stands in peaks), but not dry. Fold gently into mushroom mixture, ⅓ at a time. Bake in small baking dish at 350° F. for 30 minutes. Makes 1 luncheon serving; supplement as required.

LUNCHEON VEGETABLE PLATE

½ cup cooked cauliflower
½ cup cooked asparagus spears
½ cup cooked green beans
½ cup canned mushrooms, drained
¼ cup skim milk
¼ cup tomato juice
2 ounces cheddar cheese, diced

Arrange cooked vegetables on a plate. In small saucepan, combine skim milk, tomato juice and cheese, and heat gently until cheese melts. Pour over vegetables. Makes 1 serving.

BAKED STUFFED MUSHROOMS FLORENTINE

2 cups medium mushrooms
1½ cups cooked, chopped spinach
2 teaspoons dehydrated onion flakes, reconstituted in
   4 teaspoons water
1 teaspoon dehydrated chives, reconstituted in 2 teaspoons
   water
1 teaspoon Worcestershire
¼ teaspoon thyme
Dash red hot sauce
Salt and pepper

Wash mushrooms. Remove stems and chop them fine. Reserve whole caps. Combine spinach, chopped stems and remaining ingredients; mix well. Spoon mixture into mushroom caps. Place in baking pan holding ½ cup water (prevents mushrooms from sticking). Bake at 375° F. for about 20 minutes, or until mushrooms are tender. Makes 4 servings.

MUSTARD GREENS OR TURNIP GREENS

Both are highly nutritive. Cook washed greens in boiling water, but don't overdo the cooking or they might be bitter. Some people serve them with hot white-bread sauce (p. 221). Measure before you serve.

HOW TO PREPARE PEPPER CASES FOR STUFFING

There's a bitter taste in the skins of mature peppers (the small young ones, never), but once you know how to blister or parboil peppers, they'll always be sweet for you.

Blistered Pepper Cases: Place the raw, whole peppers under the broiler, over a low gas jet, or on charcoal briquets. Turn until skin is black and charred all around. Remove from heat, place in paper bag, tying bag to let peppers steam. After 5 minutes remove peppers from bag and peel off blistered skins with a vegetable knife. Cut out stem, and seed peppers — they are now ready to be stuffed, or sliced and served with a sprinkling of vinegar, basil and oregano.

Parboiled Pepper Cases: Cut out the stem and remove seeds. The top can be put back when the pepper is stuffed. Drop the peppers into the boiling water and let stand 3 minutes. Drain, pour on cold water, drain again and let drip dry as quickly as possible. (Using a vegetable or lettuce basket makes this an easier process.) Fill pepper cases immediately. Bake filled parboiled peppers at 350° F. in a shallow pan 20 minutes or until stuffing is piping hot.

Raw Pepper Cases: Peppers may also be stuffed raw, but they'll need to cook a little longer. Put filled peppers in a baking pan containing a little hot water, bake at 350° F. until peppers are soft. Keep replenishing water as needed, 30-40 minutes. Be sure not to overcook peppers—they will fall apart. Filled peppers can also be put under broiler or cooked on top of the stove (see p. 173).

PEPERONATA

Look for firm, shiny peppers with thick flesh, bright color; wilted or flabby ones are poor quality. Refrigerate till ready to use.

1 medium green pepper
1 medium red pepper
1 clove garlic, minced
2 teaspoons minced chives
1 medium tomato, chopped
Salt and freshly ground pepper
2 tablespoons vegetable oil

Blister peppers if they have a tough skin. Cut into strips and remove seeds. Cover with garlic, chives and chopped tomato. Sprinkle with salt and freshly ground pepper, and add the oil (1 tablespoon per serving allowed). Stir. Good as salad or vegetable. Makes 2 servings.

CHEESE-AND-GREEN-PEPPER RINGS

The golden centers of cheese and eggs, ringed with the green of the peppers, makes this a most attractive luncheon dish. Looks like a lot of work but takes only minutes and a good sharp knife. Make it ahead as a company dish.

   6 medium green peppers
   2 medium red peppers, diced
   4 ounces cheddar cheese, grated
   1 pimento, chopped
   4 hard-cooked eggs
   2 gherkins, chopped
   1 teaspoon Worcestershire
   Lettuce

Cut a slice from the top of the green peppers and discard seeds. Dice pepper tops and combine with remaining ingredients; mash together thoroughly. Pack mixture down firmly into reserved green peppers and chill in refrigerator overnight. Slice 1½ green peppers and ½ red pepper onto each of 4 plates; serve on lettuce. Makes 4 luncheon servings.

SORREL OR SOUR GRASS

Sorrel has been called the most exquisite of all vegetables, and it is widely used in French and Austrian cuisines. Wash it well, remove coarse stems, and cook in a little water in a covered pan for about 5 minutes. Serve sprinkled with salt and pepper, parsley or dill. A good accompaniment for a fish dinner. Because of the natural acidity in sorrel, never cook it with vinegar; for the same reason, cook it in an enamel pan, not in aluminum.

SCHAV (SORREL SOUP)

For summer refreshment, serve each portion of cold schav with 3 table-spoons buttermilk and ½ medium diced cucumber stirred in the soup.

2 cups sorrel (or spinach)
2 cups chicken bouillon or water
Salt and pepper
Dash mace (optional)

Wash leaves well to remove sand; drain. Shred or chop leaves into fine pieces. Add to boiling bouillon or water, cover pan and cook until leaves are soft, 5-10 minutes. Season with salt and pepper, add mace if desired. Serve hot or cold. Makes 2 servings.

SPINACH QUICHE (PIE)

2 slices bread, made into crumbs
2 tablespoons water
2 cups frozen chopped spinach
2 tablespoons dehydrated onion flakes
1 teaspoon salt
¼ teaspoon pepper
Dash nutmeg
2 eggs
1 cup evaporated skimmed milk
2 tablespoons margarine
1 ounce grated Parmesan cheese

Combine bread crumbs (reserve ¼ cup crumbs) with water, mix to a paste and press into the bottom of a pie plate or quiche dish. Bake at 400° F. for 10 minutes to make crust. Let cool. In small sauce-pan, cook spinach according to package directions, drain, squeeze dry and add onion flakes, salt, pepper, nutmeg and reserved crumbs. Remove from heat. Beat eggs and milk together; add spinach mix-ture. Stir in margarine; mix well. Transfer to pie shell, top with Parmesan cheese and bake at 400° F. for 35-40 minutes. Makes 2 luncheon servings; supplement as required.

HOT SPINACH SALAD

For the greenest vegetables, remember one rule — don't overcook. Baking soda was once added to keep vegetables green, but don't use it — it destroys nutrients.

> 4 cups fresh spinach
> 3 tablespoons chicken bouillon
> 1 tablespoon lemon juice
> ¼ teaspoon Worcestershire
> ¼ teaspoon salt
> Artificial sweetener to equal 1 teaspoon sugar

Remove stems from spinach; wash leaves thoroughly and drain. Place in a large saucepan without adding any water; cover. Steam 2 or 3 minutes, or just till leaves wilt; drain any liquid from pan. In a cup, combine bouillon, lemon juice, Worcestershire, salt and sweetener. Pour over spinach; toss to coat leaves well. Makes 4 servings.

SUMMER SQUASH

See list at beginning of this chapter for different varieties of summer squash, all moderate vegetables. The winter squash (#4 vegetables) are in the chapter that follows.

How to buy and prepare squash: One could write a cookbook about this! There are so many different kinds, but all are best when young and tender. (The skin can be easily pierced with your thumbnail.) Clean by scrubbing lightly with a vegetable brush. Do not remove the skin or the seeds (unless the latter are coarse). Squash may be cooked whole, cut into lengthwise quarters; cut into ¼-inch thick slices, or diced.

How to steam: Very young squash is superb this way. Put washed, unpeeled summer squash, sliced ¼-inch thick, into a colander or on a rack. Set colander into a deep kettle holding water which is below the level of the squash. The squash cooks by steam; it is not immersed in water. Cook covered until soft (test with a toothpick). If squash is overcooked, it loses taste and nutrients. Squash shredded on a grater and steamed for 1 or 2 minutes, served still crisp, is delectable with a dressing of lemon juice and parsley. Measure before serving.

How to boil: Slice squash and cook, covered, in a shallow skillet in a little boiling water, about ¼ to ½ cup for 2 cups of vegetables. Stir gently once or twice to lift slices on the bottom of the pan to the top. If squash is young enough, it could be cooked in 3 minutes or so. When the squash becomes translucent, it is done.

How to season: Squash is a bland vegetable and lends itself to many different seasonings. Start with the simplest — salt, pepper and minced parsley. Then try tomato juice, garlic, onions, tarragon, basil.

SQUASH (OR EGGPLANT) CREOLE

   4 cups squash (or eggplant), diced
   1 cup water
   1 envelope instant chicken broth and seasoning mix
   2 medium green peppers, diced
   2 ribs celery, diced
   1½ cups tomato juice
   1 teaspoon dehydrated onion flakes
   1 clove garlic, mashed
   ½ teaspoon salt
   Freshly ground pepper

Put diced squash into saucepan with water and seasoning mix; cook uncovered at moderate heat until squash is soft and water evaporated. Add remaining ingredients, cover pan and let cook until vegetables are done and little liquid remains. If there's too much liquid, uncover pan to cook it down. Makes 4 servings.

SQUASH SALAD

Steamed squash is splendid served cold, marinated in tarragon vinegar or Basic French Dressing (p. 227 — count 1 tablespoon vegetable oil per serving); you may serve it with hard-cooked egg or tuna fish. Young squash may be sliced thin and served raw. Or cover thin slices with boiling water and let stand 3 minutes till they soften, then drain and serve.

ZUCCHINI LUNCHEON CUSTARD

2 cups sliced zucchini
1 egg, slightly beaten
¼ cup evaporated skimmed milk
2 tablespoons finely shredded pimento
1 tablespoon dehydrated onion flakes
Dash garlic salt

Arrange zucchini in 2 individual baking pans; bake at 400° F. for 15 minutes. Combine remaining ingredients and mix well (or run in blender). Pour over zucchini in baking pans. Put pans into a larger pan holding water 1-inch deep and bake at 350° F. for 45 minutes. Makes 1 luncheon serving; supplement as required.

VARIATION
To supplement this luncheon, one ounce shredded cheese may be sprinkled over vegetables before egg mixture is poured over them. Asparagus, cauliflower, mushrooms, etc. could be used with, or in place of zucchini.

OLD-FASHIONED STEWED TOMATOES

2 medium tomatoes, peeled and diced
1 slice day-old 100% whole wheat bread, diced
Artificial sweetener to equal 1 teaspoon sugar
½ teaspoon salt
Few crushed black peppercorns
Added seasonings to taste: Pinch of basil, thyme, oregano, marjoram, parsley, dill, caraway, onion flakes, etc.

Use fresh or canned tomatoes. Heat to boiling point in small saucepan. Add bread, artificial sweetener, salt, peppercorns; stir well, and mix in any other desired seasonings. Makes 1 serving.

VARIATION
1. Marvelous baked in a small casserole over 2 small slices pineapple (canned in its own juice) plus 2 tablespoons juice. Bake at 350° F. for 10 minutes. Just before serving, you may stir 1 teaspoon margarine into tomatoes. Makes 1 serving.

2. *Cream of Tomato Soup:* Prepare Stewed Tomatoes as above. Puree tomatoes in blender, or put through strainer. Add ½ cup skim milk, heat gently and serve hot.

STUFFED TOMATOES

Take a thin slice from the smooth top end of a medium tomato without cutting all the way through. Use this top slice as a hinged lid for stuffed tomatoes. Or cut all the way through the top; dice the removed slice of tomato and use as part of the stuffing. With a spoon, scoop out the inside pulp of the tomato, leaving a firm shell; invert to drain. Prepare desired stuffing, combine with diced tomato pulp and firmly pack into the tomato shell. This can all be done several hours ahead. Two filled tomatoes make 1 serving.

HOW TO COOK STUFFED TOMATOES

Oven-Baked Tomatoes: Bake filled tomatoes in a shallow baking pan. Put a little water around tomatoes and bake at 375° F. for 15-20 minutes. Don't overdo. Tomato should be firm, stuffing hot and bubbly.

Top-of-Stove Stuffed Tomato: Put 3 tablespoons water into a small shallow saucepan or skillet. Add 2-4 stuffed tomatoes. Cover pan and cook at medium heat for 8-10 minutes. Don't let water evaporate completely — add a tablespoon or two if needed.

En Papillote: For a barbecue, wrap filled tomatoes in heavy aluminum foil; tuck ends in carefully. Grill over coals about 20 minutes.

HOW TO FILL THEM

1. For 2 tomato cases, heat ½ cup cooked enriched rice or pastina with scooped-out diced tomato pulp. Season with salt, pepper and basil. One-half teaspoon margarine or vegetable oil may be added to each baked tomato just before serving. Makes 1 serving.

2. Use ½ cup cooked, well-drained spinach seasoned with salt, lemon juice and poultry seasoning to fill 2 tomato shells. Other cooked, highly seasoned vegetables may be used as fillings, alone or in combination (mushrooms, bean sprouts, green peppers, etc.). Diced cooked chicken, lamb, and liver are also excellent as stuffings.

3. Remove top slice and pulp from 12 cherry tomatoes and mash tops with tuna fish, salt, and mayonnaise. Put back into tomato

shells. Serve on bed of watercress which has been sprinkled with finely chopped dill and celery strips (cut in matchstick pieces). Enjoy it all yourself for lunch . . . be sure to fulfill program requirements and use 4 ounces of tuna in all and no more than 1 tablespoon mayonnaise. Makes 1 serving.

GAZPACHO COCKTAIL ON THE ROCKS

1 medium cucumber, peeled
1 medium tomato, peeled
¼ cup boiling water
1 envelope instant chicken broth and seasoning mix
Dash paprika
1 teaspoon vegetable oil
Chopped chives for garnish
4-5 ice cubes

Put everything but the chives and ice cubes into the blender and run at high speed until ingredients are well blended. Pour over ice cubes in large glass. Garnish with chives. Makes 1 serving.

SAVORY APPLE-VEGETABLE CASSEROLE
You can serve this as a stuffing bed for turkey or chicken.

2 cups chopped broccoli
2 cups cauliflower florets
½ cup finely chopped celery
½ medium green pepper, finely chopped
4 teaspoons dehydrated onion flakes
2 medium apples, peeled, cored, and diced
½ cup water
1 teaspoon poultry seasoning
Salt and pepper to taste

Cook broccoli and cauliflower in separate covered pans, each holding ½ cup boiling water, until very soft. Drain (save liquid left in pot for other uses). Place cooked broccoli and cauliflower in mixing bowl with remaining ingredients and mix well with an electric or hand mixer. Turn into a 9x9x2-inch baking dish and bake at 350° F. for 30 minutes. Serve with turkey or chicken lunch or dinner. Makes 4 servings.

PICKLED VEGETABLES

Vegetables preserved by pickling add variety to your menu. Please note that we do not call for special processing in boiling water baths — these vegetables are not for long-term storage. Pickled vegetables must be stored in the refrigerator. Drain and measure or weigh all pickled vegetables before use.

Pickling Brine

    1¼ cups cider vinegar
    ¾ cup water
    ¼ teaspoon salt
    Artificial sweetener to equal 4 tablespoons sugar
    1 tablespoon pickling spices
    1 teaspoon dehydrated onion flakes (optional)
    1 small red hot pepper, sliced (optional)
    1 clove garlic, cut into quarters (optional)
    1 sprig dill (optional)

Pack the prepared vegetables closely into clean pint, quart, or half-gallon jars. Immediately after they are packed, bring the vinegar, water and salt to a boil; pour hot over the vegetables, and add other ingredients. Fill jars to ¼ inch from the top, put on cover tightly. Refrigerate for 24 hours before serving.

Preparing Vegetables for Pickling

Cauliflower florets, eggplant cut into chunks and green beans with ends cut off — all of these should be steamed until they are tender but still crisp. These vegetables may be pickled separately, or combined and pickled in mix-and-match assortments. Drain and measure before use.

These vegetables should be cut into lengthwise quarters: green peppers, red peppers, celery ribs and peeled cucumbers. Just before packing into jars, pour boiling water over them. Let stand a few minutes, then drain, pack into jars, and pour in hot pickling brine. Drain and measure before using.

Green tomatoes — wash only; do not blanch. Green tomatoes may be cut into quarters before they are packed.

You may also pickle asparagus ends (steam the tips and serve them separately as a vegetable). With a knife, pare the tough ends of the asparagus (the part you usually throw away) and peel off the outer greenish-white covering. Cut ends lengthwise in half, or quarter them, and measure. You might want to add a little more sweetener to the pickling brine.

To prepare fresh mushrooms, simmer whole mushrooms in pickling brine for 5 minutes, cool, then transfer to jar with liquid and refrigerate.

VEGETABLE LIQUID

In the best kind of vegetable cooking, there's very little water left in the pan. But we do urge you and the family to use any cooking liquid that's left, as well as the liquid from canned vegetables. Boil liquid at high heat and use in concentrated form in soups, sauces or vegetable juice drinks.

Or add to bouillon or tomato juice, chill it and serve "on the rocks," or combine a variety of liquids left from cooking vegetables, add an envelope instant onion broth and seasoning mix, heat and serve hot, with a sprinkling of chives, parsley or other herb, fresh if possible.

Please don't think this is much ado about nothing, because vegetable cooking liquids contain important food values we don't want you to miss!

Vegetables--Limited

The vegetables you never used to eat could become your favorites. If you've tasted a vegetable only once and didn't like it, it might be the cooking style (or lack of it) that you didn't like, not the vegetable. Try it again with one of our interesting flavorings. Never, never overcook any vegetable; most will become bitter. They should retain their bright color, be firmly tender, never mushy. Even squash should retain the shape of the cubes or slices (unless you're mashing or pureeing it).

Eat your quota of vegetables raw, cooked, fresh or frozen (provided they were not frozen in butter or other sauces). And, as with unlimited and moderate-amount vegetables, your quota can show up at the table in many different forms: as a traditional salad or side dish, as a soup, pudding, pie, soufflé or a colorful gelatin mold.

RULES FOR USING #4 VEGETABLES

1. You must eat 4 ounces (drained raw or cooked weight) per day, or a combination totaling that amount (for example, 1 ounce each of 4 different kinds). The #4 vegetables may be eaten only at the noon or evening meal.

2. Please note asterisks designating dark green, deep yellow and red vegetables. You must select from these marked vegetables at least 2-3 times weekly. Vary your selection of #4 vegetables from day to day.

3. These may be bought fresh, canned or frozen (except for those frozen with butter or other sauces); they may be eaten raw or cooked.

4. Drain your vegetable before you weigh it, but not *down* the drain. You may consume the liquid as is, or use it to replace water in making soups from bouillon cubes, etc.

5. The following vegetables belong to this group:

Artichoke Hearts
Bamboo Shoots
Beets
Burdock
*Brussels Sprouts
*Carrots
Celeriac (celery roots)
Jicima
Leeks
Okra
Onions
Oyster Plant (Salsify)
Parsnips
*Peas
*Pumpkin

Rutabagas
Scallions
*Squash (winter)
  Acorn
  Banana
  Butternut
  Calabaza
  Des Moines
  Gold Nugget
  Hubbard
  Peppercorn
  Table Queen or
    Danish Turban
  Turks Turban
Turnips

HOW TO STEAM VEGETABLES

This is an excellent method for preserving the flavor and nutrients in any fresh vegetable. Use it for everything — beginning with celery in the #3A group, right through to turnips in #4 — but only one vegetable in one kettle at a time. Cooking time varies with the vegetable and the way it is prepared, but the procedure is the same for all.

Prepare vegetables for cooking, and dice, slice or shred them evenly. Or leave small vegetables whole, if preferred. Put vegetable on rack, in basket, colander, etc., and set in kettle. Add just enough boiling water to cover bottom of kettle, but not enough to touch the vegetable. Cover and cook until vegetable is tender, adding more boiling water if necessary. Season to taste and serve hot.

ARTICHOKE HEARTS

1. The frozen kind, cooked according to package directions (and weighed), are delicious when served hot with 1 teaspoon melted margarine (put a few drops of margarine in each heart). Or

serve with Herb Spread (p. 223), or Tomato French Dressing (p. 228). Put the sauce into a small cupped lettuce leaf and surround with vegetable.

2. Cut 2 ounces cooked artichoke hearts into small pieces and warm in a few tablespoons of water in a small saucepan. Add a sprinkling of garlic salt and minced parsley. Use as filling for scrambled eggs, omelet, or soufflé. With a green salad — a perfect luncheon.

3. Try 2 ounces diced artichoke hearts, chilled and served in stemmed cocktail glasses, on a bed of shredded lettuce with Cocktail Sauce for Seafood (p. 216). Even better: add 4 ounces crabmeat and 2 ounces diced, cooked celeriac for a hearty luncheon. All well-chilled, of course. Makes 1 serving.

RED, WHITE AND GREEN SALAD (ARTICHOKE HEARTS, CHEESE AND TOMATO)

½ recipe Tomato Aspic (p. 240 — count 1 cup tomato juice)
4 ounces cooked or canned artichoke hearts
⅔ cup cottage cheese
½ cup diced celery
Dash onion salt
Bibb, romaine and iceberg lettuce

Prepare Tomato Aspic and pour a thin layer into a small mold which has been rinsed in cold water. Refrigerate until firm; keep remaining Aspic at room temperature. Gently open the petals of the artichoke hearts and press them lightly apart. Mash ⅓ cup of the cottage cheese and use to fill artichoke hearts. Put the hearts, cheese side down, into the mold containing the layer of aspic. Add a layer of diced celery, sprinkle with onion salt, and fill mold with remaining Aspic (it should be partly set but not firm). Place mold back into the refrigerator until firm. Unmold on bed of lettuce. Serve topped with remaining ⅓ cup of cottage cheese mashed with a tablespoon or so of water. Makes 1 luncheon serving.

PARSLEY ARTICHOKE HEARTS WITH HERBS

8 ounces frozen artichoke hearts
3 whole allspice
1 small bay leaf
½ teaspoon salt
2 tablespoons margarine, melted
2 teaspoons lemon juice
2 teaspoons minced parsley

Cook frozen artichoke hearts with allspice, bay leaf and salt, following package directions. Drain and remove allspice and bay leaf. Divide into 2 vegetable plates. For each serving, mix 1 tablespoon margarine, 1 teaspoon lemon juice and 1 teaspoon minced parsley. Serve over artichoke hearts. Makes 2 servings.

BAMBOO SHOOTS

I don't suppose this is America's favorite vegetable, but its flavor, slightly acid, is refreshing. You can buy them canned, and if you have any leftover, drain, cover with fresh cold water and refrigerate in a covered jar for up to a week. Cut small and chilled, they are a pleasant addition to a salad, and they make a nice combination with mushrooms too. We've used bamboo shoots in a number of Chinese-style casseroles throughout the book.

PICKLED BEETS

If you are using fresh beets, save the tops — they are a #3B vegetable. To cook beets, peel, slice them thin, or even put through food chopper. Cook with a minimum of water (¼ cup or so) for about 15 minutes.

1 pound sliced, cooked beets, drained
½ cup white vinegar or lemon juice
½ cup water
Artificial sweeetener to equal ¼ cup sugar (optional)
1 teaspoon salt
⅛ teaspoon pepper

Place drained beets in a large serving bowl. Combine remaining ingredients and pour over beets. Let stand in refrigerator 8-12 hours, turning beets several times. Makes 4 servings.

HAWAIIAN BEETS

> 4 ounces cooked, small, whole round or sliced beets, drained
> 2 small slices pineapple (canned in its own juice) plus
>   2 tablespoons juice
> ½ teaspoon salt
> Artificial sweetener to equal 1 teaspoon sugar (optional)

Combine beets, pineapple with juice, and salt in saucepan, and simmer until beets are glazed and piping hot. Sweeten artificially, if desired. Makes 1 serving.

BORSCH (RUSSIAN BEET SOUP)

Borsch, borscht, borsht, bortsch, borshch — there are five different spellings and five hundred ways of preparing it, so we give you a few tasty variations.

> 1 quart water
> 1 cup shredded cabbage
> 1 tablespoon dehydrated onion flakes
> 5 envelopes instant beef and/or chicken broth and
>   seasoning mix
> 8 ounces canned, shredded beets (reserve liquid)
> 2 medium tomatoes, cut up
> 1 tablespoon lemon juice
> Artificial sweetener to equal 2 teaspoons sugar

In large kettle combine water, cabbage, onion flakes and broth mix. Bring to boil, simmer and cook 30 minutes. Add beets with liquid from can, tomatoes and lemon juice; cook 15 minutes longer. Sweeten and serve hot or cold. Makes 4 servings.

VARIATIONS

1. Use peeled, shredded raw beets if desired. Cook in 1 quart water for 30 minutes before adding cabbage, then add cabbage and remaining ingredients, and cook 20 minutes longer.

2. *Some Like It Cold:* For each serving, one medium (3-ounce) hot boiled potato may be diced into each portion cold soup.

3. One fluid ounce of buttermilk may be stirred into each portion of the cold Borsch, and ½ medium diced cucumber may be added as a garnish.

BRUSSELS SPROUTS PAYSANNE

To cook these tiny cabbages whole and firm-textured, cut off stem ends and remove any wilted outer leaves. Cut a crosswise gash into the stem end of each one. For a softer texture, cut the sprouts across, in halves, quarters or slices.

    16 ounces cleaned, prepared Brussels sprouts
    2 cloves garlic, mashed or pounded to a paste with coarse salt
    4 tablespoons vegetable oil

Steam (p. 286) or cook Brussels sprouts in boiling salted water to cover until tender, 10-15 minutes. Drain well. Transfer to 4 small pottery bowls. Combine garlic and oil and divide mixture equally over cooked vegetables. Makes 4 servings.

BURDOCK

Burdock is cultivated in Japan as a root vegetable; the Iroquois Indians are said to have dried the roots, too, for winter use. In contemporary America, however, it is regarded as a weed. But as it has so much food value, and is so widely available along the waysides, we hope it will become more popular. The peeled root and the young flower stems or leaves, according to some recipes, are boiled and seasoned to taste.

COOKED SWEET CARROTS

Fresh carrots bought with their tops on — firm, smooth and bright orange in color — are as delicious as a confection. Frozen whole baby carrots usually have good flavor and are a boon for busy cooks.

    8 ounces carrots
    ½ cup boiling water or chicken bouillon
    ¼ teaspoon salt (optional)
    Artificial sweetener to equal 1 teaspoon sugar (optional)

Wash carrots and scrub with brush. Add them whole, diced, grated, shredded, or cut into julienne strips, to saucepan. Cover with hot liquid (omit salt if you use chicken bouillon), put lid on pan and cook until tender. Young sliced or shredded carrots should be cooked in about 10 minutes; if whole, 15-20 minutes; if old, 25-30 minutes. Do not overcook. They should be crisp and sweet but, if you wish, add artificial sweetener. If you have cooked young carrots whole, you can put a sprig of parsley at the root end to simulate carrot tops for decoration. Makes 2 servings.

BRAISED CARROTS, CELERY AND PEAS

    1 stalk celery
    4 ounces carrots, diced
    4 ounces peas
    2 teaspoons dehydrated onion flakes
    1 cup chicken bouillon
    1 tablespoon minced parsley
    ½ teaspoon dried mint
    1 tablespoon margarine

Cut off top leaves and tough ends of celery, and recove coarse outer ribs. (Save leaves and outer ribs for making soup.) Cut celery stalk in half crosswise, then quarter lengthwise. Transfer to shallow flameproof oven-to-table casserole and cover with boiling salted water. Parboil celery for 5 minutes. Drain immediately, cool under cold running water and drain again. Remove celery from casserole and set aside. Add carrots, peas, onion flakes and chicken bouillon to casserole, and bring to boil. Return celery to casserole and bake covered at 375° F. for 30 minutes. Sprinkle with parsley and mint and stir in margarine at the table. Makes 2 servings.

PUREE OF CARROT AND RICE SOUP
An adaptation of Potage Crécy, from classical French cuisine.

    8 ounces carrots, sliced thin
    ½ cup sliced celery
    1 tablespoon dehydrated onion flakes
    1½ cups chicken bouillon
    Salt and pepper
    ¼ teaspoon thyme
    1 cup cooked enriched rice

Cook carrot, celery, onion flakes and chicken bouillon in covered saucepan for about 15 minutes, or until vegetables are soft. Puree in blender, add salt, pepper and thyme, and serve immediately over ½ cup rice in each of two soup bowls. Makes 2 servings.

CARROT AND FRUIT MELANGE

4 ounces cooked, diced carrots
½ cup cooked enriched rice, or ½ cup canned bean sprouts, drained and rinsed
3 tablespoons chicken bouillon or water
1 medium tangerine, cut in segments, or sections cut from 1 small orange, or 1 medium red apple (unpeeled), cored and diced
1 teaspoon brown sugar replacement
2 teaspoons lemon juice
1 teaspoon margarine

Combine cooked carrots and rice or bean sprouts in small saucepan with bouillon. Heat gently. Remove from heat, stir in fruit sections, add brown sugar replacement, lemon juice or margarine. Makes 1 serving.

CARROT AND PINEAPPLE MOLD

1 envelope (1 tablespoon) unflavored gelatin
¼ cup water
¼ cup hot water
2 small slices pineapple (canned in its own juice) plus 2 tablespoons juice
4 ounces coarsely grated raw carrots
2 teaspoons lemon or lime juice
½ teaspoon salt

Soften gelatin in water, stir in hot water to dissolve it. Dice pineapple or crush in blender with juice. Combine gelatin and pineapple with other ingredients and pour into small wet mold. Refrigerate until set. To unmold, dip outside of mold in very warm water almost to the top, run a knife around the inside, and hold serving plate upside-down on top of mold, then invert. Makes 1 serving.

PICKLED CARROTS

Cut carrots into long strips. Steam strips until tender, but still firm and crisp. Pack tightly into pint or quart jars and fill to ¼ inch from the top with hot Pickling Brine (p. 283). Put on lid and seal tight. Store in refrigerator; use after 24 hours. Drain and weigh before use.

CELERIAC (CELERY ROOT) COCKTAIL

Appearances deceive — this rough-looking root has a subtle, mild and sweet flavor, reminiscent both of potato and celery.

8 ounces scrubbed, sliced and peeled celery root
Lemon juice
1 cup finely-shredded lettuce
1 recipe Cocktail Sauce, for Seafood (p. 216 — count 6 fluid ounces tomato juice per serving)
2 tablespoons mayonnaise

Cut celery root into slices and brush with lemon juice. Steam until tender when pierced with fork. Serve in two stemmed seafood-cocktail glasses on a bed of lettuce. Combine cocktail sauce and mayonnaise, mix well, and divide into the cocktail glasses. Makes 2 servings.

JICIMA

This crisp Mexican vegetable (pronounced heé-kee-mah) is mild and slightly sweet; you may use it like water chestnuts in salads or with seafood. Here are some tasty ways to prepare it:

1. Try it raw as an appetizer, sliced and weighed and sprinkled with lime juice, chili powder and salt.
2. Make a *Crunchy Chicken Salad* with 4 ounces cooked, skinned, boned, diced chicken; ¼ medium green pepper, diced; 1 large slice pineapple (canned in its own juice); 2 ounces diced jicima and 1 tablespoon mayonnaise mixed with the 2 tablespoons pineapple juice. Makes 1 serving.
3. Steamed jicima may be sprinkled with a little lemon juice and served with chicken or fish. It is also a pleasant luncheon served with ⅔ cup cottage cheese.

4. For a dessert, try a hot *Jicima Fruit Compote*. Boil 4 ounces diced jicima with 1 teaspoon lemon juice, artificial sweetener to taste and 1 stick cinnamon, until jicima is soft. Then add 1 sliced apple or ½ cup pitted sweet cherries and a dash dehydrated orange peel; cover and simmer for 2 minutes. Serve hot.

OKRA

Native to Africa, but now grown in our Southern states, young pods are juicy, not dry and woody as are the overmature plants. In addition to fresh, okra is also available canned or frozen.

If pods are young, they may be cooked whole. Cut away stem ends before or after they are cooked; weigh serving. If mature, cut pods into thick crosswise slices. Cook okra in boiling salted water, drain and serve with Maitre d'Hotel Spread (p. 223) or lemon juice and 1 tablespoon margarine.

You'll find okra included in our Jerusalem Chicken with Okra (p. 183) and Bluefish Stew Port au Prince (p. 102).

OKRA GUMBO
The gelatinous okra pods make a fine thickener for soup.

> 4 ounces diced okra
> 1 medium green pepper, diced
> 1 medium tomato, diced
> 2 cups water
> 2 envelopes instant chicken broth and seasoning mix
> 2 teaspoons dehydrated onion flakes

Combine in saucepan and cook covered until vegetables are soft. Makes 2 servings.

ONIONS—FRESH AND DEHYDRATED

Fresh onions are a #4 vegetable. You may prefer to replace it, as a seasoning, with dehydrated onion flakes or chives (which are unlimited). The dehydrated flakes should be reconstituted in water or liquid if they are used without cooking (when added to salads, for example). Rehydrate 1 teaspoon flakes in about a tablespoon of water.

Water-Fried Onion Rings: Here is a good procedure for "frying" onions without fat. Peel a 4-ounce onion, and cut in slices ⅓-inch thick. Separate slices into rings, or cut each slice to the center to make long strings. Sprinkle with salt, and "water-fry" in heated heavy iron or non-stick skillet. To do this, cover with 1 cup water and ½ envelope instant chicken broth and seasoning mix (gives color to the onion). Cook until onion is soft and liquid is evaporated; if onion is not golden, let it brown lightly in dry pan. A delectable addition to broiled liver or steak meals.

CREAMED ONION AND SPINACH CASSEROLE

> 16 ounces braised onions, drained, see below
> ⅓ cup instant non-fat dry milk
> Dash nutmeg and white pepper
> 1 envelope instant chicken broth and seasoning mix
> 2 cups cooked, chopped spinach

Combine all ingredients except spinach in blender. Blend until smooth. Add spinach to onion mixture. Turn into 1-quart casserole and bake at 350° F. for 20 minutes or until bubbly. Makes 4 servings.

To braise onions: peel them and put them into a shallow oven-to-table casserole, half-covered with boiling water. Simmer, covered, over low heat for 30 minutes, until onions are tender, turning once.

TANGY ONION AND ORANGE SALAD

> Lettuce
> 4 ounces sliced onions
> 1 small orange, divided into segments
> 1 tablespoon vegetable oil
> 1 tablespoon wine vinegar
> 1 tablespoon capers

Toss ingredients together in small salad bowl. Makes 1 serving.

ONION SOUP EN CASSEROLE

    16 ounces onions, sliced thin
    1 quart water
    5 envelopes instant beef broth and seasoning mix, or
       5 beef bouillon cubes
    1 teaspoon "legal" steak sauce
    Dash celery salt
    Pepper
    4 slices toast (optional)
    2 ounces grated Parmesan cheese (optional)

In flameproof casserole, cook onions in boiling water with beef broth mix, steak sauce and celery salt, until onions are soft (about 10 minutes). Put casserole into 450° F. oven and cook uncovered until bubbly. Sprinkle with pepper and serve hot. For lunch, divide Parmesan cheese over toast and place on top of casserole. Bake until cheese is melted. Makes 4 servings.

VARIATION

Cream of Onion Soup: Cook onions in 3 cups water. When onions are soft, stir in 1 cup evaporated skimmed milk and heat in oven. Makes 4 servings.

SALSA

Use this favorite Mexican relish with eggs, steak or hamburger.

    4 ounces sweet onion, or scallions
    4 peeled green chili peppers
    2 medium tomatoes
    ½ clove garlic, or ½ teaspoon garlic salt
    ½ teaspoon monosodium glutamate
    ¼ teaspoon salt

Chop onions, chili peppers, tomatoes and garlic very fine, so that they are no longer identifiable separately. Add monosodium glutamate and salt. Let stand ½ hour before using (or keep several days in screw-top jar in refrigerator. It can also be frozen). Makes 4 servings.

OYSTER PLANT CREAM SOUP

This plant that looks like a parsnip and tastes like an oyster can sometimes be found fresh in Italian produce markets. It's occasionally grown in backyard gardens, and you can find it canned in many gourmet departments (an import from France). It's also called salsify.

4 ounces cooked or canned, drained oyster plant (see note)
1 cup chicken bouillon
½ cup watercress leaves
1 teaspoon dehydrated onion flakes
¼ cup evaporated skimmed milk
Salt and pepper
Dash red hot sauce

In saucepan, heat oyster plant, bouillon, watercress leaves and onion flakes. Cook for 10 minutes, then pour (without draining) into blender container, and puree. Put back in saucepan with milk, salt, pepper and red hot sauce; heat gently but do not boil. Makes 1 serving.

NOTE: To cook fresh oyster plant, scrape off the skin and drop immediately into acidulated water (2 teaspoons vinegar to 2 cups water) to prevent discoloration. Cook till tender in small amount of boiling salted water.

OYSTER PLANT ROCKEFELLER (IN CLAM SHELLS)

4 ounces canned, drained oyster plant, cut in 2-inch pieces
¼ cup cooked spinach
1 teaspoon dehydrated onion flakes, reconstituted in
    1 tablespoon water
½ teaspoon minced tarragon or parsley
Dash celery salt and cayenne pepper
Dash red hot sauce
½ slice bread, made into crumbs (optional)
2 teaspoons vegetable oil

Arrange oyster plant pieces in decorative clam shells (the number you need depends on their size) or ramekins. In blender container combine spinach, onion flakes, tarragon or parsley, celery salt, cayenne pepper and red hot sauce; blend until smooth. Blend in bread crumbs, if desired, and oil. Spread this mixture over the oyster plant pieces, and bake at 450° F. until piping hot, about 10-15 minutes. Makes 1 serving.

PARSNIPS

An excellent vegetable, too little known (except in some ethnic cuisines as a soup stock ingredient). It looks like a white carrot, and can be cooked just like carrots. Scrape with a vegetable brush to clean; weigh, slice and drop them immediately into acidulated water (parsnips discolor easily too). Transfer to ¼ cup boiling water, cover and cook until tender. Serve with a sprinkling of artificial sweetener or minced parsley, or both.

PARSNIPS A LA GREQUE

4 ounces scraped parsnips
Lemon juice
¾ cup chicken bouillon
2 teaspoons tarragon vinegar or lemon juice
Dash parsley, dill or fennel seeds
1 clove garlic
1 tablespoon vegetable oil

Slice parsnips, and immediately brush with lemon juice. Drop into saucepan with remaining ingredients, except oil, and cook until parsnips are tender and liquid almost evaporated. Discard garlic clove. Use immediately or cool at room temperature. Serve sprinkled with oil. Makes 1 serving.

MINTED HOLIDAY PEAS

1 cup diced celery
½ cup water
1 tablespoon dehydrated onion flakes
1 envelope instant vegetable broth and seasoning mix
1 teaspoon dried mint
¼ teaspoon imitation butter flavoring
1 cup cooked or canned mushroom stems and pieces
   (reserve liquid)
16 ounces cooked peas
½ cup pimentos, cut in strips (optional)

Combine celery, water, onion flakes, broth mix, mint, butter flavoring and mushroom liquid in saucepan, and simmer until celery is tender. Add cooked peas, garnish with mushrooms and pimentos, if desired; heat thoroughly. Makes 4 servings.

GREEN PEAS FRANCAISE

Fresh vegetables are sweet when just cooked; if you're using canned, frozen or not-so-fresh vegetables, a dash of artificial sweetener at serving time will perk up the flavor.

> ½ head lettuce
> 8 ounces shelled fresh peas
> 2 teaspoons dehydrated onion flakes
> Dash artificial sweetener (optional)
> ¼ teaspoon imitation butter flavoring
> Salt and pepper

Shred lettuce into a saucepan, add peas and onion flakes and 3-4 tablespoons water (just enough to moisten — the lettuce provides the extra moisture). Cover pan and cook until peas are done, about 15 minutes. Add sweetener and butter flavoring. Salt and pepper at the table. This may also be baked in a casserole as part of an oven meal. Allow 45 minutes at 325° F. Makes 2 servings.

VARIATION

Spiced Peas: Follow directions above but omit onion flakes and add a small stick of cinnamon, ¼ teaspoon ginger and artificial sweetener to equal 1 teaspoon sugar.

PUREE OF PEAS

Delicious used as stuffing for 1 cup baked mushroom caps.

> 1 pound frozen green peas
> Dash onion powder and chopped chives

Cook the peas as per package directions, using a minimum of water. Puree in blender, sprinkle with onion powder and chives, and serve as a vegetable. Makes 4 servings.

VARIATION

Cream of Pea Soup: Pour puree into saucepan, add 1 cup skim milk, and heat gently, but do not boil. Stir frequently. Makes 4 servings.

PUMPKIN CHIFFON TARTLETS

Most cooks use canned pumpkin, but it can be prepared fresh, of course. Wash and cut in half crosswise, remove seeds, string, and peel. Cook in salted boiling water until tender, or steam until very soft. Mash well or puree in blender. Happy Thanksgiving!

16 ounces cooked or canned pumpkin
4 tablespoons brown sugar replacement
¼ teaspoon rum extract
⅛ teaspoon nutmeg
⅛ teaspoon cinnamon
⅛ teaspoon ginger
2 envelopes (2 tablespoons) unflavored gelatin
¼ cup water
1 cup evaporated skimmed milk
Artificial sweetener to equal 4 teaspoons sugar

Combine first 6 ingredients in large bowl; mix well. Set aside. Sprinkle gelatin over water in small saucepan to soften. Place over low heat and stir until gelatin has dissolved, about 3 minutes. Set aside. Combine milk and artificial sweetener in bowl; mix with rotary beater. Slowly pour in gelatin mixture and continue beating until stiff peaks form. Fold ¾ of this into pumpkin mixture. Divide equally into 4 individual dessert molds. Top each portion with equal amounts of remaining gelatin mixture. Chill until firm. Makes 4 servings.

SCALLIONS AND LEEKS

Treat these like their cousin, the onion. Scallions, known as spring or raw green onions in various parts of the country, may be eaten raw or braised in a little water. Chopped, they're great in salads.

Leeks are often used as a flavoring in soups and chowders; their delicate flavor makes them a delicious vegetable too. Wash the leaves carefully, as they often have sand caught in them. Trim off root end, discard most of green stem, slit lengthwise, and cook in a shallow covered pan with ½ cup boiling water and ½ envelope instant chicken broth and seasoning mix. Turn leeks once. Cook 7 or 8 minutes, till tender; test by inserting a knife at the thick root end. Drain and weigh. Serve with cooking liquid.

WINTER SQUASH

Winter squash, with their fanciful names, acorn, banana, butternut, Hubbard and Danish turban or table queen, are plentiful through the colder months. Try them all — they're so simple to prepare. Be sure to remove seeds and stringy fibers.

Cut winter squash into slices and steam in a colander (not touching water) until tender. Serve with margarine.

Or cut squash in half, sprinkle with water, and bake at 400° F. until tender, about 20 minutes for banana squash to 45 minutes for Hubbard. Hard-shelled winter squash will have to be scooped out of its shell, before it is weighed. The pulp may be mashed and served in the squash shell or "boat," as some call it. If desired, sprinkle salt, pepper, cinnamon, nutmeg, artificial sweetener or brown sugar replacement on squash right before serving. Margarine may be stirred into hot squash too.

BUTTERNUT SQUASH AND APPLE FLUFF

    16 ounces peeled, sliced butternut (or other winter) squash
    4 medium cooking apples, peeled, cored and sliced
    ½ cup water or dietetic carbonated beverage (any flavor)
    Pinch salt
    ½ cup evaporated skimmed milk
    3 tablespoons brown sugar replacement
    ½ teaspoon cinnamon
    Dash nutmeg, cloves and ginger

In saucepan combine squash, apples, water or beverage and salt; bring to boil and cook 15 minutes, or until squash and apples are soft. Mash well or puree in blender with remaining ingredients. Transfer to baking dish. Bake uncovered at 350° F. for 20-30 minutes. Makes 4 servings.

TURNIPS

If you can find young white ones, scrub them clean with a vegetable brush (don't peel). Serve raw in a salad, or cut, dice and steam or cook in a small amount of water. Four ounces (by weight) equals 1 serving.

Rutabagas are yellow turnips, less subtle in flavor than the white. Peel them, cut in chunks, weigh 4 ounces, cover with boiling water and cook until tender, 10-15 minutes. Turnips may be seasoned with artificial sweetener and cinnamon or dehydrated onion flakes softened in water. If you are not keen on turnips, you might try mashing together 4 ounces freshly boiled turnips and 1 medium (3-ounce) potato. Season with salt and pepper and add 1 tablespoon margarine. Makes 1 serving.

TURNIPS COOKED IN STOCK

    1 pound peeled white turnips
    ¾ cup water
    1 envelope instant chicken broth and seasoning mix
    2 teaspoons lemon juice
    1 slice bread, made into crumbs

Cut turnips into thin slices. In saucepan, bring water, broth mix and lemon juice to boil. Add turnip slices, and simmer covered, until tender. Drain and serve. To make sauce, combine ½ cup liquid from cooking vegetable with bread crumbs. Season to taste and serve hot over cooked vegetable. Makes 4 servings.

In recipes for more than one serving, divide mixture evenly so every portion has an equal amount of each ingredient. For soups and stews:

    1. Drain the liquid and set aside
    2. Divide solid ingredients evenly, and
    3. Add equal amounts of the liquid to each portion

BAKED VEGETABLE AND POTATO CASSEROLE

All vegetables should be scrubbed and peeled, if necessary, before they are weighed. If frozen vegetables are used, add them to the casserole after 20 minutes. They have been parboiled and need less cooking than fresh ones.

    4 ounces carrots, diced
    4 ounces jicima, or oyster plant, diced
    4 ounces okra, or parsnips, diced
    4 ounces turnip, diced
    4 medium (3-ounce) potatoes, diced
    ½ cup diced celery
    2 teaspoons dehydrated onion flakes
    Generous dash of paprika
    2 cups vegetable bouillon
    2 tablespoons chopped chives or parsley

In casserole, combine carrots, jicima, okra, turnip, potatoes and celery. Stir in onion flakes and sprinkle with paprika. Pour in vegetable bouillon, cover casserole, and bake at 325° F. until vegetables are soft, 40-50 minutes. Just before serving, stir in chopped chives or parsley. Divide evenly; serve in bowls. Makes 4 servings.

MIXED COOKED VEGETABLE SALAD

    3 ounces cooked, diced carrots
    3 ounces cooked peas
    2 ounces bamboo shoots, sliced
    1 cup cooked cauliflower, separated into florets
    1 cup cooked, sliced green beans
    Fresh or dried herbs to taste (dill, parsley, marjoram, basil, etc.)
    2 recipes Mayonnaise Sauce (p. 226 — count 1 tablespoon mayonnaise and 1 fluid ounce evaporated skimmed milk per serving), or 1⅓ cups cottage cheese

Combine vegetables and herbs, and toss gently, to avoid mashing the vegetables. Divide into 2 salad bowls, and just before serving, pour Mayonnaise Sauce equally into each bowl (for a satisfying luncheon salad, use cottage cheese). Makes 2 servings.

Leveling and Maintenance Plans

You've almost done it! Just 10 pounds short of goal, you transfer to our Leveling Plan. And when the 10 pounds are off, and you are where you should be, we aim to keep your figure uncluttered forever with our Maintenance Plan. There are Leveling and Maintenance Plans for Men, Women and Youth.

LEVELING PLAN

Read every word carefully and see how much more you are getting. Even though the plan follows the format of the Basic Program, there are some adjustments in quantity and choices.

1. DIETETIC PRODUCTS
Notice the change here.
Restrict artificial sweeteners to about 20 calories per day.

2B. LIMITED ITEMS
Be careful to make the adjustment in these items.
Reduce bouillon cubes, instant mixes for broth and seasoning to 1 cube or 1 envelope of instant mix per day. Reduce unflavored gelatin to 1 envelope (1 tablespoon) per day.

3. VEGETABLES
B. Moderate Amounts
Reduce to 2 cups raw or 1 cup cooked unless otherwise specified, e.g. 1 medium tomato.

4. VEGETABLES
Use the cup or package (or can) equivalent of 4 ounces. These vegetables are now in 2 groups. Group A contains all the #4 vegetables on the Program with the exception of Group B (listed below).

Group B
Select up to 3 times a week:

Brussels sprouts	Onions	Pumpkin
Burdock	Parsnips	Scallions
Leeks	Peas	Squash (winter)

Bonus
Tomato juice, reduce to 1 cup (8 fluid ounces),
    or 1 tomato and 1 cucumber,
    or 2 pickles

5. FRUITS
    MAN: reduce fruit to 3 daily.
    YOUTH: reduce fruit to 4 daily.

Look at the new additions, and add as follows:

List #1
Grapefruit sections, ¾ cup
Orange sections, ¾ cup
Papaya, diced (½-inch cubes), ¾ cup

List #2
Fig, 1 medium
Kiwi, 1 medium
Pineapple (canned in its juice), ½ cup chunks or crushed
Pomegranate, 1 medium

List #3
Select up to 4 times weekly; do not choose the same fruit every day. On days you choose from this list:
    WOMAN: Do not include an apple or pear among your fruits;
    MAN AND YOUTH: Do not include more than 2 apples or 2 pears among your fruits.
Apricot halves, dried, 4
Mango, ½ medium
Persimmon (2-inch diameter), 1 or 3 small
Prunes, dried, 2
Watermelon, 1 wedge (4-inch x 4-inch x 8-inch)—not more than 2 pounds with rind

List #4

Weekly, if desired:

Avocado, ¼ medium

Avocado, diced, ⅓ cup

6. FISH, MEAT AND POULTRY

WOMAN AND YOUTH: Reduce to 3 ounces at noon and 4 ounces at evening.

MAN: Reduce to 3 ounces at noon and 6 ounces at evening.

Group A

Fish at least 3 times a week. The "once-a-week" category remains the same.

Groups B and C

These become one group. Do not select any one item from this group more than 3 times a week, except chicken.

7. LIVER

Choose at least once a week (or more often). It need not be considered in the combined Group B and C choice.

8. BREAD AND CEREAL

MAN AND YOUTH: Reduce bread to 3 slices daily.

a) Add cracked wheat, rye or pumpernickel.

b) Add weekly, *if desired:*

One (1) medium-size hamburger bun or frankfurter roll may be used in place of one slice of bread.

c) If cereal is eaten at breakfast, the bread may be omitted and used at another meal or between meals. The bread at lunch may also be omitted and used in the same way.

9. WEEKLY CHOICE GROUP

This category is no longer daily. It becomes a *weekly choice*. Omit 1 slice of bread and select one:

Beans, lima, ½ cup

Corn:

  1 medium ear

  ½ cup cream style

  ½ cup whole kernel

Cowpeas (and/or black-eyed peas), ½ cup

Hominy grits (enriched), ¾ cup cooked

Pasta (enriched):

  ½ cup noodles, cooked

  ⅔ cup macaroni or spaghetti, cooked

Potato, 1 baked or boiled (about 6 ounces)

Rice (enriched), ½ cup cooked

11. EGGS AND CHEESE
Reduce hard cheese to 2 ounces weekly.

12. MILK
> YOUTH: Reduce to 3 glasses (8 fluid ounces each) skim milk,
> or 1½ glasses (12 fluid ounces) evaporated skimmed milk,
> or 2¼ glasses (18 fluid ounces) buttermilk

LEVELING MENU PLAN

MORNING:
Choice of:
> Cheese, 1 ounce hard or 2 ounces farmer,
>   or ¼ cup cottage or pot cheese
> or Fish, 2 ounces
> or Egg, 1
> or Cereal, 1 ounce with skim milk

Bread, 1 slice
Beverage (if desired)

NOON:
Choice of:
> Fish, meat or poultry, 3 ounces
> or Cheese, 2 ounces hard or 4 ounces farmer
> or ⅔ cup cottage or pot cheese
> or Eggs, 2

At least one #3 vegetable
4 ounces #4 vegetable (if desired)
> WOMAN AND MAN: 1 slice bread
> YOUTH: 2 slices bread

Beverage (if desired)

EVENING:
Choice of:
> WOMAN AND YOUTH: Fish, meat or poultry, 4 ounces
> MAN: Fish, meat or poultry, 6 ounces

4 ounces #4 vegetable (if not eaten at noon meal)
Reasonable amounts of #3 vegetables
> MAN: 1 slice bread

Beverage (if desired)

DAILY:

1 tablespoon vegetable oil, margarine or mayonnaise,
   or 2 tablespoons imitation (or diet) margarine

WOMAN OR MAN: 2 glasses (8 fluid ounces each) skim milk,
               or 1 glass (8 fluid ounces) evaporated skimmed
               milk,
               or 1½ glasses (12 fluid ounces) buttermilk

YOUTH: 3 glasses (8 fluid ounces each) skim milk,
         or 1½ glasses (12 fluid ounces) evaporated skimmed
         milk,
         or 2¼ glasses (18 fluid ounces) buttermilk

WOMAN AND MAN: 3 fruits

YOUTH: 4 fruits

2 #3 vegetables

4 ounces #4 vegetable

WEEKLY:

Liver at least once
4 eggs
Fish at least three times

OPTIONAL, DAILY:

Bouillon or broth
Tomato Juice
Coffee or Tea
Water

MAINTENANCE PLAN

Food choices follow the same menu pattern as in the "Leveling
Plan." Guidance is given on how to choose foods to maintain your
weight for life. Adjustments are as follows:

6. FISH, MEAT AND POULTRY
Group C

Choose only once a week, if desired:

Bacola (dried salted codfish)	Ham, boiled or cured	Luncheon meat
		Pork
Beef, corned	Herring (fresh or pickled)	Salami
Bologna		Sardines
Duck	Liverwurst	Tongue

7. LIVER
May be eaten every other week or once a week, if desired.

11. Eggs and Cheese
Do not use more than 4 ounces of hard cheese weekly.

MORNING:
Juice or Fruit
Choice of:

>Cheese, 1 ounce hard or 2 ounces farmer,
>>or ¼ cup cottage or pot cheese
>or Fish, 2 ounces
>or Egg, 1
>or Cereal, 1 ounce with skim milk

Bread, 1 slice
Additions as allowed
Beverage (if desired)

NOON:
Choice of:

>Fish, meat or poultry, 3 ounces,
>or Cheese, 2 ounces hard or 4 ounces farmer,
>or ⅔ cup cottage or pot cheese,
>or Eggs, 2

#3 vegetable, at least one
#4 vegetable (if desired)
WOMAN AND MAN: 1 slice bread
YOUTH: 2 slices bread
Additions as allowed
Beverage (if desired)

EVENING:
Choice of:

>WOMAN AND YOUTH: Fish, meat or poultry, 4 ounces
>MAN: Fish, meat or poultry, 6 ounces

#3 vegetable
#4 vegetable (if not eaten at noon meal)
MAN: 1 slice bread
Additions as allowed
Beverage (if desired)

DAILY:
1 tablespoon vegetable oil, margarine or mayonnaise,
or 2 tablespoons imitation (or diet) margarine
WOMAN AND MAN: 2 glasses (8 fluid ounces each) skim milk,
or 1 glass (8 fluid ounces) evaporated skimmed
milk,
or 1½ glasses (fluid ounces) buttermilk
YOUTH: 3 glasses (8 fluid ounces each) skim milk,
or 1½ glasses (12 fluid ounces) evaporated skimmed milk
or 2¼ glasses (18 fluid ounces) buttermilk
WOMAN AND MAN: 3 fruits
YOUTH: 4 fruits
2 #3 vegetables
1 #4 vegetable

OPTIONAL:
Bouillon or broth
Tomato Juice
Coffee or Tea
Water

Goal Weights

The weights have been established by recognized authorities. If you are uncertain about your frame, consider it medium. Remove shoes and have someone measure your height using a flat ruler extending from the top of your head to a wall. Use a standard measuring scale. Weigh yourself once a week only and always under similar conditions—on the same scale and at the same time of day.

CHILDREN UNDER 12 YEARS OF AGE: Goal weights must be determined by the child's pediatrician. No standard goal is listed for children.

FOR MEN

HEIGHT	SMALL FRAME	MEDIUM FRAME	LARGE FRAME
5'0"	118	126	134
5'1"	121	129	137
5'2"	124	132	140
5'3"	127	135	143
5'4"	131	139	147
5'5"	134	142	150
5'6"	138	146	154
5'7"	142	150	158
5'8"	146	154	162
5'9"	150	158	166
5'10"	154	162	170
5'11"	158	166	176
6'0"	164	172	182
6'1"	170	178	188
6'2"	179	184	194
6'3"	184	190	200

FOR WOMEN

HEIGHT	SMALL FRAME	MEDIUM FRAME	LARGE FRAME
4'9"	106	114	122
4'10"	108	116	124
4'11"	110	118	126
5'0"	113	121	129
5'1"	116	124	132
5'2"	120	128	136
5'3"	123	132	140
5'4"	127	136	144
5'5"	130	139	148
5'6"	134	142	152
5'7"	138	146	156
5'8"	142	150	160
5'9"	146	154	163
5'10"	150	158	166
5'11"	154	162	170
6'0"	158	166	174

FOR BOYS

HEIGHT	12 YRS.	13 YRS.	14 YRS.	15 YRS.	16 YRS.	17 YRS.	18 YRS.
4'2"	58						
4'3"	61						
4'4"	64	64					
4'5"	68	68					
4'6"	71	71	72				
4'7"	74	74	74				
4'8"	77	78	78	80			
4'9"	81	82	83	83			
4'10"	85	85	86	87			
4'11"	89	89	90	90	90		
5'0"	92	93	94	95	96		
5'1"	96	97	99	100	103	106	
5'2"	101	103	103	104	107	111	116
5'3"	106	107	108	110	113	118	123
5'4"	109	111	113	115	117	121	126
5'5"	114	117	118	120	122	127	131
5'6"		119	122	125	128	132	136
5'7"		124	128	130	134	136	139
5'8"			134	134	137	141	143
5'9"			137	139	143	146	149

FOR GIRLS

HEIGHT	12 YRS.	13 YRS.	14 YRS.	15 YRS.	16 YRS.	17 YRS.	18 YRS.
4'2"	62						
4'3"	65						
4'4"	67						
4'5"	69	71					
4'6"	71	73					
4'7"	75	77	78				
4'8"	79	81	83				
4'9"	82	84	88	92			
4'10"	86	88	93	96	101		
4'11"	90	92	96	100	103	104	
5'0"	95	97	101	105	108	109	111
5'1"	100	101	105	108	112	113	116
5'2"	105	106	109	113	115	117	118
5'3"	110	110	112	116	117	119	120
5'4"	114	115	117	119	120	122	123
5'5"	118	120	121	122	123	125	126
5'6"		124	124	125	128	129	130
5'7"		128	130	131	133	133	135
5'8"		131	133	135	136	138	138
5'9"			135	137	138	140	142

Daily Food Record

To help you keep track of your daily and weekly use of limited foods, rule a notebook page into 8 columns. List the following headings across the page:

Food   Mon.   Tues.   Wed.   Thurs.   Fri.   Sat.   Sun.

List the following headings down the page, in the Food column:

Bread
Cereal
Cheese, Hard
Cheese, Soft
Daily Choice
Eggs
Fats
Fish
Shellfish
Fruit #1
Fruit #2
Fruit #3

Liver
Meat Group B
Meat Group C
Milk
Vegetabl. #3B
Vegetabl. #4
Bouillon Cubes
Dietetic Bev.
Extracts
Gelatin
Tomato Juice

Change food headings as necessary when you reach Leveling (Daily Choice becomes Weekly Choice, etc.) Keep accurate count of ingredients.

Weekly Weight Record

You can keep track of your weight in the notebook too. At the top of the page, record the following:

Starting date and time:
Starting weight:
Goal weight:
Weight to Leveling (10 pounds before goal):

Rule the remainder of the page into 3 columns with the following headings across the page:

Date & Time   Weight   Net Change

Fill in your weekly weight and weight loss, even after you reach Goal and transfer to Leveling and Maintenance.

Index

320